The
Gun Control
Debate

THE
GUN CONTROL
DEBATE

A Documentary History

Edited by MARJOLIJN BIJLEFELD

Primary Documents in American History and Contemporary Issues

GREENWOOD PRESS
Westport, Connecticut • London

Library of Congress Cataloging-in-Publication Data

The gun control debate : a documentary history / edited by Marjolijn
 Bijlefeld.
    p. cm.—(Primary documents in American history and
 contemporary issues series, ISSN 1069-5605)
   Includes bibliographical references (p.   ) and index.
   ISBN 0-313-29903-X (alk. paper)
   1. Gun control—United States—History—Sources. 2. Firearms—Law
 and legislation—United States—History—Sources. I. Bijlefeld,
 Marjolijn, 1960-   . II. Series.
 HV7436.G865   1997
 363.3'3'0973—dc21   96-53518

British Library Cataloguing in Publication Data is available.

Copyright © 1997 by Marjolijn Bijlefeld

All rights reserved. No portion of this book may be
reproduced, by any process or technique, without the
express written consent of the publisher.

Library of Congress Catalog Card Number: 96-53518
ISBN: 0-313-29903-X
ISSN: 1069-5605

First published in 1997

Greenwood Press, 88 Post Road West, Westport, CT 06881
An imprint of Greenwood Publishing Group, Inc.

Printed in the United States of America

The paper used in this book complies with the
Permanent Paper Standard issued by the National
Information Standards Organization (Z39.48–1984).

10 9 8 7 6 5 4 3 2 1

Copyright Acknowledgments

Amendment"; this material was originally published as an article, the full text of which appears at 62 *Tennessee Law Review* 443 (1995); this excerpt is reprinted by permission of the author and the Tennessee Law Review Association, Inc.

Document 47 is taken from Randy E. Barnett, Foreword: "Guns, Militias, and Oklahoma City"; this material was originally published as an article, the full text of which appears at 62 *Tennessee Law Review* 443 (1995); this excerpt is reprinted by permission of the author and the Tennessee Law Review Association, Inc.

Excerpts from Documents 51, 55, and 68 are taken from Richard Gardiner, "To Preserve Liberty—A Look at the Right to Keep and Bear Arms," *Northern Kentucky Law Review* 10, no. 1 (1982), and appear courtesy of *Northern Kentucky Law Review*.

Excerpts from Documents 56 and 69 are taken from Martin C. Ashman, "Handgun Control by Local Government," *Northern Kentucky Law Review* 10, no. 1 (1982), and appear courtesy of *Northern Kentucky Law Review*.

Excerpts from Documents 59 and 113 are taken from UNDER FIRE: THE NRA AND THE BATTLE FOR GUN CONTROL by Osha Gray Davidson. © 1993 by Osha Gray Davidson. Reprinted by permission of Henry Holt & Co., Inc.

Excerpts from Documents 60, 78, 83, 89, 99, 106, 110, 120, 151, 161, 174, and Appendix VI appear courtesy of the National Rifle Association of America.

Excerpts from Documents 61, 82, 129, 165, and 178 are from the book *Guns, Crime, and Freedom* by Wayne LaPierre. Copyright © 1994 by Regnery Publishing, Inc. All rights reserved. Reprinted by special permission of Regnery Publishing, Inc., Washington, D.C.

Excerpts from Document 62 are taken from Jack Anderson, *Inside the NRA: Armed and Dangerous, an Expose* (Beverly Hills, CA: Dove Books, 1996), and appear courtesy of Dove Books.

Excerpts from Documents 85 and 115 are taken from Clayton E. Cramer and David B. Kopel, " 'Shall Issue': The New Wave of Concealed Handgun Permit Laws"; this material was originally published as an article, the full text of which appears at 62 *Tennessee Law Review* 679 (1995); this excerpt is reprinted by permission of the Tennessee Law Review Association, Inc.

Excerpts from Document 86, taken from David McDowall, Colin Loftin, and Brian Wiersema, "Easing Concealed Firearms Laws: Effects on Homicide in Three States"; Document 94, taken from James B. Jacobs and Kimberly A. Potter, "Keeping Guns out of the 'Wrong' Hands: The Brady Law and the Limits of Regulation"; Document 95, taken from Philip J. Cook, Stephanie Molliconi and Thomas B. Cole, "Regulating Gun Markets"; Document 152, taken from Gary Kleck and Marc Gertz, "Armed Resistance to Crime: The Prevalence and Nature of Self-Defense with a Gun"; Document 153, taken from David Hemenway, Sara J. Solnick, and Deborah R. Azrael, "Firearms and Community Feelings of Safety"; Document 154, taken from Tom W. Smith and Robert J. Smith, "Changes in Firearms Ownership among Women, 1980–1994"; Document 186, taken from Alfred Blumstein, "Youth Violence, Guns, and the Illicit-Drug Industry"; and Document 187, taken from Beth Bjerregaard and Alan Lizotte, "Gun Ownership and Gang Membership," appear in *The Journal of Criminal Law and Criminology* 86, no. 1 (Fall 1995) and are reprinted courtesy of *The Journal of Criminal Law and Criminology*.

Excerpts from Document 87 are taken from David B. Kopel, "The Untold Triumph of Concealed-Carry Permits," *Policy Review*, no. 78 (July/August 1996), and are reprinted courtesy of David B. Kopel.

Excerpts from Document 88 are taken from John R. Lott, Jr., and David B. Mustard, "Crime, Deterrence, and Right-to-Carry Concealed Handguns," *Journal of Legal Studies* 26, no. 1 (January 1997), and are reprinted with permission of the *Journal of Legal Studies*; John R.

Excerpts from Document 125 are taken from Brandon S. Centerwall, "Homicide and the Prevalence of Handguns: Canada and the United States, 1976–1980," *American Journal of Epidemiology* 124 (December 1, 1991), and are reprinted with the permission of the *American Journal of Epidemiology* and Brandon S. Centerwall.

Excerpts from Document 127 are taken from Karl P. Adler, "Firearm Violence and Public Health: Limiting the Availability of Guns," *Journal of the American Medical Association* 271, no. 16 (April 27, 1994): 1281–1282, and are reprinted with permission of the *Journal of the American Medical Association*.

Excerpts from Document 130 are taken from Charles Marwick, "A Public Approach to Making Guns Safer," *Journal of the American Medical Association* 273, no. 22 (June 14, 1995): 1743–1744, and are reprinted with permission of the *Journal of the American Medical Association*.

Excerpts from Document 131 are taken from Daniel M. Sosin et al., "Trends in Death Associated with Traumatic Brain Injury," *Journal of the American Medical Association* 273, no. 22 (June 14, 1995): 1778–1780, and are reprinted with permission of the *Journal of the American Medical Association*.

Excerpts from Document 132 are taken from Kenneth W. Kizer et al., "Hospitalization Charges, Costs, and Income for Firearm-Related Injuries at a University Trauma Center," *Journal of the American Medical Association* 273, no. 22 (June 14, 1995): 1768–1773, and are reprinted with permission of the *Journal of the American Medical Association*.

Excerpts from Document 134 are taken from Stephen W. Hargarten et al., "Characteristics of Firearms Involved in Fatalities," *Journal of the American Medical Association* 275, no. 1 (January 3, 1996): 42–45, and are reprinted with permission of the *Journal of the American Medical Association*.

Excerpts from Document 135 are taken from Stephen P. Teret, "The Firearm Injury Reporting System Revisited," *Journal of the American Medical Association* 275, no. 1 (January 3, 1996): 70, and are reprinted with permission of the *Journal of the American Medical Association*.

Excerpts from Document 143 are taken from Garen J. Wintemute, Stephen P. Teret, Jess F. Kraus, and Mona W. Wright, "The Choice of Weapons in Firearms Suicides," *American Journal of Public Health* (July 1988), and reprinted with permission of the *American Journal of Public Health*.

Excerpts from Document 144 are adapted from HEALTH AFFAIRS, Frank Zimring, "Policy Research on Firearms and Violence," *Health Affairs* 12, no. 4 (Winter 1993): 114–115. Copyright 1993. The PEOPLE-TO-PEOPLE HEALTH FOUNDATION, INC., Project HOPE.

Excerpts from Document 147 are taken from James D. Wright, "Second Thoughts about Gun Control," *The Public Interest*, no. 91 (Spring 1988), and are reprinted with permission of *The Public Interest*.

Document 148 is excerpted with permission of Macmillan Reference USA, a Division of Simon & Schuster, from THE CITIZEN'S GUIDE TO GUN CONTROL by Franklin E. Zimring and Gordon Hawkins. Copyright © 1987 by Macmillan Publishing Company.

Excerpts from Document 149 are taken from Don B. Kates, Jr., "The Value of Civilian Arms Possession as Deterrent to Crime or Defense against Crime, *American Journal of Criminal Law* 18, no. 113 (1991), and are reprinted with permission of the *American Journal of Criminal Law*.

Excerpts from Document 155 are taken from Garen J. Wintemute, "The Relationship between Firearm Design and Firearm Violence: Handguns in the 1990s," *Journal of the American Medical Association* 275 (June 12, 1996): 1749–1753, and are reprinted with permission of the *Journal of the American Medical Association*.

Excerpts from Document 156 are taken from Arthur L. Kellerman et al., "Weapon Involvement in Home Invasion Crimes," *Journal of the American Medical Association* 273, no. 22 (June 14, 1995): 1759–1762, and are reprinted with permission of the *Journal of the American Medical Association*.

Excerpts from Document 163 are taken from "Assault Weapons as a Public Health Hazard in the United States," *Journal of the American Medical Association* 267, no. 22 (June 10, 1992): 3067–3070, and are reprinted with permission of the *Journal of the American Medical Association*.

Excerpts from Document 164 are taken from Edgar A. Suter, " 'Assault Weapons' Revisited—An Analysis of the AMA Report," *Journal of the Medical Association of Georgia* (May 1994), and are reprinted with permission of the *Journal of the Medical Association of Georgia*.

Excerpts from Document 177 are taken from John F. Harris, "Clinton Draws Bead on Dole's Assault Weapons Retreat," *Washington Post* (July 11, 1996). Copyright © 1996 The Washington Post. Reprinted with permission.

Excerpts from Document 197 are taken from Joan Biskupic, "High Court Plans Review of Brady Handgun Law," *Washington Post* (June 18, 1996). Copyright © 1996 The Washington Post. Reprinted with permission.

Excerpts from Document 199 are reprinted with the permission of the Educational Fund to End Handgun Violence.

Excerpts from Document 204 are taken from Joshua M. Horwitz, "*Kelly v. R.G. Industries:* A Cause of Action for Assault Weapons," 15 U. Dayton L. Rev 125–139 (1989), and are reprinted with the permission of the *University of Dayton Law Review*, William S. Hein and Co., Inc., and Joshua M. Horwitz.

Excerpts from Appendix V are taken from material produced by Handgun Control Inc., and are reprinted with permission of Handgun Control Inc.

Contents

Series Foreword

This series is designed to meet the research needs of high school and college students by making available in one volume the key primary documents on a given historical event or contemporary issue. Documents include speeches and letters, congressional testimony, Supreme Court and lower court decisions, government reports, biographical accounts, position papers, statutes, and news stories.

The purpose of the series is twofold: (1) to provide substantive and background material on an event or issue through the texts of pivotal primary documents that shaped policy or law, raised controversy, or influenced the course of events, and (2) to trace the controversial aspects of the event or issue through documents that represent a variety of viewpoints. Documents for each volume have been selected by a recognized specialist in that subject with the advice of a board of other subject specialists, school librarians, and teachers.

To place the subject in historical perspective, the volume editor has prepared an introductory overview and a chronology of events. Documents are organized either chronologically or topically. The documents are full text or, if unusually long, have been excerpted by the volume editor. To facilitate understanding, each document is accompanied by an explanatory introduction. Suggestions for further reading follow the document or the chapter.

It is the hope of Greenwood Press that this series will enable students and other readers to use primary documents more easily in their research, to exercise critical thinking skills by examining the key documents in American history and public policy, and to critique the variety of viewpoints represented by this selection of documents.

Introduction

What, exactly, is gun control and why is it a topic of so much debate? Gun control has many meanings, as can be seen by the approximately 20,000 gun laws on the books today. Some are tax and licensing laws; some control who is ineligible to buy a gun; and some are discharge laws, for example, that spell out where guns may not be fired. Some gun control goes even further and includes prohibitions on sales of certain kinds of guns or ammunition or bans on handgun sales in cities, such as Washington, D.C.

While the term "gun control" implies restriction, the debate is much like that immutable force of physics: For every action, there is an equal and opposite reaction. Today, those on opposite sides of the issue argue for seemingly opposite goals: One side might wish to see a law passed that makes it more difficult for individuals to purchase guns; the other might argue for laws that make it easier for gun owners to acquire permits to carry concealed weapons.

There are approximately 200 million privately owned firearms in this country, according to the federal Bureau of Alcohol, Tobacco and Firearms (BATF). For some people, owning a gun is simply a part of life, a tool for hunting or target shooting, or the chosen means of self-protection. For others, guns represent something more insidious—a tool to be feared—especially when they fall into the wrong hands.

Most people have some opinion on gun control, based on their upbringing and experiences. In fact, many people have quite strong opinions on whether the laws governing access to guns should be stricter or less so.

Noting that, it is not hard to see why there is little middle ground in the gun control debate. People advocating stricter laws are often categorized as those looking for an easy answer to the complex problems of crime. They are also seen as sympathetic to a system in which the government has greater control over what we do and say than ever before.

On the other hand, people who oppose gun laws are often viewed as a group willing to endanger the public so they can continue to enjoy their own pursuits. They are feared as advocates of vigilantism, even anarchy.

Those characterizations are stereotypical. Avid hunters can back waiting periods and background checks; some who want to see handgun sales limited may personally own shotguns or rifles.

Just as with any social and political issue, those who most often speak and are sought out to express their views are those from opposite ends of the spectrum. The middle ground view is muffled by the cries of those who have more at stake than a single piece of legislation. In our search for a quick answer, we want to know whether a waiting period, for example, is a good thing or a bad thing.

One aspect in the debate that remains tragically the same is the amount of gun violence in this country. But even here, the two sides in the gun control debate attribute this to different reasons.

One side says that we live in a violent society; guns are just the tools—just as knives and clubs might be—of criminals. The problem is not with guns, but with those who are reckless or wield them for unlawful purposes. The occasions where someone is killed or injured unintentionally are the unfortunate price society pays so that individuals can choose their own methods of self-protection. The answer, they say, is crime control, not gun control.

The other side argues that guns, particularly handguns, have an escalating effect on violence. Fights that might have been settled with a fist turn deadly when a gun is present. This side argues that further limitations on guns are needed to protect society. Restricting access to guns can positively impact the rate of intentional violence and significantly minimize the rate of unintentional injuries and death.

The crux of America's gun control debate is firmly rooted in the actions and words of our Founding Fathers more than 200 years ago. Nearly every discussion or debate on gun control focuses on, or at least touches upon, the meaning of the Second Amendment to the U.S. Constitution: "A well-regulated militia, being necessary to the security of a free state, the right of the people to keep and bear arms shall not be infringed." Even after all these years, judicial, scholarly, and political interpretation of that phrase differs.

The gun control debate obviously is not new, but it goes through cycles of popularity depending on the social and political climate. In the wake of high profile shootings, such as the 1968 assassinations of Martin Luther King, Jr., and Sen. Robert Kennedy, gun control took center stage in the public debate.

In the past decade, the gun control debate has increasingly gained attention—perhaps as high profile shootings keep it at the fore of people's minds. There seems to be a perception that violent crime is on the increase, even though statistics generally do not bear this out. However, for many people, perception is reality. Stories of drive-by shootings, innocent victims of gang warfare, and hot-tempered drivers in traffic jams likely fuel this feeling.

The gun control debate is always intermingled with a mix of passionate emotions, especially fear—fear of crime, fear of a society out of control, fear of excessive government regulation. Each side fervently believes it is right. That might explain why so many monikers are used to describe the two sides in the gun control debate. This volume will refer to them, whenever possible, simply as "gun control advocates" and "gun control opponents."

Part I

Historical Background

THE CONSTITUTION AND THE SECOND AMENDMENT

While the Founding Fathers of this country were developing the system of government, as set forth in the Constitution, many feared that a standing army controlled by a strong central government would leave them helpless. The federal Constitution contained no provisions to prohibit a standing army or allow states to create their own militias. The Constitution was signed by 39 men from the 12 states represented at the Constitutional Convention on September 17, 1787; three delegates refused to sign because of the absence of a bill of rights. Two years later, the First Congress agreed on 12 proposed amendments to the Constitution. During this time, debate focused on a standing army versus a state militia and citizens' rights, and even obligations, to carry arms.

Before addressing arms and the militia in the Bill of Rights, however, two militia clauses were included in the U.S. Constitution.

DOCUMENT 1: Militia Clauses of the U.S. Constitution

The Congress shall have Power . . .

To provide for calling forth the Militia to execute the Laws of the Union, suppress Insurrections and repel Invasions;

To provide for organizing, arming, and disciplining, the Militia, and for governing such Part of them as may be employed in the Service of the United States, reserving to the States respectively, the Appointment of the Officers, and the Authority of training the Militia according to the discipline prescribed by Congress.

Source: U.S. Constitution, Article I, section 8, clauses 15, 16.

One of the inspirations for including a right to bear arms clause came from the English Bill of Rights.

DOCUMENT 2: English Bill of Rights (1689)

That the subjects which are Protestants, may have arms for their defense suitable to their conditions, and as allowed by law.

Source: English Bill of Rights, enacted December 16, 1689.

The exact wording of the amendment here went through debate and various revisions before it was incorporated in the Bill of Rights. In his book, historian Edward Dumbauld listed the various amendments offered.

DOCUMENT 3: *The Bill of Rights*, Edward Dumbauld (1957)

Amendment offered in Congress by James Madison, June 8, 1789: The right of the people to keep and bear arms shall not be infringed; a well armed and well regulated militia being the best security of a free country: but no person religiously scrupulous of bearing arms shall be compelled to render military service in person.

Amendment reported by the Select Committee, July 28, 1789: A well regulated militia, composed of the body of the people, being the best security of a free State, the right of the people to keep and bear arms shall not be infringed, but no person religiously scrupulous shall be compelled to bear arms.

Amendment passed by the House of Representatives, August 24, 1789: A well regulated militia, composed of the body of the People, being the best security of a free State, the right of the People to keep and bear arms, shall not be infringed, but no one religiously scrupulous of bearing arms shall be compelled to render military service in person.

Source: Edward Dumbauld, *The Bill of Rights* (1957; reprint, Westport, Conn.: Greenwood Press, 1979), 206–22.

Other proposals were offered. For example, Samuel Adams proposed that the "constitution never be construed to authorize Congress to prevent the people of the United States, who are peaceable citizens, from keeping their own arms."

The version passed by the Senate on September 9, 1789, became the one proposed by Congress to the states for ratification. It is now the Second Amendment.

DOCUMENT 4: The Second Amendment

A well-regulated militia, being necessary to the security of a free state, the right of the people to keep and bear arms shall not be infringed.

Source: Bill of Rights.

At the end of 1791, Virginia became the 11th of 14 states to ratify the Bill of Rights, making it part of the Constitution. A sampling of the debates that ensued during these years follows.

Much of the friction during the framing of the Constitution and the Bill of Rights was between the Federalists and Anti-Federalists. Federalists favored a strong and active central government. Although Federalists later became a political party, in the early years, federalism was more of a concept. Early Federalists were those who advocated ratification of the Constitution. Key among them was Alexander Hamilton.

DOCUMENT 5: The Plan Presented by Alexander Hamilton (1787)

No state to have any forces land or naval—and the Militia of the states to be under the sole and exclusive direction of the United States the offices of which to be appointed and commissioned by them.

Source: The Plan Presented by Alexander Hamilton, June 18, 1787, as cited by Michael Kammen, ed., *The Origins of the American Constitution, A Documentary History* (New York: Penguin, 1986), 38.

Another Federalist was James Madison, an influential writer and law-yer from Virginia who went on to become president.

DOCUMENT 6: "The Alleged Danger from the Powers of the Union to the State Governments Considered," *Federalist* No. 45, James Madison (1788)

But if the Union, as has been shown, be essential to the security of the people of America against foreign danger; if it be essential to their se-curity against contentions and wars among the different States; if it be essential to guard them against those violent and oppressive factions which embitter the blessings of liberty, and against those military estab-lishments which must gradually poison its very fountain; if, in a word, the Union be essential to the happiness of the people of America, is it not preposterous, to urge as an objection to a government, without which the objects of the Union cannot be attained, that such a government may derogate from the importance of the governments of the individual States? Was, then, the American Revolution effected, was the American Confederacy formed, was the precious blood of thousands spilt, and the hard-earned substance of millions lavished, not that the people of Amer-ica should enjoy peace, liberty, and safety, but that the government of the individual States, that particular municipal establishments, might en-joy a certain extent of power, and be arrayed with certain dignities and attributes of sovereignty? We have heard of the impious doctrine in the Old World, that the people were made for kings, not kings for the peo-ple. Is the same doctrine to be revived in the New, in another shape that the solid happiness of the people is to be sacrificed to the views of po-litical institutions of a different form? It is too early for politicians to presume on our forgetting that the public good, the real welfare of the great body of the people, is the supreme object to be pursued; and that no form of government whatever has any other value than as it may be fitted for the attainment of this object. Were the plan of the convention adverse to the public happiness, my voice would be, Reject the plan. Were the Union itself inconsistent with the public happiness, it would be, Abolish the Union. In like manner, as far as the sovereignty of the States cannot be reconciled to the happiness of the people, the voice of every good citizen must be, Let the former be sacrificed to the latter.

Source: Federalist No. 45.

In the next essay, James Madison suggests that, even in the worst case scenario of tyrant after tyrant ruling the country, "it would not be going too far to say, that the State governments, with the people on their side, would be able to repel the danger."

DOCUMENT 7: "The Influence of the State and Federal Governments Compared from the New York Packet," *Federalist* No. 46, James Madison (1788)

[To a U.S. army of about 25,000 or 30,000 men] would be opposed a militia amounting to near half a million of citizens with arms in their hands, officered by men chosen from among themselves, fighting for their common liberties, and united and conducted by governments possessing their affections and confidence. It may well be doubted, whether a militia thus circumstanced could ever be conquered by such a proportion of regular troops. Those who are best acquainted with the last successful resistance of this country against the British arms, will be most inclined to deny the possibility of it. Besides the advantage of being armed, which the Americans possess over the people of almost every other nation, the existence of subordinate governments, to which the people are attached, and by which the militia officers are appointed, forms a barrier against the enterprises of ambition, more insurmountable than any which a simple government of any form can admit of. Notwithstanding the military establishments in the several kingdoms of Europe, which are carried as far as the public resources will bear, the governments are afraid to trust the people with arms. And it is not certain, that with this aid alone they would not be able to shake off their yokes. But were the people to possess the additional advantages of local governments chosen by themselves, who could collect the national will and direct the national force, and of officers appointed out of the militia, by these governments, and attached both to them and to the militia, it may be affirmed with the greatest assurance, that the throne of every tyranny in Europe would be speedily overturned in spite of the legions which surround it. Let us not insult the free and gallant citizens of America with the suspicion, that they would be less able to defend the rights of which they would be in actual possession, than the debased subjects of arbitrary power would be to rescue theirs from the hands of their oppressors. Let us rather no longer insult them with the supposition that they can ever reduce themselves to the necessity of making the experiment, by a blind and tame submission to the long train of insidious measures which must precede and produce it. The argument under the present head may be put into a very concise form, which appears altogether conclusive. Either the mode in which the federal government is to be constructed will render it sufficiently dependent on the people, or it will not.

Source: Federalist No. 46, Tuesday, 29 January 1788.

   Federalists found their philosophical and political sparring partners in the Anti-Federalists. This group opposed ratification of the Constitution and encouraged the creation of the Bill of Rights. It, too, had prominent and influential men at its helm, including Patrick Henry of Virginia, Elbridge Gerry of Massachusetts, and George Mason, a key author of the Virginia Declaration of Rights and state constitution. Gerry and Mason were delegates to the Constitutional Convention but refused to sign the document.
   Several writings appeared at the time in opposition to the Federalist Papers, including "Essays of Brutus." Historian and editor Michael Kammen notes leading scholars have most often attributed these Anti-Federalist writings to Robert Yates, an Albany, New York, lawyer.

DOCUMENT 8: Essay of Brutus (1787)

   A free republic will never keep a standing army to execute its laws. It must depend upon the support of its citizens. But when a government is to receive its support from the aid of the citizens, it must be so constructed as to have the confidence, respect and affection of the people. Men who, upon the call of the magistrate, offer themselves to execute the laws, are influenced to do it either by affection to the government, or from fear; where a standing army is at hand to punish offenders, every man is actuated by the latter principle, and therefore, when the magistrate calls, will obey: but where this is not the case, the government must rest for its support upon the confidence and respect which the people have for their government and laws.

Source: Essay of Brutus, 18 October 1787, as cited in Michael Kammen, ed., *The Origins of the American Constitution, A Documentary History* (New York: Penguin, 1986), 310–11.

DOCUMENT 9: Essay of Brutus (1787)

   In the bills of rights of the states it is declared, that a well regulated militia is the proper and natural defense of a free government—That as standing armies in time of peace are dangerous, they are not to be kept up, and that the military should be kept under strict subordination to, and controlled by the civil power.

The same security is as necessary in this constitution, and much more so; for the general government will have the sole power to raise and to pay armies, and are under no control in the exercise of it; yet nothing of this is to be found in this new system.

Source: Essay of Brutus, 1 November 1787, as cited in Michael Kammen, ed., *The Origins of the American Constitution, A Documentary History* (New York: Penguin, 1986), 316, 317.

In the 1789 debate in Congress on James Madison's proposed Bill of Rights, Elbridge Gerry, the Massachusetts Anti-Federalist, argued that a state militia was necessary: "to prevent the establishment of a standing army, the bane of liberty. . . . Whenever governments mean to invade the rights and liberties of the people, they always attempt to destroy the militia in order to raise an army upon their ruins."

The following entry was written by Noah Webster, an editor who advocated a strong central government.

DOCUMENT 10: "An Examination of the Leading Principles of the Federal Constitution," Noah Webster (1787)

Another source of power in government is a military force. But this, to be efficient, must be superior to any force that exists among the people, or which they can command; for otherwise, this force would be annihilated, on the first exercise of acts of oppression. Before a standing army can rule, the people must be disarmed; as they are in almost every kingdom in Europe. The supreme power in America cannot enforce unjust laws by the sword; because the whole body of the people are armed, and constitute a force superior to any band of regular troops that can be, on any pretense, raised in the United States. A military force, at the command of Congress, can execute no laws, but such as the people perceive to be just and constitutional, for they will possess the *power*, and jealousy will instantly inspire the *inclination*, to resist the execution of a law which appears to them unjust and oppressive.

Source: Noah Webster, "An Examination into the Leading Principles of the Federal Constitution," in *Pamphlets on the Constitution of the United States, Published during Its Discussion by the People, 1787–1788*, ed., P. Ford, 1888, 56.

The following entry was written by an Anti-Federalist senator from Virginia, one of the signers of the Declaration of Independence.

DOCUMENT 11: Richard Henry Lee (1788)

But, say gentlemen, the general militia are for the most part employed at home in their private concerns, cannot well be called out, or be depended upon; that we must have a select militia [essentially a National Guard] that is, as I understand it, particular corps or bodies of young men, and of men who have but little to do at home, particularly armed and disciplined in some measure, at the public expense, and always ready to take the field. These corps, not much unlike regular troops, will ever produce an inattention to the general militia; and the consequence has ever been, and always must be, that the substantial men, having families and property, will generally be without arms, without knowing the use of them, and defenseless; whereas, to preserve liberty, it is essential that the whole body of the people always possess arms, and be taught alike, especially when young, how to use them . . .

Source: R. Lee, *Additional Letters from the Federal Farmer* (1788).

DOCUMENT 12: Tench Coxe (1789)

As civil rulers, not having their duty to the people duly before them, may attempt to tyrannize, and as the military forces which must be occasionally raised to defend our country, might pervert their power to the injury of their fellow citizens, the people are confirmed by the next article in their right to keep and bear their private arms.

Source: Philadelphia Federal Gazette, 18 June 1789.

DOCUMENT 13: Roger Sherman (July 1789)

The militia shall be under the government of the laws of the respective States, when not in the actual Services of the United States, but such rules as may be prescribed by Congress for their uniform organization and discipline shall be observed in officering and training them, but military service shall not be required of persons religiously scrupulous of bearing arms.

Source: James Madison Papers.

The following entry reports the debate in the House of Representatives. The speakers cited are Rep. Elbridge Gerry, an Anti-Federalist from Massachusetts who refused to sign the Constitution and protested its ratification; Rep. Joshua Seney, a Maryland Federalist; Rep. James Jackson, a Federalist from Georgia; Rep. William Loughton Smith, a Federalist from South Carolina who had studied law in London during the American Revolution; Rep. Roger Sherman from Connecticut, an ardent supporter for ratification; Rep. John Vining, a Delaware Federalist; Rep. Michael Jenifer Stone of Maryland; and Rep. Egbert Benson, a New York Federalist.

DOCUMENT 14: Debates in House of Representatives (August 17, 1789)

The third clause of the fourth proposition in the report was taken into consideration, being as follows; "A well regulated militia, composed of the body of the people, being the best security of a free state; the right of the people to keep and bear arms shall not be infringed, but no person, religiously scrupulous, shall be compelled to bear arms."

Mr. Gerry

This declaration of rights, I take it, is intended to secure the people against the maladministration of the government; if we could suppose that in all cases the rights of the people would be attended to, the occasion for guards of this kind would be removed. Now I am apprehensive, sir, that this clause would give an opportunity to the people in power to destroy the constitution itself. They can declare who are those religiously scrupulous, and prevent them from bearing arms.

What, sir, is the use of a militia? It is to prevent the establishment of a standing army, the bane of liberty. Now it must be evident, that under this provision, together with their other powers, congress could take such measures with respect to a militia, as make a standing army necessary. Whenever government mean to invade the rights and liberties of the people, they always attempt to destroy the militia, in order to raise an army upon their ruins. This was actually done by Great Britain at the commencement of the late revolution. They used every means in their

power to prevent the establishment of an effective militia to the east-
ward. The assembly of Massachusetts, seeing the rapid progress that
administration were making, to divest them of their inherent privileges,
endeavored to counteract them by the organization of the militia, but
they were always defeated by the influence of the crown.

Mr. Seney

Wished to know what question there was before the committee, in
order to ascertain the point upon which the gentleman was speaking?

Mr. Gerry

Replied, that he meant to make a motion, as he disapproved of the
words as they stood. He then proceeded. No attempts that they made
were successful, until they engaged in the struggle which emancipated
them at once from their thralldom. Now, if we give a discretionary
power to exclude those from militia duty who have religious scruples,
we may as well make no provision on this head; for this reason he
wished the words to be altered so as to be confined to persons belonging
to a religious sect, scrupulous of bearing arms.

Mr. Jackson

Did not expect that all people of the United States would turn Quakers
or Moravians, consequently one part would have to defend the other, in
case of invasion; now this, in his opinion, was unjust, unless the constitution secured an equivalent, for this reason he moved to amend the
clause, by inserting at the end of it "upon paying an equivalent to be
established by law."

Mr. Smith

Enquired what were the words used by the conventions respecting
this amendment; if the gentleman would conform to what was proposed
by Virginia and Carolina, he would second him: He thought they were
to be excused provided they found a substitute.

Mr. Jackson

Was willing to accommodate; he thought the express was, "No one,
religiously scrupulous of bearing arms, shall be compelled to render military service in person, upon paying an equivalent."

Mr. Sherman

Conceived it difficult to modify the clause and make it better. It is
well-known that those who are religiously scrupulous of bearing arms,
are equally scrupulous of getting substitutes or paying an equivalent;
many of them would rather die than do either one or the other—but he
did not see an absolute necessity for a clause of this kind. We do not
live under an arbitrary government, said he, and the states respectively
will have the government of the militia, unless when called into actual

service; besides, it would not do to alter it so as to exclude the whole of any sect, because there are men amongst the Quakers who will turn out, notwithstanding the religious principles of the society, and defend the cause of their country. Certainly it will be improper to prevent the exercise of such favorable dispositions, at least whilst it is the practice of nations to determine their contests by the slaughter of their citizens and subjects.

Mr. Vining

Hoped the clause would be suffered to remain as it stood, because he saw no use in it if it was amended so as to compel a man to find a substitute, which, with respect to the government, was the same as if the person himself turned out to fight.

Mr. Stone

Enquired what the words "Religiously scrupulous" had reference to, was it of bearing arms? If it was, it ought so to be expressed.

Mr. Benson

Moved to have the words "But no person religiously scrupulous shall be compelled to bear arms" struck out. He would always leave it to the benevolence of the legislature—for, modify it, said he, as you please, it will be impossible to express it in such a manner as to clear it from ambiguity. No man can claim this indulgence of right. It may be a religious persuasion, but it is no natural right, and therefore ought to be left to the discretion of the government. If this stands part of the constitution, it will be a question before the judiciary, on every regulation you make with respect to the organization of the militia, whether it comports with this declaration or not? It is extremely injudicious to intermix matters of doubt with fundamentals.

I have no reason to believe but the legislature will always possess humanity enough to indulge this class of citizens in a matter they are so desirous of, but they ought to be left to their discretion.

The motion for striking out the whole clause being seconded, was put, and decided in the negative, 22 members voting for it, and 24 against it.

Mr. Gerry

Objected to the first part of the clause, on account of the uncertainty with which it is expressed: A well regulated militia being the best security of a free state, admitted an idea that a standing army was a secondary one. It ought to read "a well regulated militia, trained to arms," in which case it would become the duty of the government to provide this security, and furnish a greater certainty of its being done.

Source: The Congressional Register, 17 August 1789, as cited in *Creating the Bill of Rights: The Documentary Record from the First Federal Congress*, ed. Helen E. Veit,

Kenneth R. Bowling, and Charlene Bangs Bickford (Baltimore: Johns Hopkins University Press, 1991), 182–84.

Some scholars argue that the "militia" is the people—those armed private citizens called together when circumstances dictate. Indeed, much has been written about the scrappy fighters whose dedication to the goal helped secure victory. But that view was not universally held.

For example, George Washington wrote a letter to the president of the Congress just before the enlisted soldiers' terms were about to expire (all at the same time) encouraging Congress to offer more pay and greater benefits. Aside from fearing wholesale desertion of his army, he also worried about the capability of the militia men and the jealousy they invoked by flaunting rules—for which soldiers would be punished.

DOCUMENT 15: Letter of George Washington to the President of Congress (September 24, 1776)

To place any dependence upon Militia, is, assuredly, resting upon a broken staff. Men just dragged from the tender scenes of domestic life; unaccustomed to the din of arms; totally unacquainted with every kind of military skill, which being followed by a want of confidence in themselves, when opposed to troops regularly trained, disciplined, and appointed, superior in knowledge, and superior in arms, makes them timid and ready to fly from their own shadows. Besides, the sudden change in their manner of living, (particularly in the lodging) brings on sickness in many; impatience in all, and such an unconquerable desire of returning to their respective homes that it not only produces shameful, and scandalous desertions among themselves, but infuses the like spirit in others . . .

These . . . are but a small part of the inconveniences which might be enumerated and attributed to militia; but there is one that merits particular attention, and that is the expense. Certain I am, that it would be cheaper to keep 50,000 or 100,000 men in constant pay than to depend upon half the number, and supply the other half occasionally by militia . . .

The jealousies of a standing army, and the evils to be apprehended from one, are remote; and in my judgment, situated and circumstanced as we are, not at all to be dreaded; but the consequence of wanting one, according to my ideas, formed from the present view of things, is certain, and inevitable ruin; for if I was called upon to declare upon oath, whether the militia have been most serviceable or hurtful upon the whole; I should subscribe to the latter.

Source: Writings of Washington, Letter of 24 September 1776, vol. 6 (Washington, D.C.: U.S. Government Printing Office, June 1932).

In her 1994 book, *To Keep and Bear Arms,* historian Joyce Lee Malcolm concluded that there was no question that the amendment was intended as an individual right. The following entry is just one of those she uses to support that view. William Rawle was George Washington's candidate for the nation's first attorney general.

DOCUMENT 16: William Rawle (1829)

No clause in the constitution could by any rule of construction be conceived to give congress a power to disarm the people. Such a flagitous attempt could only be made under some general pretense by a state legislature. But if in any blind pursuit of inordinate power, either should attempt it, this amendment may be appealed to as a restraint on both.

Source: William Rawle, *A View of the Constitution of the United States of America,* 2d ed. (Philadelphia, 1829).

DOCUMENT 17: "Commentaries on the Constitution of the United States," Justice Joseph Story (1833)

The right of the citizens to keep and bear arms has justly been considered as the palladium of the liberties of a republic; since it offers a strong moral check against the usurpation and arbitrary power of rulers; and will generally, even if these are successful in the first instance, enable the people to resist and triumph over them.

And yet, though this truth would seem so clear, and the importance of a well regulated militia would seem so undeniable, it cannot be disguised that, among the American people, there is a growing indifference to any system of militia discipline, and a strong disposition, from a sense of its burdens, to be rid of all regulations. How it is practicable to keep the people duly armed, without some organization, it is difficult to see. There is certainly no small danger that indifference may lead to disgust, and disgust to contempt; and thus gradually undermine all the protection intended by this clause.

Source: Joseph Story, "Commentaries on the Constitution of the United States," 1833, as cited in *The Founders' Constitution*, ed. P. Kurland and R. Lerner, 1987, 677, 678.

By its very design, the U.S. Constitution was never intended to be the sole document spelling out all laws for the new country. For flexibility's sake, it was designed as a framework from which government would create new and adapt existing laws. So in the two centuries following the framing of the Constitution, legal scholars and politicians have focused on the limitations and rights set out by the Second Amendment. The following entry was written by Judge Thomas Cooley.

DOCUMENT 18: "General Principles of Constitutional Law in the United States of America," Judge Thomas Cooley (1898)

It may be supposed from the phraseology of this provision that the right to keep and bear arms was only guaranteed to the militia; but this would be an interpretation not warranted by the intent. The militia, as has been elsewhere explained, consists of those persons who, under the law, are liable to the performance of military duty, and are officered and enrolled for service when called upon. But the law may make provision for the enrollment of all who are fit to perform military duty for a small number only, or it may wholly omit to make any provision at all, and if the right were limited to those enrolled, the purpose of this guaranty might be defeated altogether by the action or neglect to act of the government it was meant to hold in check. The meaning of the provision undoubtedly is, that the people, from whom the militia must be taken, shall have the right to keep and bear arms, and they need no permission or regulation of law for that purpose. But this enables the government to have a well-regulated militia; for to bear arms implies something more than the mere keeping; it implies the learning to handle and use them in a way that makes those who keep them ready for their efficient use; in other words, it implies a right to meet for voluntary discipline in arms, observing in doing so the laws of public order.

Source: "General Principles of Constitutional Law in the United States of America," *The Founders Constitution*, 3rd ed. (Chicago: University of Chicago Press), 298–99.

STATE DECLARATIONS OF RIGHTS

States in the new nation retained much of their sovereignty. In drafting their own constitutions and bills of rights during the American Revolution, many states' leaders included language on the right to keep and bear arms. A few examples follow. A full listing can be found in Appendix I.

DOCUMENT 19: Virginia Declaration as Proposed by Thomas Jefferson

No freeman shall ever be debarred the use of arms.

Source: Papers of Thomas Jefferson, vol. 1, 344.

This was not the language chosen for the Virginia statute. Selected instead was wording written by George Mason.

DOCUMENT 20: Virginia Declaration of Rights (June 12, 1776)

That a well regulated militia, composed of the body of the people, trained to arms, is the proper, natural and safe defense of a free state; that standing armies, in time of peace, should be avoided, as dangerous to liberty; and that in all cases the military should be under strict subordination to, and governed by, the civil power.

Source: Virginia Constitution, Article I, section 13.

DOCUMENT 21: Pennsylvania Declaration of Rights (1776)

That the people have a right to bear arms for the defense of themselves and the state; and as standing armies in the time of peace are dangerous to liberty, they ought not to be kept up; and that the military should be kept under strict subordination to, and governed by, the civil power.

Source: Pennsylvania Constitution, Article I, section 21.

DOCUMENT 22: North Carolina Declaration of Rights (1776)

That the people have a right to bear arms, for the defense of the State; and as standing armies, in time of peace, are dangerous to liberty, they ought not to be kept up; and that the military should be under strict subordination to, and governed by, the civil power.

Source: North Carolina Constitution, Article I, section 30.

DOCUMENT 23: Massachusetts Declaration of Rights (1780)

The people have a right to keep and to bear arms for the common defense.

Source: Massachusetts Declaration of Rights, Part I, Article XVII.

ADDITIONAL READING

Atherton, Herbert M., and J. Jackson Barlow. *1791–1991: The Bill of Rights and Beyond*. Washington, D.C.: Commission on the Bicentennial of the United States Constitution, 1991.

Cottrol, Robert J., ed. *Gun Control and the Constitution. Sources and Explorations on the Second Amendment*. New York: Garland Publishing Inc., 1994.

Cramer, Clayton E. *For the Defense of Themselves and the State: The Original Intent and Judicial Interpretation of the Right to Keep and Bear Arms*. Westport, Conn.: Praeger Publishers, 1994.

Kammen, Michael, ed. *The Origins of the American Constitution, a Documentary History*. New York: Viking Penguin, 1986.

Malcolm, Joyce Lee. *To Keep and Bear Arms: The Origins of an Anglo-American Right*. Cambridge: Harvard University Press, 1994.

Northern Kentucky Law Review 10, no. 1 (1982).

U.S. Senate. *The Right to Keep and Bear Arms*. Report of the Subcommittee on the Constitution of the Committee on the Judiciary. Washington, D.C.: February 1982.

Veit, Helen E., Kenneth R. Bowling, and Charlene Bangs Bickford, eds. *Creating the Bill of Rights: The Documentary Record from the First Federal Congress*. Baltimore: Johns Hopkins University Press, 1991.

Part II

Modern Views on the Second Amendment

Times have certainly changed since the late 18th century when the wording and intent of the Constitution and Bill of Rights were being considered. Yet scholars, politicians, and the public continue to debate the Second Amendment. At issue is the question of whether the framers of the Constitution intended the amendment as a collective right or an individual right. Gun control advocates argue that the right is a collective one provided to a well-regulated militia, such as the National Guard. Gun rights advocates maintain the right is granted to individuals, not just to organized and/or state-sanctioned militias.

American society today is so different from what the Founding Fathers could have imagined. While most Americans do not fear our government will use its army to ensure absolute, tyrannical power, there are factions that firmly believe they must maintain their weapons to protect themselves in case of such an event. One group that watches developments in the new militia is the Militia Watchdog. On its World Wide Web home page, it notes:

The militia movement arose in the 1990s as a reaction to a perception among the radical right that a corrupt federal government had begun or would soon begin to confiscate the weapons of free-thinking American patriots. The incompetence and malfeasance of government agents at Ruby Ridge in 1992 and Waco in 1993 became rallying cries for the nascent movement; the Brady Law and the assault weapons ban added much fuel to the fire.

The bombing of the federal building in Oklahoma City in 1995 focused attention on these militia groups—and also generated publicity for them. The Militia Watchdog notes that by the summer of 1996, some form of militia group had formed in every state.

Finally, whereas arms in the late 1700s were viewed as essential tools for hunting and defense, our forefathers could not have envisioned modern life or the number of intentional and unintentional killings and woundings in which firearms play a part.

A focus of much of the debate centers on the first half of the amendment, "A well-regulated militia, being necessary to the security of a free state . . ." Is the right to bear arms interconnected with the militia? What exactly does "well-regulated" mean: for example, does it mean regulated by the state or well drilled?

The following documents are a sampling of recent scholarly opinions on the meaning of the Second Amendment.

DOCUMENT 24: *E. Adams v. Williams* (1972)

A powerful lobby dins into the ears of our citizenry that these gun purchases are constitutional rights protected by the Second Amendment. . . . There is under our decisions no reason why stiff state laws governing the purchase and possession of pistols may not be enacted. There is no reason why pistols may not be barred from anyone with a police record. There is no reason why a state may not require a purchaser of a pistol to pass a psychiatric test. There is no reason why all pistols should not be barred to everyone except the police.

Source: E. Adams v. Williams, 407 U.S. 143, 92 S. Ct. 1921, 322 Ed. 612.

DOCUMENT 25: "Standing Armies and Armed Citizens: An Historical Analysis of the Second Amendment," Roy G. Weatherup, J.D. (1975)

In the last angry decades of the twentieth century, members of rifle clubs, paramilitary groups and other misguided patriots continue to oppose legislative control of handguns and rifles. These ideological heirs of the vigilantes of the bygone western frontier era still maintain that the Second Amendment guarantees them a personal right to "keep and bear arms." But the annals of the Second Amendment attest to the fact that its adoption was the result of a political struggle to restrict the power of the national government and to prevent the disarmament of state militias. Not unlike their English forbears [sic], the American revolutionaries had a deep fear of centralized executive power, particularly when standing armies were at its disposal. The Second Amendment was adopted to prevent the arbitrary use of force by the national government against the states and the individual.

Delegates to the Constitutional Convention had no intention of establishing any personal right to keep and bear arms. Therefore the "individualist" view of the Second Amendment must be rejected in favor of the "collectivist" interpretation, which is supported by history and a handful of Supreme Court decisions on the issue . . .

The contemporary meaning of the Second Amendment is the same as it was at the time of its adoption. The federal government may regulate the National Guard, but may not disarm it against the will of state legislatures. Nothing in the Second Amendment, however, precludes Congress or the states from requiring licensing and restriction of firearms; in fact, there is nothing to stop an outright congressional ban on private ownership of all handguns and all rifles.

Source: Hastings Constitutional Law Quarterly 2 (Fall 1975): 1000–1001.

DOCUMENT 26: Statement of the Association of the Bar of the City of New York (1982)

A constitutional provision concerning the right to "bear Arms" is directed at checking power. The question is what the framers of the Constitution intended. There are basically three relationships which could have been intended to be affected: (1) the individual against the world; (2) the populace against the government, whether state or federal; and (3) the state government against the federal government. The first possibility, that the framers were concerned with the right of individuals to protect their homes and their persons from whatever depredations might confront them, appears to be without historical support.

Some have argued that the militia was regarded as the populace at large—or at least those members of the populace capable of bearing arms. To these commentators, militia meant the "unorganized militia," so that the Second Amendment must be read as permitting the populace to maintain arms as a check against excesses of any or all government. . . . Whatever the merits of the "unorganized militia" analysis may be, however, it has never found judicial favor.

The federal courts have long regarded the Second Amendment as concerned only with the "organized militia" maintained by the states.

Source: Committee on Federal Legislation, the Association of the Bar of the City of New York, in *The Right To Keep and Bear Arms*, Report of the Subcommittee on the Constitution of the Committee on the Judiciary, U.S. Senate. Washington, D.C.: Government Printing Office, February 1982.

This point, too, is one of contention. Among those saying that an understanding of English history is integral to understanding the development of the U.S. provision on bearing arms is Professor Joyce Lee Malcolm. She is the author of a book and several law review articles on this topic.

DOCUMENT 27: "The Right of the People to Keep and Bear Arms: The Common Law Tradition," Joyce Lee Malcolm (1983)

The right of Englishmen to have arms was a very real and an individual right. For all able-bodied men there was also the civic duty to bear arms in the militia. The twin concepts of a people armed and a people trained to arms were linked, but not inseparably.

If one applies English rights and practice to the construction of the Second Amendment to the United States Constitution, it is clear that the Amendment's first clause is an amplifying rather than a qualifying clause, and that a general rather than a select militia was intended. In fact, every American colony formed a militia that, like its English model, comprised all able-bodied male citizens. This continued to be the practice when the young republic passed its first uniform militia act under its new constitution in 1792. Such a militia implied people armed and trained to arms.

The Second Amendment should properly be read to extend to every citizen the right to have arms for personal defense. This right was a legacy of the English, whose right to have arms was, at base, as much a personal right as a collective duty. It is significant that the American right to keep arms was unfettered, unlike the English right, which was limited in various ways throughout its development.

Thus, in guaranteeing the individual right to keep and bear arms, and the collective right to maintain a general militia, the Second Amendment amplified the tradition of the English Bill of Rights for the purpose of preserving and protecting government by and for the people.

Source: Hastings Constitutional Law Quarterly 10, no. 285 (Winter 1983): 313–14.

In testimony before a congressional committee in April 1995, Professor Malcolm told U.S. Rep. John Conyers that there is plenty of historical support that the framers were, indeed, concerned about the right of individuals to protect themselves. She said, "It is very hard, sir, to find a historian who now believes that it is only a collective right. That as it has become more thoroughly researched, there is a general consensus that in fact it is an individual right. That's why this is so lopsided. There is no one for me to argue against anymore."

However, the arguments do continue.

DOCUMENT 28: "To Keep and Bear Their Private Arms: The Adoption of the Second Amendment 1787–1791," Stephen P. Halbrook, Ph.D., J.D. (1982)

In recent years it has been suggested that the Second Amendment protects the "collective" right of states to maintain militias, but not the right of "the people" to keep and bear arms. If anyone entertained this notion in the period in which the Constitution and Bill of Rights were debated and ratified, it remains one of the most closely guarded secrets of the eighteenth century, for no known surviving writing of the 1787–1791 period states that thesis. Instead, "the people" in the Second Amendment meant the same as it did in the first, fourth, ninth and tenth amendments, i.e., each and every free person. A select militia as the only privileged class entitled to keep and bear arms was considered an execrative to a free society as would be select spokesmen approved by government and the only class entitled to freedom of the press. Nor were those who adopted the Bill of Rights willing to clutter it with details such as nonpolitical justifications for the right (e.g., self-protection and hunting) or a list of what everyone knew to be common arms, such as muskets, scatterguns, pistols and swords. In light of contemporary developments, perhaps the most striking insight made by those who originally opposed the attempt to summarize all the rights of a freeman in a bill of rights was that, no matter how it was worded, artful misconstruction would be employed to limit and destroy the very rights sought to be protected.

Source: Northern Kentucky Law Review 10, no. 1 (1982).

DOCUMENT 29: "The Ideological Origins of the Second Amendment," Robert E. Shalhope (1982)

Whether the armed citizen is relevant to late–twentieth-century American life is something that only the American people—through the Supreme Court, their state legislatures, and Congress—can decide. Those who advocate some measure of gun control are not without powerful arguments to advance on behalf of their position. The appalling and unforeseen destructive capability of modern weapons, the dissolving of the connection between an armed citizenry and the agrarian setting that figured so importantly . . . , the distinction between the right to keep arms and such measures as "registration," the general recognition of the responsibility of succeeding generations to modify the constitutional inheritance to meet new conditions—all will be serviceable in the ongoing debate. But advocates of the control of firearms should not argue that the Second Amendment did not intend for Americans of the late eighteenth century to possess arms for their own personal defense, for the defense of their states and their nation, and for the purpose of keeping their rulers sensitive to the rights of the people.

Source: The Journal of American History 69 (1982): 613–14.

DOCUMENT 30: "State Firearms Regulation and the Second Amendment," Warren Spannaus, J.D., Attorney General for the State of Minnesota from 1971 to 1983 (July 1983)

The federal government is obliged by many provisions of the Constitution to respect the basic rights of man. Some civil limitations were imposed on the government in the original document. . . . However, the greatest limitations preventing the federal government from intruding into personal rights were added in 1791, with the ratification of the first ten amendments, the Bill of Rights. By those amendments the basic rights of conscience, the fundamental guarantees of fair procedure for persons accused of crime, and the rights to private property are guaranteed to be protected from intrusion by the federal government.

However, none of the rights of personal freedom, conscience, or private property are absolute. For instance, while the constitutional guarantee of freedom of religion is extensive, it does not serve to protect acts judged to be morally wrong, such as polygamous marriages. Similarly, the freedom of speech which is often defended by the courts does not extend to the seditious utterances of a conspiracy . . .

Conflicting interests or parties are likely to place different interpretation on particular provisions of the Constitution. Accordingly, the United States Supreme Court is the authoritative interpreter of the Constitution, as well as of the intentions of its authors. The federal courts, and ultimately the Supreme Court as final expositor of the United States Constitution, mark the boundaries of authority between state and nation, state and state, and government and its citizens . . .

Source: Hamline Law Review 6 (July 1983): 383–90.

One of the authors of the following document, Dennis A. Henigan, is director of the Legal Action Project of Handgun Control, Inc.

DOCUMENT 31: "The Second Amendment in the Twentieth Century: Have You Seen Your Militia Lately?" Keith A. Ehrman and Dennis A. Henigan (1989)

The key developments in the history of the militia have been: the arming of the militias by the federal government; the split between an organized and unorganized militia; the passage of the militias from state authority to largely federal authority; and the rise of the army as the main defense force in the country. What effect have these changes had on the Second Amendment's current status?

The Second Amendment was ratified to ensure each state's ability to maintain an effective militia and to arm its militia if the federal government failed to do so. Thus, the right of an individual to possess a firearm is protected by the Second Amendment only if the individual's possession of the firearm is necessary to ensure a viable state militia.

. . . The federal government is responsible for arming and equipping the present day state militia, the National Guard. No state still requires its citizens to supply weapons for its militia. Consequently, possession of a weapon by an individual no longer bears any relationship to an effective militia. So long as privately owned firearms are not needed to supply the militia, and the National Guard remains armed by the federal government, the guarantee encompassed in the Second Amendment imposes no restrictions on federal legislations seeking to regulate ownership or possession of arms by individuals.

Some . . . commentators claim that the National Guard cannot be the independent state militia contemplated in 1789. Those militias were to be tools largely of the states, ready to fight the federal government. Today, the federal government has ultimate authority and control over the militia. Still other pro-gun commentators urge that the militia is important only in its "idealized" form of common citizens having arms. Without unrestricted access to guns, there is no possibility of an anonymous armed citizenry able to rise against a tyrannical government. These commentators all conclude that the present-day organized militia is not sufficient to guarantee the security of the people, as was intended by the Second Amendment. The underlying premise of this viewpoint is that citizens should be allowed to keep weapons in order to exercise the "right" to overthrow an oppressive government.

A major problem with these arguments is that they assume the Second Amendment drafters viewed the militia as an anonymous "armed citizenry at large," rather than as some form of state-organized, state-trained unit. But the Second Amendment was not designed to ensure that every citizen would have weapons. The Second Amendment was designed to assure the states and citizens that they could maintain effective state militias. However, the states and citizens demonstrated during the 1800s that they did not want to exercise this prerogative.

Even if the present-day National Guard is not the exact equivalent of the colonial militia, this is so simply because of the passage of time. The militia of the 1700s no longer exists. In the late eighteenth and early nineteenth centuries, the Second Amendment might well have prevented the federal government from passing extensive legislation affecting private ownerships of firearms. Such laws could have seriously impaired the effectiveness of the states to maintain their militias, given the statutes of the time and the poor manner in which the states armed their militias. Today, however, the state militias are well armed. So long as the federal government continues to provide arms, and so long as privately owned weapons are not needed for militia purposes, gun legislation should raise no constitutional problems.

Source: University of Dayton Law Review 15 (1989): 5–58.

DOCUMENT 32: "Federal and State Constitutional Guarantees to Arms," *University of Dayton Law Review Report* (1989)

The Second Amendment should be interpreted according to well-established rules governing interpretation of constitutional guarantees when determining if a particular statute is unconstitutional. Reasonable time, place, and manner restrictions may be imposed on the exercise of fundamental rights, provided the restrictions are narrowly tailored. Courts must balance the justification put forward by the state against the character and magnitude of the asserted injury to the constitutionally protected right. . . .

The bearing of arms in a public place is different from the keeping of arms in the home on account of the home's special zone of privacy. Reasonable time, place, and manner regulations may be placed on bearing arms in a public place. For example, people may be prevented from bringing arms into court. However, the peaceful bearing of arms in a motor vehicle or on a street could not be prohibited. A constitutional right may not be curtailed simply because some people find its exercise disagreeable or offensive.

The framing of the right to arms reveals an awareness of crime. Nevertheless, the guarantee promises that the right "shall not be infringed." The Framers also knew the obvious: certain persons have always been treated differently and do not enjoy the full array of rights. In accord with this understanding are decisions holding that a convicted felon may be prevented from voting or holding office in a union. The collateral consequences of a felony conviction go beyond deprivation of the right to keep and bear arms. . . . Nevertheless, while courts adhere to these well-known exceptions in construing other constitutional guarantees, the right to arms has often been treated with disfavor. The command that the people have a right to keep and bear arms is simply ignored. Courts simply look at the preamble or precatory language of the Second Amendment, ignore the rest of the language, and interpret it to guarantee the right of a state to have a military force. However, the right of a state to have and train military of constabulary forces does not depend on the Second Amendment right of the people to keep and bear arms . . .

The Second Amendment need not be rendered moribund because some courts have ignored its command and the political and social ideas that prevailed at the time of its framing. *Stare decisis* is a rule that has less power in constitutional cases. Courts are obligated to overrule erroneous precedent. Even a line of cases covering nearly a century has been branded as "an unconstitutional assumption of powers by courts of the United States which no lapse of time or respectable array of opinion should make us hesitate to correct." . . .

. . . The solid majority of gun owners are noncriminal, and their guns create no social problems. . . . Hence, fairness demands that gun owners not be used as scapegoats for society's shortcomings. Reliance on the state for protection is an illusory remedy. Neither the police nor the state has a duty to protect the individual citizen. The burden falls on the citizen to defend himself and his family. The Framers intended that the citizen be armed and not be left defenseless. An armed people also serve as a deterrent against crime.

Gun control laws have at least five political functions: (1) increase citizen reliance on government and tolerance of increased police powers and abuse; (2) facilitate repressive action by government; (3) help prevent opposition to government; (4) lessen pressure for major or radical reform; (5) allow selective enforcement against dissidents. In our imperfect world the servants of the state have committed outrages. Nevertheless, they are always exempted from gun laws designed to disarm the people. Crime, regardless of who commits it, "must be prevented by the penitentiary and gallows, and not by a general deprivation of a constitutional privilege."

Source: University of Dayton Law Review 15 (1989): 59–90.

DOCUMENT 33: "The Embarrassing Second Amendment," Sanford Levinson (1989)

No one has ever described the Constitution as a marvel of clarity, and the Second Amendment is perhaps one of the worst drafted of all its provisions. What is special about the Amendment is the inclusion of an opening clause—a preamble, if you will—that seems to set out its purpose. No similar clause is a part of any other Amendment, though that does not, of course, mean that we do not ascribe purposes to them . . .

A standard move of those legal analysts who wish to limit the Second Amendment's force is to focus on its "preamble" as setting out a restrictive purpose. . . . This purposive reading quickly disposes of any notion that there is an "individual" right to keep and bear arms. The right, if such it be, is only a state's right. The consequence of this reading is obvious: the national government has the power to regulate—to the point of prohibition—private ownership of guns, since that has, by stipulation, nothing to do with preserving state militias . . .

This is not a wholly implausible reading, but one might ask why the Framers did not simply say something like "congress shall have no power to prohibit state-organized and directed militias." Perhaps they in fact meant to do something else . . .

I, for one, have been persuaded that the term "militia" did not have the limited reference that . . . many modern legal analysts assign to it. There is strong evidence that "militia" refers to all of the people, or at least all of those treated as full citizens of the community. Consider, for example, the question asked by George Mason, one of the Virginians who refused to sign the Constitution because of its lack of a Bill of Rights: "Who are the Militia? They consist now of the whole people." . . .

The standard argument in favor of strict control and, ultimately, prohibition of private ownership focuses on the extensive social costs of widespread distribution of firearms. . . . It is hard to disagree . . . ; it appears almost crazy to protect as a constitutional right something that so clearly results in extraordinary social costs with little, if any, compensating social advantage . . .

. . . And yet . . .

Circumstances may well have changed in regard to individual defense, although we ignore at our political peril the good-faith belief of many Americans that they cannot rely on the police for protection against a variety of criminals. . . .

. . . what it means to take rights seriously is that one will honor them even when there is significant social cost in doing so. If protecting freedom of speech, the rights of criminals defendants, or any other part of the Bill of Rights were always (or even most of the time) clearly costless to the society as a whole, it would truly be impossible to understand why they would be as controversial as they are. The very fact that there are often significant costs—criminals going free, oppressed groups having to hear viciously racist speech and so on—helps to account for the observed fact that those who view themselves as defenders of the Bill of Rights are generally antagonist[ic] to prudential arguments. Most often, one find[s] them embracing version[s] of textual, historical, or doctrinal argument that dismiss as almost crass and vulgar any insistence that times might have changed [and] made too "expensive" the continued adherence to a given view. "Cost-benefit" analysis, rightly or wrongly, has come to be viewed as a "conservative" weapon to attack liberal rights. Yet one find[s] that the tables are strikingly turned when the Second Amendment comes into play. Here it is "conservatives" who argue in effect that social costs are irrelevant and "liberals" who argue for a notion of the "living Constitution" and "changed circumstances" that would have the practical consequence of removing any real bite from the Second Amendment . . .

For too long, most members of the legal academy have treated the Second Amendment as the equivalent of an embarrassing relative, whose mention brings a quick change of subject to other, more respectable, family members. That will no longer do. It is time for the Second Amendment to enter full scale into the consciousness of the legal academy.

Source: Yale Law Journal 99 (1989): 637–59.

DOCUMENT 34: "Encroachments of the Crown on the Liberty of the Subject: Pre-Revolutionary Origins of the Second Amendment?" Stephen P. Halbrook, J.D. (1989)

[H]istory demonstrates that, to the patriots who were interested in preserving civil liberty, the mere possibility in 1786 that the government would seize arms gave rise to a robust philosophical defense of what was considered a fundamental, personal right. When in 1774 the rulers of Boston dared even to consider disarming the inhabitants, thousands of armed citizens felt justified in assembling and marching to the town to demonstrate their opposition. The founders considered a ban on importation of firearms and ammunition to violate the individual's right to obtain and possess arms . . .

Unfortunately, scholars have never analyzed the "arbitrary encroachments of the Crown on the liberty of the subject" which gave rise to the second amendment, perhaps because that hidden history could conflict with the questionable premise that banning firearms would not infringe on individual rights. Prohibitionists assert that there is no evidence of a pre-Revolutionary American belief in a person's right to bear arms or of American protest against British infringement of this right.

To restate the postulate of social philosophers, the failure to select a topic for study, or consignment of the history of a concept to the Orwellian memory hole, implies a value judgment as well. When the concept subject to this treatment is a guarantee in the Bill of Rights, it remains to be seen whether the libertarian hopes of the Revolutionary Founding Fathers will be realized in the third century of the American body politic.

Source: University of Dayton Law Review 15 (1989): 91–124.

DOCUMENT 35: "The Right to Be Armed: A Constitutional Illusion," Dennis A. Henigan (December 1989)

The [National Rifle Association's] NRA's version of the "right to keep and bear arms" is, in short, nothing more than a constitutional illusion created by mass advertising to further a political objective. However strong this constitutional fantasy is in the minds of the NRA's leadership, and however potent a political tool it has been, it remains a mirage nonetheless, which disappears when approached by real judges faced with deciding the constitutionality of real laws . . .

Source: San Francisco Barrister (December 1989): 11–14.

DOCUMENT 36: "The Right to Bear Arms," Warren E. Burger, Chief Justice of the United States from 1969 to 1986 (January 14, 1990)*

That Second Amendment clause must be read as though the word "because" was the opening word of the guarantee. Today, of course, the

*Reprinted with permission from Parade, copyright © 1990.

"state militia" serves a very different purpose. A huge national defense establishment has taken over the role of the militia of 200 years ago.

Some have exploited these ancient concerns, blurring sporting guns—rifles, shotguns and even machine pistols—with all firearms, including what are now called "Saturday night specials." There is, of course, a great difference between sporting guns and handguns. Some regulation of handguns has long been accepted as imperative; laws relating to "concealed weapons" are common. That we may be "over-regulated" in some areas of life has never held us back from more regulation of automobiles, airplanes, motorboats and "concealed weapons."

Let's look at the history.

First, many of the 3.5 million people living in the 13 original Colonies depended on wild game for food, and a good many of them required firearms for their defense from marauding Indians—and later from the French and English. Underlying all these needs was an important concept that each able-bodied man in each of the 13 independent states had to help or defend his state.

The early opposition to the idea of national or standing armies was maintained under the Articles of Confederation; that confederation had no standing army and wanted none. The state militia—essentially a part-time citizen army, as in Switzerland today—was the only kind of "army" they wanted. From the time of the Declaration of Independence through the victory at Yorktown in 1781, George Washington, as the commander-in-chief of these volunteer militia armies, had to depend upon the states to send those volunteers.

When a company of New Jersey militia volunteers reported for duty to Washington at Valley Forge, the men initially declined to take an oath to "the United States," maintaining, "Our country is New Jersey." Massachusetts Bay men, Virginians and others felt the same way. To the American of the 18th century, his state was his country, and his freedom was defended by his militia.

The victory at Yorktown—and the ratification of the Bill of Rights a decade later—did not change people's attitudes about a national army. They had lived for years under the notion that each state would maintain its own military establishment, and the seaboard states . . . their own navies as well. These people, and their fathers and grandfathers before them, remembered how monarchs had used standing armies to oppress their ancestors in Europe. Americans wanted no part of this. A state militia, like rifle and powder horn, was as much a part of life as the automobile is today; pistols were largely for officers, aristocrats—and dueling.

Against this background, it was not surprising that the provision concerning firearms emerged in very simple terms with the significant predicate—basing the right on the *necessity* for a "well regulated militia," a state army.

In the two centuries since then—with two world wars and some lesser ones—it has become clear, sadly, that we have no choice but to maintain a standing national army while still maintaining a "militia" by way of the National Guard, which can be swiftly integrated into the national defense forces.

Americans also have a right to defend their homes, and we need not challenge that. Nor does anyone seriously question that the Constitution protects the right of hunters to own and keep sporting guns for hunting game any more than anyone would challenge the right to own and keep fishing rods and other equipment for fishing—or to own automobiles. To "keep and bear arms" for hunting today is essentially a recreational activity and not an imperative of survival, as it was 200 years ago; "Saturday night specials" and machine guns are not recreational weapons and surely are as much in need of regulation as motor vehicles.

Americans should ask themselves a few questions. The Constitution does not mention automobiles or motorboats, but the right to keep and own an automobile is beyond question; equally beyond question is the power of the state to regulate the purchase or the transfer of such a vehicle and the right to license the vehicle and the driver with reasonable standards. In some places, even a bicycle must be registered, as must some household dogs.

If we are to stop this mindless homicidal carnage, is it unreasonable:

1) to provide that, to acquire a firearm, an application be made reciting age, residence, employment and any prior criminal convictions?

2) to require that this application lie on the table for 10 days (absent a showing for urgent need) before the license would be issued?

3) that the transfer of a firearm be made essentially as with that of a motor vehicle?

4) to have a "ballistic fingerprint" of the firearm made by the manufacturer and filed with the license record so that, if a bullet is found in a victim's body, law enforcement might be helped in finding the culprit?

These are the kind of questions the American people must answer if we are to preserve the "domestic tranquility" promised in the Constitution.

Source: Parade Magazine, 14 January 1990.

In the following entry, two attorneys present the view that there is a racial element to the discussion of the Second Amendment.

DOCUMENT 37: "The Second Amendment: Toward an Afro-Americanist Reconsideration," Robert J. Cottrol, J.D., and Raymond T. Diamond, J.D. (1991)

Throughout American history, black and white Americans have had radically different experiences with respect to violence and state protection. Perhaps another reason the Second Amendment has not been taken very seriously by the courts and the academy is that for many of those who shape or critique constitutional policy, the state's power and inclination to protect them is a given. But for all too many black Americans, that protection historically has not been available. Nor, for many, is it readily available today. If in the past the state refused to protect black people from the horrors of white lynch mobs, today the state seems powerless in the face of the tragic black-on-black violence that plagues the mean streets of our inner cities, and at times seems blind to instances of unnecessary police brutality visited upon minority populations . . .

The history of blacks, firearms regulations, and the right to bear arms should cause us to ask new questions regarding the Second Amendment. These questions will pose problems both for advocates of stricter gun controls and for those who argue against them. Much of the contemporary crime that concerns Americans is in poor black neighborhoods and a case can be made that greater firearms restrictions might alleviate this tragedy. But another, perhaps stronger case can be made that a society with a dismal record of protecting a people has a dubious claim on the right to disarm them. Perhaps a reexamination of this history can lead us to a modern realization of what the framers of the Second Amendment understood: that it is unwise to place the means of protection totally in the hands of the state, and that self-defense is also a civil right.

Source: The Georgetown Law Journal 809, no. 2 (December 1991): 309–61.

Dennis A. Henigan, Handgun Control, Inc. attorney and director of the Legal Action Project at the Center to Prevent Handgun Violence, said that the debate at the time was not about whether individuals should be armed to fight the power of federal and state governments, but that the federal government had been given "excessive power over the military force which state governments relied upon for their security."

DOCUMENT 38: "Arms, Anarchy, and the Second Amendment," Dennis A. Henigan (1991)

Of particular interest on this issue are the debates in the Virginia ratification convention, both because this was the convention in which the
militia issue was most extensively discussed and because it no doubt
had a profound influence on the Virginian James Madison, who authored
the Second Amendment. The Virginia debate is replete with expressions
of fear that federal control over the militias would destroy them.

George Mason argued that the power given Congress to "organize,
arm and discipline" the militia would allow Congress to destroy the
militia by "rendering them useless—by disarming them . . . Congress
may neglect to provide for arming and disciplining the militia; and the
state governments cannot do it, for Congress has an exclusive right to
arm them . . ." Patrick Henry also was concerned about the arming of
the state militia. He stated that "necessary as it is to have arms, and
though our Assembly has, by a succession of laws for many years, endeavored to have the militia completely armed, it is still far from being
the case. When this power is given up to Congress . . . how will your
militia be armed?" Mason and Henry proposed that, "if Congress should
refuse to find arms for [the militia], this country may lay out their own
money to purchase them." Federalist James Madison countered this argument by maintaining that the Congressional power to arm the militia
was not exclusive, and thus Congress lacked the power to paralyze the
state militia. Similarly, John Marshall asked: "If Congress neglect our
militia, we can arm them ourselves. Cannot Virginia import arms? Cannot she put them into the hands of her militia-men?" Significantly, there
is not a word in the Virginia debates about the need to ensure that the
people are armed to ensure the potential for revolution against state or
federal governmental excesses.

These speakers took it for granted that the arming of the militia was
a governmental function; the issue being debated is the need to affirm
the states' concurrent power with the federal government to furnish arms
to the militia. It is difficult for the insurrectionist theory to account for
this debate at all. If the militia is simply the collection of citizens with
their own arms, why all the concern about whether the central government's power to arm the militia is exclusive, or rather concurrent with
the states' power? More fundamentally, if the function of the militia is
to check the excesses of state and federal government by ensuring the

potential for armed revolt by the people, how could the militia also be dependent on those same governments for its arms?

Source: Valparaiso University Law Review 26 (1991): 117, 118.

DOCUMENT 39: "The Right of the People or the Power of the State: Bearing Arms, Arming Militias, and the Second Amendment," Stephen P. Halbrook, J.D. (1991)

Every term in the Second Amendment's substantive guarantee—which is not negated by its philosophical declaration about a well regulated militia—demands an individual rights interpretation. The terms "right," "the people," "keep and bear," and "infringed" apply only to persons, not states. Moreover, the Framers, supporters, and opponents of the original Constitution all agreed on the political ideal of an armed populace, and the unanimous interpretation of the Bill of Rights in Congress and by the public was that the Second Amendment guaranteed the individual right to keep and bear arms. Indeed, the very amendment which would have made explicit the state power to maintain a militia failed completely. The language and historical intent of the Second Amendment mandate recognition of the individual right to keep and bear firearms and other personal weapons. Like those who oppose flag burning as symbolic protest, opponents of this right have the option of pressing for an amendment to a Bill of Rights no longer seen as worthwhile.

Source: Valparaiso University Law Review 26 (1991): 206–207.

DOCUMENT 40: "Civic Republicanism and the Citizen Militia: The Terrifying Second Amendment," David C. Williams (1991)

The republican framers of the Second Amendment were painfully aware that ultimate political power would lie with those who controlled the means of force. As a result, they sought to arm not a narrow slice of society that might seize the government for its own end, but rather all the citizens in a state, in the form of a universal militia, which would always act in the common good. In republican thinking, this militia had an ambiguous status. On the one hand, it was a creature of the state apparatus, inasmuch as the state gathered it, ensured it was universal, trained it in the use of arms, and mobilized it against foreign invasion or domestic insurrection. On the other hand, it was composed of all of the citizens, deriving its legitimacy from them and being virtually synonymous with them . . .

The right to arms belonged to all, but as a collective right, a right of the universal militia and not of separate private individuals. Republicans feared government and sought to give the people ways to resist it, but they also feared the self-interest that lurked in each individual's breast. They feared the militia less than either private persons or the government because they identified the militia with the body of the people—a rhetorical construct that by definition could not betray the common good because the common good was its good. That construct was utopian and artificial even at the time. Militia members had separate and different interests, and the militia never truly represented the whole body of the people. But as a regulative ideal, the concept of the militia offers a guide to interpreting the Second Amendment.

The Amendment expresses a hope that the means of force could be vested in those who would express universal good. But with the passage of two centuries, it has become increasingly difficult to identify such a body. We have no modern analogue of the universal militia. Private gun owners represent a partial interest, and so does the National Guard. By the same token, it has become increasingly difficult to identify a "common" interest among radically heterogeneous citizens . . .

Source: The Yale Law Journal 101 (1991): 551–615.

The last few entries have focused on different interpretations of the Second Amendment. Some scholars argue that the individual rights interpretation is so clear that it should be known as the "Standard Model." Opponents, like attorney Dennis Henigan who calls it the "insurrectionist theory," argue that such a reading could encourage anarchy. Law professor Glenn Harland Reynolds notes that the Tennessee Constitution contains an "explicit recognition of the right—and in fact the duty—of citizens to rebel against a tyrannical government."

DOCUMENT 41: Tennessee Constitution

That all power is inherent in the people and all free governments are founded on their authority, and instituted for their peace, safety, and happiness; for the advancement of those ends they have at all times an unalienable and indefeasible right to alter, reform, or abolish the government in such manner as they may think proper.

That government being instituted for the common benefit, the doctrine of non-resistance against arbitrary power and oppression is absurd, slavish and destructive of the good and happiness of mankind.

Source: Tennessee Constitution, Article I, sections 1 and 2.

Professor Reynolds, who wrote that the Standard Model is consistent with both the text of the Constitution and its historical framework, also noted that an individual's right to bear arms does not exclude restrictions.

DOCUMENT 42: "A Critical Guide to the Second Amendment," Glenn Harlan Reynolds (1995)

Discussion of the right to keep and bear arms seems to lead inevitably to questions of whether the existence of such a right necessitates the right to own, for instance, a howitzer or a nuclear weapon. Writers adhering to the Standard Model, which stresses fidelity to the purposes and history of the Second Amendment, have arrived at fairly convincing answers to such questions by drawing on those sources.

The right to keep and bear arms is no more absolute than, say, the right to free speech. Just as the demand "your money or your life" is not protected by the First Amendment, so the right to arms is not without limits. But the right to arms is no more undone by this fact than freedom of speech is undone by the fact that that right is not absolute either . . .

Because one purpose of the right is to allow individuals to form up into militia units at a moment's notice, the kinds of weapons protected are those in general military use, or those that, though designed for civilians, are substantially equivalent to those military weapons. Because another purpose is the defense of the home, Standard Model writers also import common law limitations on the right to arms, as they existed at the time of the framing. Under the common law, individuals had a right to keep and bear arms, but not such arms as were inherently a menace to neighbors, or that had an unavoidable tendency to terrify the community. Thus, weapons such as machine guns, howitzers, or nuclear weapons would not be permitted. Note however that the much-vilified "assault rifle" would be protected under this interpretation—not in spite of its military character, but because of it. The "recreational and sporting uses" often cited by both sides in the contemporary gun control debate, on the other hand, are not relevant. They are cited by those who favor gun control in the hopes of not arousing the fears of hunters and target shooters, and by those who oppose gun control in the hopes of mobilizing those same groups. But they have nothing to do (directly) with the purpose of maintaining an armed citizenry. Recreation and sport, to the extent they are protected at all, are covered only penumbrally; the Second Amendment is not about sport or recreation . . .

Standard Model scholars dominate the academic literature on the Second Amendment almost completely. But their views are much less represented in the more popular media, where the "states' rights" view seems still to be dominant. Perhaps this reflects the notorious "liberal bias" of the media, though frankly I doubt that. Instead, I am afraid that it has to do with a central failing of American academia: the strong tendency of academics to talk to one another rather than to outsiders. In some fields, this is inevitable, simply because no one else is interested. But that cannot be the case where the subject is one as controversial and contested as the right to keep and bear arms. Instead, I think it has to do with the reluctance of legal academics to "go public" with their views . . .

Legal academics cannot force Americans to learn, but we can at least do our best to see that they have the opportunity, by taking our knowledge public [and] talking about our work to people who aren't law professors or law students.

If the Standard Model scholars had done more of this over the past few years, the public debate would be very different.

Source: Tennessee Law Review 62 (Spring 1995): 461, 478, 479–80, 507–8.

DOCUMENT 43: *To Keep and Bear Arms: The Origins of an Anglo-American Right*, Joyce Lee Malcolm (1994)

. The Second Amendment was meant to accomplish two distinct goals, each perceived as crucial to the maintenance of liberty. First, it was meant to guarantee the individual's right to have arms for self-defense and self-preservation. Such an individual right was a legacy of the English Bill of Rights. This is also plain from American colonial practice, the debates over the Constitution, and state proposals for what was to become the Second Amendment. . . .

These privately owned arms were meant to serve a larger purpose as well, albeit the American framers of the Second Amendment, like their

English predecessors, rejected language linking their right to "the common defense." ...

The second and related objective concerned the militia, and it is the coupling of these two objectives that has caused the most confusion. ... The argument that today's National Guardsmen, members of a select militia, would constitute the only persons entitled to keep and bear arms has no historical foundation. Indeed, it would seem redundant to specify that members of a militia had the right to be armed. A militia could scarcely function otherwise. ... The amendment guaranteed that the right of "the people" to have arms not be infringed. Whatever the future composition of the militia, therefore however well or ill armed, was not crucial because the people's right to have weapons was to be sacrosanct.

Source: To Keep and Bear Arms: The Origins of an Anglo-American Right (Cambridge: Harvard University Press, 1994), 162–63.

DOCUMENT 44: *For the Defense of Themselves and the State,* Clayton E. Cramer (1994)

The history of the right to keep and bear arms is disappointing. In spite of overwhelming evidence concerning original intent, much of the judicial interpretation of the Second Amendment and the state analogs has been repeated efforts to avoid the original intent and explicit language of these protections. In this century especially, original intent has increasingly been formally abandoned by the courts as a basis for constitutional interpretation ...

The Supreme Court has a number of choices, if various assault weapon ban cases reach it. The Court can recognize the Second Amendment as a limitation on the powers of the Federal Government only, precluding any federal ban. ...

The Court can recognize the Second Amendment as incorporated under the Fourteenth Amendment ...

The Supreme Court has the option to continue ducking decisions about the Second Amendment—and allow circuit courts to make decisions that would have seemed incomprehensible to the Framers—as they did when they denied the appeal of *Quilici v. Village of Morton Grove* and upheld the Appeals Court's decision that handguns are not military weapons ...

Finally, the Supreme Court has a fourth option—to hear a case, overturn the existing precedents of *U.S. v. Cruikshank* (1876) and *Presser v. Illinois* (1886), and ignore the overwhelming number of state supreme court decisions that have recognized "the right to keep and bear arms" as an individual right.

Source: Clayton E. Cramer, *For the Defense of Themselves and the State: The Original Intent and Judicial Interpretation of the Right to Keep and Bear Arms* (Westport, Conn.: Praeger Publishers, 1994), 269–74.

Beyond the direct wording of the Second Amendment, some scholars have also focused on the Fourteenth Amendment, saying it broadens the rights of the Second Amendment.

DOCUMENT 45: Fourteenth Amendment of the U.S. Constitution (1868)

No state shall make or enforce any law which shall abridge the privileges or immunities of citizens of United States; nor shall any state deprive any person of life, liberty, or property, without due process of law; nor deny to any person within its jurisdiction the equal protection of the laws.

Source: U.S. Constitution, Amendment 14, section 1.

The Fourteenth Amendment has been used to extend the personal rights granted in the Bill of Rights from infringement by state governments. Yet, whether the Fourteenth Amendment incorporates the Second Amendment is something legal scholars argue over.

In the following entry, attorney Stephen P. Halbrook explains how the Fourteenth Amendment, which became law shortly after the Civil Rights Act of 1866, extended as personal rights to all citizens those guarantees in the Bill of Rights.

DOCUMENT 46: *The Fourteenth Amendment and the Right to Keep and Bear Arms: The Intent of the Framers*, Stephen P. Halbrook, J.D. (1982)

In the understanding of Southern Democrats and Radical Republicans alike, the right to keep and bear arms, like other Bill of Rights freedoms, was made applicable to the states by the Fourteenth Amendment.

The framers of the Fourteenth Amendment and of the civil rights acts of Reconstruction, rather than predicating the right to keep and bear arms on the needs of an organized state militia, based it on the right of the people individually to possess arms for protection against any oppressive force—including racist or political violence by the militia itself or by other state agents such as sheriffs. At the same time, the militia was understood to be the whole body of the people, including blacks. . . . With the passage of the Fourteenth Amendment, the right and privilege individually to keep and bear arms was protected from both state and federal infringement.

Source: Report of the Subcommittee on the Constitution of the Committee on the Judiciary, U.S. Senate, 97th Cong., 2d sess., 1982, 68–82.

ADDITIONAL READING

Amar Akhil. "The Bill of Rights as a Constitution." *Yale Law Journal* 100 (1990): 1131–164.

———. "The Bill of Rights and the 14th Amendment." *Yale Law Journal* 101 (1992).

Bordenet, Bernard J. "The Right to Possess Arms: The Intent of the Framers of the Second Amendment." *University of West Los Angeles Law Review* 21 (1990).

Brown, Wendy. "Guns, Cowboys, Philadelphia Mayors, and Civic Republicanism: On Sanford Levinson's *The Embarrassing Second Amendment*." *Yale Law Journal* 99 (1989).

Cantrell, Charles L. "The Right of the Individual to Bear Arms." *Wisconsin Bar Bulletin* 53 (October 1980).

Caplan, David I. "Restoring the Balance: Second Amendment Revisited." *Fordham Urban Law Journal* 5 (1976): 31–53.

———. "Handgun Control: Constitutional or Unconstitutional?" *North Carolina Central Law Journal* 5 (1976).

———. "The Right of the Individual to Bear Arms: A Recent Judicial Trend." *Detroit College of Law Review* (1982): 789–823.

Cottrol, Robert J., and Raymond T. Diamond. "The Fifth Auxiliary Right." *Yale Law Journal* 104 (1995).

Cramer, Clayton E. "The Racist Roots of Gun Control." *Kansas Journal of Law & Public Policy* (Winter 1995).

Cress, Lawrence D. "An Armed Community: The Origins and Meaning of the Right to Bear Arms." *The Journal of American History* 71 (1984).

Dowlut, Robert. "The Right to Arms: Does the Constitution or the Predilection of Judges Reign?" *Oklahoma Law Review* 36 (1983): 65–105.

———. "The Current Relevancy of Keeping and Bearing Arms." *University of Baltimore Law Forum* 15 (1984).

———. "Federal and State Constitutional Guarantees to Arms." *University of Dayton Law Review* 15 (1989).

Dowlut, Robert, and Janet Knoop. "State Constitutions and the Right to Keep and Bear Arms." *Oklahoma City University Law Review* 36 (1982): 177–241.

Gifford, Dan. "The Conceptual Foundations of Anglo-American Jurisprudence in Religion and Reason." *Tennessee Law Review* 62 (1995).

Gottlieb, Alan. "Gun Ownership: A Constitutional Right." *Northern Kentucky Law Review* 10 (1982).

Halbrook, Stephen P. "The Jurisprudence of the Second and Fourteenth Amendments." *George Mason University Law Review* 4 (1981): 63–96.

———. "To Keep and Bear Their Private Arms: The Adoption of the Second Amendment 1789–1791." *Northern Kentucky Law Review* 10 (1982): 13–39.

———. *That Every Man Be Armed—The Evolution of a Constitutional Right*. Albuquerque: University of New Mexico Press, 1984.

———. "The Right to Bear Arms in the First State Bills of Rights: Pennsylvania, North Carolina, Vermont and Massachusetts." *Vermont Law Review* 10 (1985): 255–320.

———. "What the Framers Intended: A Linguistic Analysis of the Right to 'Bear Arms.' " *Law & Contemporary Problems* 49 (1986).

———. *A Right to Bear Arms: State and Federal Bills of Rights and Constitutional Guarantees*. Westport, Conn.: Greenwood Press, 1989.

———. "Encroachment of the Crown on the Liberty of the Subject: Pre-Revolutionary Origins of the Second Amendment." *University of Dayton Law Review* 15 (1989).

———. "The Right of the People or the Power of the State: Bearing Arms, Arming Militias, and the Second Amendment." *Valparaiso Law Review* 26 (1991): 131–207.

———. "Rationing Firearms Purchases and the Right to Keep Arms: Reflections on the Bills of Rights of Virginia, West Virginia, and the United States." *West Virginia Law Review* 96 (1993): 1–83.

———. "Congress Interprets the Second Amendment: Declarations by a Co-Equal Branch on the Individual Right to Keep and Bear Arms." *Tennessee Law Review* 62 (1995).

———. "Second-Class Citizenship and the Second Amendment in the District of Columbia." *George Mason University Civil Rights Law Journal* 5 (1995): 105–78.

———. "Personal Security, Personal Liberty, and 'The Constitutional Right to Bear Arms': Visions of the Framers of the Fourteenth Amendment." *Seton Hall Constitutional Law Journal* 5 (1995): 341–434.

Hardy, David T. "Armed Citizens, Citizen Armies: Toward a Jurisprudence of the Second Amendment." *Harvard Journal of Law and Public Policy* (1986): 559–638.

———. *Origin and Development of the Second Amendment*. Southport, Conn.: Blacksmith Corporation, 1986.

———. "The Second Amendment and the Historiography of the Bill of Rights." *Journal of Law & Politics* 4 (1987).

Hayes, Stuart R. "The Right to Keep and Bear Arms, a Study in Judicial Misinterpretation." *William and Mary Law Review* 2 (1960).

Henigan, Dennis A., E. Bruce Nicholson, and David Hemenway. "In Conversation with the Editors of Aletheia Press." *Guns and the Constitution: The*

Myth of Second Amendment Protection for Firearms in America. Northampton, Mass.: Aletheia Press, 1995.

Johnson, Nicholas J. "Beyond the Second Amendment: An Individual Right to Arms Viewed through the Ninth Amendment." *Rutgers Law Journal* 24 (1992): 1–81.

———. "Shots across No Man's Land: A Response to Handgun Control, Inc.'s Richard Aborn." *Fordham Urban Law Journal* 22, no. 2 (1995).

Kates, Don B., Jr. "Handgun Prohibition and the Original Meaning of the Second Amendment." *Michigan Law Review* 82 (1983).

———. "The Second Amendment and the Ideology of Self-Protection." *Constitutional Commentary* 9 (1992).

Levine, Ronald B., and David B. Saxe. "The Second Amendment: The Right to Bear Arms." *Houston Law Review* 7 (1969).

Lund, Nelson. "The Second Amendment, Political Liberty, and the Right to Self-Preservation." *Alabama Law Review* 39 (1987).

Malcolm, Joyce Lee. *Disarmed: The Loss of the Right to Bear Arms in Restoration England.* Cambridge, Mass.: The Mary Ingraham Bunting Institute of Radcliffe College, 1980.

———. Essay Review. *George Washington University Law Review* 54 (1986).

McClure, James A. "Firearms and Federalism." *Idaho Law Review* 7 (1970).

Moncure, Thomas. "Who Is the Militia—The Virginia Ratification Convention and the Right to Bear Arms." *Lincoln Law Review* 19 (1990).

The Right to Keep and Bear Arms. Report of the Subcommittee on the Constitution of the Committee on the Judiciary, U.S. Senate. Washington, D.C.: Government Printing Office, February 1992.

"The Right to Keep and Bear Arms: A Necessary Constitutional Guarantee or an Outmoded Provision of the Bill of Rights?" *Albany Law Review* 31 (1967).

Scarry, Elaine. "War and the Social Contract: The Right to Keep and Bear Arms." *Pennsylvania Law Review* 139 (1991).

Shalhope, Robert E. "The Ideological Origins of the Second Amendment." *The Journal of American History* 69 (1982): 559–614.

———. "The Armed Citizen in the Early Republic." *Law & Contemporary Problems* 49 (1986).

Sprecher, Robert A. "The Lost Amendment." *American Bar Association* 51 (1965). (2 parts.)

Van Alstyne, William. "The Second Amendment and the Personal Right to Arms." *Duke Law Journal* 43 (1994).

Whisker, James B. *Our Vanishing Freedom: The Right to Keep and Bear Arms.* McLean, Va.: Heritage House, 1972.

———. "Historical Development and Subsequent Erosion of the Right to Keep and Bear Arms." *West Virginia Law Review* 78 (1976): 171–90.

———. *The Citizen Soldier and United States Military Policy.* Croton-on-Hudson, NY: North River Press, 1979.

Young, David E., ed. *The Origin of the Second Amendment: A Documentary History of the Bill of Rights, 1787–1792.* Ontonagon, Mich.: Golden Oak Books, 1995.

Part III

The Second Amendment Goes to Court

The Second Amendment and gun control laws are not debated only in classrooms and scholarly journals. They occasionally get taken to court.

In the United States, the Supreme Court is where the bullet meets the backstop. While the public generally believes the Second Amendment grants an individual the right to bear arms, case law over the last 100 years has generally been interpreted differently.

Although no *federal* gun control law has even been overturned on the basis that it violates the Second Amendment of the U.S. Constitution, in some cases, debate continues over interpretation of court decisions. Indeed, there is even disagreement with the previous statement.

Expressing that view is law professor Randy E. Barnett, who summarizes the frustration felt by those who believe the courts have overlooked the intent of the framers.

DOCUMENT 47: Foreword: "Guns, Militias, and Oklahoma City," Randy E. Barnett (1995)

Yet though the Second Amendment does explicitly protect the right of the people to keep and bear arms, it has yet to be deemed by the Court to be a fundamental right. And it has yet to be applied by the federal judiciary to the states via the Fourteenth Amendment, notwithstanding the fact that it was among the privileges or immunities that the . . . Congress specifically contemplated when it proposed that amendment. The lengths to which the political establishment has gone to deny that this enumerated right is fundamental and that it applies to the states via the Fourteenth Amendment suggests to millions of reasonable law-abiding citizens that the Constitution is being willfully interpreted in a politically partisan way by those who disagree with the *merits* of the Second Amendment. At a minimum, it is hard to dismiss the frustration of such persons as unreasonable or irrational.

Source: Tennessee Law Review 62, no. 3 (Spring 1995): 443, 450–51.

Those who share this opinion often point to cases, such as an 1846 case in Georgia, in which the court held that the federal Second Amendment was binding on the state.

DOCUMENT 48: *Nunn v. State* (1846)

The right of the whole people, old and young, men, women and boys, and not militia only, to keep and bear arms of every description, and not such merely as are used by the militia, shall not be infringed, curtailed or broken in upon, in the smallest degree; and all this for the important end to be attained [by] the rearing up and qualifying [of] a well-regulated militia, so vitally necessary to the security of a free state. Our opinion is, that any law, state or federal, is repugnant to the Constitution, and void, which contravenes this right, originally belonging to our forefathers . . .

Source: Nunn v. State, 1 Ga. (1 Kel.) 243 (1846).

One case that gun rights supporters often point to is *Dred Scott v. Sandford*, the 1857 case in which the Supreme Court decided that an African American slave could not become an American citizen.

Although it is not cited in later court cases more directly on point with gun control, it is often included in the gun control discussion because of the following passage.

DOCUMENT 49: *Dred Scott v. Sandford* (1857)

It would give to persons of the Negro race, who were recognized as citizens in any one State of the Union, the right to enter every other State whenever they pleased, . . . and it would give them the full liberty of speech in public and in private upon all subjects upon which its own citizens might speak, to hold public meetings upon political affairs, and to keep and carry arms wherever they went.

Source: Dred Scott v. Sandford, 60 U.S. (19 How.) 417, 1857.

However, many other scholars begin their discussion of court cases with an 1875 U.S. Supreme Court decision.

DOCUMENT 50: *U.S. v. Cruikshank* (1875)

The right there specified is that of "bearing arms for a lawful purpose." This is not a right granted by the Constitution. Neither is it in any manner dependent upon that instrument for its existence. The second amendment declares that it shall not be infringed; but this, as has been seen, means no more than that it shall not be infringed by Congress. This is one of the amendments that has no other effect than to restrict the powers of the national government . . .

Source: U.S. v. Cruikshank, 92 U.S. 542 (1875).

Although later courts have cited this case in decisions on later gun control issues, debate over its interpretation and meaning continues. For example, the National Rifle Association's general counsel wrote the following in 1982.

DOCUMENT 51: "To Preserve Liberty—A Look at the Right to Keep and Bear Arms," Richard Gardiner (1982)

In *United States v. Cruikshank*, the first case in which the Supreme Court had the opportunity to interpret the second amendment, the Court plainly recognized that the right of the people to keep and bear arms was a right which existed prior to the Constitution when it stated that such a right "is not a right granted by the Constitution . . . [n]either is it in any manner dependent upon that instrument for its existence." The indictment in *Cruikshank* charted, inter alia, a conspiracy by Klansmen to prevent blacks from exercising their civil rights, including the bearing of arms for lawful purposes. The Court held, however, that because the right to keep and bear arms existed independent of the Constitution, and the second amendment guaranteed only that the right to keep and bear arms shall not be infringed *by Congress*, the federal government had no power to punish a violation of the right by a private individual; rather, citizens had "to look for their protection against any violation by their fellow-citizens" of their right to keep and bear arms to the police power in the state. Thus, the second amendment did not apply in *Cruikshank* since the violation alleged was by fellow-citizens, not the federal government.

Source: "Second Amendment Symposium: Rights in Conflict in the 1980s," *Northern Kentucky Law Review* 10, no. 1 (1982).

The second case to be heard in federal courts was *Presser v. Illinois.* Herman Presser was indicted in September 1879 for violating sections of the Illinois Military Code.

DOCUMENT 52: Military Code of Illinois (1879)

It shall not be lawful for any body of men whatever, other than the regular organized volunteer militia of this State and the troops of the United States, to associate themselves together as a military company or organization, or to drill or parade with arms in any city, or town, of this State, without the license of the Governor thereof, which license may at any time be revoked.

Source: Military Code of Illinois, 1879, Act of 28 May 1879, Laws of 1879.

The indictment charged that Presser did belong to and therefore could not parade and drill with an unlicensed military company in Chicago and was neither a part of the regular organized volunteer militia of the state nor a troop of the United States. Presser led the march on horseback, holding a cavalry sword.

The court rejected the argument that Presser's Second Amendment rights were violated.

DOCUMENT 53: *Presser v. Illinois* (1886)

We think it clear that the sections under consideration, which only forbid bodies of men to associate together as military organizations, or to drill or parade with arms in cities and towns unless authorized by law, do not infringe the right of the people to keep and bear arms. But a conclusive answer to the contention that this amendment prohibits the legislation in question lies in the fact that the amendment is a limitation only upon the power of Congress and the national government, and not upon that of the States. It was so held by this court in the case of *United States v. Cruikshank.*

Source: *Presser v. Illinois*, 116 U.S. 252 (1886).

Later courts and gun control supporters have pointed to this decision as an affirmation of the Second Amendment's collective right. Gun control opponents point to a section found later in the same court decision.

DOCUMENT 54: *Presser v. Illinois* (1886)

It is undoubtedly true that all citizens capable of bearing arms constitute the reserved military force or reserve militia of the United States as well as of the States, and, in view of this prerogative of the general government, as well as of its general powers, the States cannot, even laying the constitutional provision in question out of view, prohibit the people from keeping and bearing arms, so as to deprive the United States of their rightful resource for maintaining the public security, and disable the people from performing their duty of the general government. But, as already stated, we think it clear that the sections under consideration do not have this effect.

Source: *Presser v. Illinois*, 116 U.S. 252 (1886).

The following documents represent some of the scholarly debate regarding the impact and interpretation of this decision.

DOCUMENT 55: "To Preserve Liberty—A Look at the Right to Keep and Bear Arms," Richard Gardiner (1982)

The idea of the armed people maintaining "public security" mentioned in this passage from *Presser* was based upon the common law concept that individuals had the right and, in fact, the duty, not only to resist malefactors, such as robbers and burglars, but to aid in the enforcement of criminal laws and to use deadly force, if necessary, to do so. Disarming individuals would, of course, deprive them of their ability to protect themselves and others, and of their ability to perform their duty to maintain "public security" (or, in the words of the second amendment, the "security of a free State"). Likewise, disarming individuals would deprive them of their ability to perform "their duty to the general government," i.e., the duty to contribute to the common defense, a duty which can most effectively be carried out if individuals are familiar with the use of firearms.

Presser, moreover, plainly suggests that the second amendment applies to the States through the fourteenth amendment and thus that a State cannot forbid individuals to keep and bear arms. To understand why, it is first necessary to fully appreciate the statutory scheme the Court had before it.

Source: "Second Amendment Symposium: Rights in Conflict in the 1980s," *Northern Kentucky Law Review* 10, no. 1 (1982).

DOCUMENT 56: "Handgun Control by Local Government," Martin C. Ashman, J.D. (1982)

In *Presser v. Illinois*, the United States Supreme Court considered a claim that the State of Illinois infringed the Second Amendment rights of men associated in a fraternal military association by prohibiting their drills with arms. The Court rejected this claim and expressed its opinion that no substantive "right to bear arms" was infringed by banning private military drills. However, the Court determined to base its ruling on an even more fundamental ground: "A conclusive answer to the contention that this amendment prohibits the legislation in question lies in the fact that the amendment is a limitation only upon the power of Congress and the National government, and not upon that of the States."

The *Presser* Court similarly rejected the argument that the Fourteenth Amendment, through its Privileges and Immunities Clause, adopted a "right to bear arms" as one of the attributes of citizenship. Finally, the Court denied the claim that the Due Process Clause of the Fourteenth Amendment invalidated the state legislation, ruling that this argument "is so clearly untenable as to require no discussion."

In short, the Court in *Presser* unequivocally held that the Second Amendment does not reach state and local governments, either directly or through the Fourteenth Amendment.

Source: "Second Amendment Symposium: Rights in Conflict in the 1980s," *Northern Kentucky Law Review* 10, no. 1 (1982).

The next case also has an interesting history. The case was dismissed before a federal court, essentially on a technicality. However, in explaining the dismissal, the judges did write that they could not see how the defendant's Second Amendment rights were infringed.

DOCUMENT 57: *Miller v. Texas* (1894)

In his motion for a rehearing, however, defendant claimed that the law of the State of Texas forbidding the carrying of weapons, and authorizing the arrest without warrant of any person violating such law . . . was in conflict with the Second and Fourth Amendments to the Constitution of the United States. We have examined the record in vain, however, to find where the defendant was denied the benefit of any of these provisions, and even if he were, it is well settled that the restrictions of these amendments operate only upon the Federal power, and have no reference whatever to proceedings in state courts.

Source: Miller v. Texas, 153 U.S. 535 (1894).

It was many years before another federal court case was heard involving the Second Amendment.

In the meantime, however, there were a series of cases heard on the state level in which state courts ruled that a particular law restricting weapons did impede on that state constitution's clause protecting an individual's right to bear arms.

The National Rifle Association supplied the following partial listing and summary of such cases.

DOCUMENT 58: The Right to Keep and Bear Arms: Court Decisions Voiding Restrictive or Prohibitive Arms Laws, National Rifle Association

Bliss v. Commonwealth, 12 Ky. (2 Littl) 90, 13 Am. Dec. 251 (1822)
Struck down concealed carrying law involving a sword in a cane as unconstitutional.

Nunn v. State, 1 Ga. (1 Kelly) 243 (1846)
Struck down pistol carrying law as too restrictive.

Smith v. Ishenhour, 43 Tenn (3 Cold.) 214 (1866)
Struck down gun confiscation law as unconstitutional.

Andrews v. State, 50 Tenn. (3 Heisk.) 165, 8 AM. Rep. 8 (1871)
Struck down pistol carrying law as too restrictive.

Wilson v. State, 33 Ark. 557, 34 Am. Rep. 52 (1878)
Struck down pistol carrying law as too restrictive.

Jennings v. State, 5 Tex. App. 298 (1878)
Struck down law requiring forfeiture of pistol after misdemeanor conviction as unconstitutional.

In re Brickey, 8 Idaho 587, 70 P. 609 (1902)
Struck down pistol carrying law as too restrictive.

State v. Rosenthal, 75 Vt. 295, 55 A, 610 (1903)
Struck down pistol carrying ordinance as too restrictive.

In re Reilly, 31 Ohio Dec. 364 (Cp.P. 1919)
Struck down law forbidding hiring armed security guards.

State v. Kerner, 181 N.C. 574, 107 S.E. 222 (1921)
Struck down pistol carrying license and bond requirement as too restrictive.

People v. Zerillo, 219 Mich. 635, 189 N.W. 927 (1922)
Struck down restrictive pistol possession law.

Glasscock v. City of Chattanooga, 157 Tenn. 518, 111 S.W. 2d 678 (1928)
Struck down gun carrying law as too restrictive.

People v. Nakamura, 99 Colo. 262, 62P. 2d 246 (1936) (en banc)
Struck down prohibitive firearms possession law.

City of Las Vegas v. Moberg, 82 N.M. 626, 485 P.2d 737 (Ct. App. 1971)
Struck down restrictive gun carrying law.

City of Lakewood v. Pillow, 180 Colo. 20,510 P.2d 744 (1972) (en banc)
Struck down gun law on sale, possession and carrying as too restrictive.

State v. Kessler, 289 Or. 359, 614 P. 2d 94 (1980)
Struck down prohibition of possession of a club.

State v. Blocker, 291 Or. 255, 630, P.2d 824 (1981)
Struck down prohibition of carrying a club.

State v. Delgado, 298 Or. 395, 692 P.2d 610 (1984)
Struck down prohibition of possession of a switchblade.

Barnett v. State, 72 Or. App. 585, 695 P.2d 991 (1985)
Struck down prohibition of possession of a black jack.

State ex. rel. City of Princeton v. Buckner, 180 W. Va. 457, 377 S.E.2d 139 (1988)
Struck down a gun carrying law as too restrictive.

Source: National Rifle Association.

Part IV

The National Rifle Association

The major advocate of gun rights in this country has been the National Rifle Association, incorporated in November 1871. Its formation occurred after founders William Conant Church and Gen. George Wingate encouraged the inclusion of marksmanship in military training. With funding from the state of New York (the organization has been officially separate from the military since its inception), it began sponsoring target shooting competitions.

DOCUMENT 59: *Under Fire: The NRA and the Battle for Gun Control*, Osha Gray Davidson (1993)

Gradually, almost imperceptibly, the National Rifle Association changed from a quasi-governmental league devoted to military preparedness to a truly national group catering to the needs of all sportsmen carrying guns. It is much more difficult to say with any certainty when the group became a lobby. From the beginning, the NRA was in the business of swaying legislation to benefit its members and itself. The group had moved its headquarters to Washington, D.C. in 1907, but that had been primarily to be closer to the military brass. Not that the gun group supported governmental controls on gun ownership. When calls for such legislation swept the urban East in 1911 the NRA denounced the trend in strong terms.

"A warning should be sounded to legislators against passing laws which on the face of them seem to make it impossible for a criminal to get a pistol, if the same laws would make it very difficult for an honest man and a good citizen to obtain them," wrote James Drain, the organization's president. "Such laws have the effect of arming the bad man and disarming the good one to the injury of the community."

Source: Osha Gray Davidson, *Under Fire: The NRA and the Battle for Gun Control* (New York: Henry Holt, 1993), 28–29.

The National Rifle Association analyzes its own effectiveness as a public interest group in the following 1986 document. In it, the writers explain how the NRA did not establish a lobbying arm until 1975, when it created the Institute for Legislative Action (ILA), followed by other entities, such as the NRA Political Victory Fund—a political action committee, and its legal and research arm, the Firearms Civil Rights Legal Defense Fund. The paper also explains how the NRA worked with Congress in these early years, lobbying in support of moderate gun control.

DOCUMENT 60: "The NRA and Criminal Justice Policy: The Effectiveness of the National Rifle Association as a Public Interest Group," Paul H. Blackman, Ph.D., Research Coordinator, and Richard E. Gardiner, J.D., Assistant General Counsel (1986)

In the 1970s, however, the NRA began to notice that legislation which it had earlier supported had failed to curb crime, or in any way impair criminal access to firearms. In addition, the NRA noticed that the legislation adversely affected the firearms freedoms of the law-abiding . . .

The NRA further noted that the failure of allegedly moderate legislation did not persuade the advocates of "gun control" that such measures were not the answer. . . . This resulted in calls for additional "moderate" or "reasonable" legislation. As a threat, should the NRA continue to fight tooth and nail against "moderate" and "reasonable" legislation, the specter of legislation described as anything other than moderate was raised.

In 1977, after a purge of the leadership by the life members, the NRA Board of Directors officially agreed to stop compromising. The result is the legislative, political, and legal activism for which the NRA now has its reputation . . .

The political strength of the NRA is, plainly and simply, the result of its membership, a membership committed to the goals of the Association. While it is, of course, difficult to summarize the motivations of some 3.1

million individuals, undoubtedly one of the reasons for such commitment is the fact that members stand to lose not only their property but their very freedom since it will be <u>they</u>, not the violent criminal, who will be subject to prison sentences if "gun control" legislation is enacted. But, maybe even more importantly, our members' commitment arises from their concern over the erosion of what they see as their traditional and historic rights to decide how to live their own lives and how to dispose of their hard-earned wages, an erosion that has occurred not because <u>they</u> have done anything, but because a very few others have abused <u>their</u> rights . . .

For obvious reasons, crime control measures are easier to lobby for or against if the law-enforcement community is on your side. . . . On some issue, too, law enforcement will be automatically divided, as would any other field which involved both management and labor, jurisdictional disputes, and the like. Moreover, the law-enforcement community has often been at odds with civil rights and civil liberties organizations and with the media supporters of those organizations . . .

The small segment of the law-enforcement community which generally supports "gun control" legislation tends to fit into what the police themselves perceive as an "anti-cop" mold . . .

There is one issue on which many police are divided between the NRA's position and that of anti-gun organizations, the so-called "cop killer" bullet, which led to more extensive expressions of anti-gun sentiments by leaders of numerous police organizations. . . . It is not clear to what extent the organizations had any support from their law-enforcement officer members. Their lobbying techniques did not include the ordinary grass-roots approach, used effectively by the NRA and other groups. . . . For most purposes, departmental policies preclude independent expression of views by subordinate officers except as individuals and in private communication to policymakers, not publicly or in formal testimony. Those private expressions of support for firearms freedom by law-enforcement personnel, to their congressmen and to other policymakers, help to make it clear to those policymakers where the sentiments of law enforcement lie, whether in concert with the formal expressions of law-enforcement organizations or against . . .

Clearly, in lobbying it is best to have public opinion—particular[ly] aware and active public opinion—on one's side. That is one of the reasons the National Rifle Association is so effective. The public believes that guns are (a) constitutionally protected, (b) an effective means for protection from criminals, (c) that gun control laws do not impede the ability of criminals to obtain and use guns for criminals purposes but (d) interfere with the law abiding, and (e) that the way to cut crime is to punish criminals. Public opinion is not enough to guarantee victory, particularly in legislative bodies, but it helps.

Proponents of more restrictive gun laws attempt to disparage NRA's claim to public support, or even gun-owner support, by suggesting a commercial basis for the NRA, calling it an industry lobby.... Depending upon the issue, NRA and the firearms industry may be in agreement or disagreement; for that matter, industry itself may be divided. Domestic manufacturers and importers may be divided on importation issues; long gun manufacturers stand to benefit from restrictive handgun legislation; and so on . . .

In fact the NRA's financial strength is from the voluntary contributions of its members. Industry advertises in the magazines the NRA produces just as it advertises in any publication read by persons large percentages of whom are apt to buy firearms and related products, including, of course, law enforcement publications. The advertising revenues are used to offset the cost of the publication of the magazines, accounting for about 10–12% of the cost of producing the American Rifleman and the American Hunter magazines. None of the revenues thus produced go to the lobbying arm of the NRA; and no corporate contributions are sought or accepted by the PAC. The NRA is a grass-roots lobby, whose source of strength lies in the support of gun owners and of the public in general.

Source: NRA, paper presented at the annual meeting of the American Society of Criminology, Atlanta, Georgia, 29 October–1 November 1986.

In his recent book, NRA executive vice president Wayne LaPierre summed up the goal and stance of the organization.

DOCUMENT 61: *Guns, Crime, and Freedom*, Wayne LaPierre (1994)

Are there any limits on either the kinds of arms the Second Amendment guarantees or the kinds of people it protects?

Neither felons nor children under eighteen, of course, have the right to own arms—any more than they have the right to vote. This restriction is based on solid historical reasons. The National Rifle Association, moreover, has for over seventy years supported laws to prohibit gun ownership by those who have been convicted of violent felonies.

By the same token, the NRA has for decades supported and helped pass tough penalties to keep those who misuse guns in prison where they belong. The NRA was among the earliest and strongest proponents of "Three Strikes and You're Out" laws which would put repeat violent offenders in jail *permanently*.

Yet the anti-individual rights crowd accuses the NRA of claiming the Second Amendment guarantees guns for all—including criminals—and all weapons—including weapons of war like bazookas and bombs. Such has never been the case, and there is no reason for anyone to believe otherwise.

Source: Wayne LaPierre, *Guns, Crime and Freedom* (Washington, D.C.: Regnery, 1994), 17.

However, the strength of the NRA's lobbying is well known in Washington. The organization often generously funds opponents of gun control laws—and targets supporters of stricter laws for defeat in future elections. That is essentially the aim of a lobby, after all. But critics say the organization is controlled by unyielding zealots who do not represent the membership.

DOCUMENT 62: *Inside the NRA: Armed and Dangerous, an Expose*, Jack Anderson (January 1996)

Unhappily, however, the current leadership of the NRA has changed a fellowship of sportsmen, target shooters, and hunters into an intransigent right-wing political organization that is not representative of its membership and serves them ill. What is worse, its fanatical propaganda serves the nation ill. Worse still, its unholy alliance with many members of Congress taints the legislative process. It is inconceivable that many members of the NRA know what the organization is doing and still support it—either that or the NRA has assembled as its membership 3.5 million fanatic-fringe extremists who are wholly out of touch with reality.

I don't think the latter is true . . .

Former president George Bush resigned his membership in the NRA in May 1995 after its executive vice president, Wayne LaPierre, distributed a letter calling agents of the Bureau of Alcohol, Tobacco and Firearms "jack-booted thugs." The former president was not alone in his contempt for LaPierre's rabid rhetoric. Colorado Senator Ben Nighthorse Campbell, elected as a Democrat but now a Republican, also resigned his NRA membership, as did General Norman Schwarzkopf. Michigan Congressman John D. Dingell, a longtime opponent of gun control, resigned his seat on the NRA board of directors.

Senator Campbell said of the NRA, "They've become abusive, accusatory, sick, violent, threatening bullies. They want absolute subservience, and they're not going to get it from me."

General Schwarzkopf said, "[The NRA has become] very inflexible and almost radical; they appeal to a fringe element of gun owners."

Source: Jack Anderson, *Inside the NRA: Armed and Dangerous, an Expose* (Beverly Hills, Calif.: Dove Books, 1996), pp. 15–16.

In the wake of such incidents as Waco and Ruby Ridge, it became apparent that it is not only gun owners and militia members who feel that government is encroaching on their freedoms. So in the fund-raising letter to which Jack Anderson referred, the NRA tried to tap into that distrust. It should be noted that some different rules apply in fundraising. Many organizations know that in these efforts, they are reaching members who are already sympathetic to their cause. Therefore, many organizations pick a convenient "enemy" and pump up the rhetoric and sense of urgency. Liberals, conservatives, Democrats, Republicans, gun control advocates, and gun rights supporters all use this tactic.

DOCUMENT 63: NRA Fund-raising Letter (Spring 1995)

It doesn't matter to them [gun control advocates in Congress] that the semi-auto ban gives jack-booted government thugs more power to take away our Constitutional rights, break in our doors, seize our guns, destroy our property, and even injure or kill us . . .

Fact No. 2: If the anti-gunners fail to achieve their goals in Congress, they have a fall-back position in Bill Clinton, the most anti-gun President in American history. In two short years, Bill Clinton launched two successful attacks on the Constitution. He signed two gun control bills into law. He has sworn to veto any repeal of the semi-auto ban and any restoration of our Constitutional rights. His Interior and Agriculture Departments have set their sights on closing hunting lands.

And his Environmental Protection Agency is attempting to take jurisdiction over existing uses of lead. This, of course, includes gun ranges and spent shot. What's more, gun owners aren't the only ones Clinton's EPA has set its sights on. They're after fishermen, too. They want to BAN the use of small lead fishing sinkers and, of gravest concern, they want to stop the home casting of these sinkers.

If fishing sinkers are on the Clinton bureaucrat's list, you know what's next: lead shot, lead bullets, bullet casting and reloading . . .

Fact No. 3: President Clinton's army of anti-gun government agents continues to intimidate and harass law-abiding citizens.

In Clinton's administration, if you have a badge, you have the government's go-ahead to harass, intimidate, even murder law-abiding citizens.

Source: NRA fund-raising letter cited in *Congressional Record*, 9 May 1995 (Senate), pp. S6294–S6297.

In a May 3, 1995, letter to Sen. Carl Levin, who had complained specifically about the language of Fact No. 3, the NRA president defended the fund-raising appeal:

DOCUMENT 64: Letter from Thomas L. Washington, NRA President, to Sen. Carl Levin (May 3, 1995)

While I concede that some of the language in the NRA fundraising letter you refer to might have been rhetorically impassioned—as is most political direct mail—that in no way disparages the NRA, nor diminishes the seriousness of the alleged federal law enforcement abuses to which the letter refers. And it is certainly in no way related to the terrorist bombing in Oklahoma City.

You asked if we can "honestly justify" rhetoric decrying such abuses of federal power. That's what we want to find out. In January 1994, the American Civil Liberties Union, the National Rifle Association and others wrote to President Clinton, petitioning him to appoint a commission to investigate 25 Documented cases of alleged federal law enforcement abuse. Our request was ignored. So again in January 1995, the ACLU, NRA and others petitioned the President. All we ask is a full, fair and open examination the facts—a request that, so far, has been denied.

This isn't just some petty gripe against the enforcement of anti-gun laws by the Bureau of Alcohol, Tobacco and Firearms. On the contrary, the inquiry we requested was to focus on all 53 federal law enforcement agencies, and on charges ranging from the denial of basic civil rights, to the confiscation and destruction of property, to the improper use of deadly force against unarmed civilians.

. . . Let's get all the facts out on the table regarding these cases. If the accusations against federal law enforcement are baseless, let's expose them as such and vindicate the officers accused. If, on the other hand, particular officers are operating outside the rule of law, let's find them, remove them and prosecute them for the good of the whole. Whatever the case, let's put the grievances to rest once and for all.

Source: NRA response, cited in *Congressional Record*, 9 May 1995 (Senate), pp. S6294–S6297.

Sen. John H. Chaffee of Rhode Island added his objections on the Senate floor.

DOCUMENT 65: Comments of Senator John Chaffee (May 9, 1995)

The apocalypse described in this fundraising letter is not familiar to me. The Government described in these pages is not familiar to me. This is not a description of reality. It is a description of terror designed for one purpose: to provoke a visceral reaction against the U.S. Government—and at the end of the day, to raise money.

There are many powerful and ugly words used in this letter. They are insulting to American law enforcement and to American citizens. Why does Mr. LaPierre use them? I suppose in order to tap into the rage that some feel against the U.S. Government, to feed that rage, and to use that rage to gain donations.

Source: *Congressional Record*, 9 May 1995 (Senate), pp. S6294–S6297.

The NRA remains the most recognized organization for firearms owners, but there are others. Up until recently, most of the others were equally—or more—adamant in their opposition to restrictions on firearms and ammunition. But in 1993, a new organization, the American Firearms Association (AFA), was formed, founded by ex–NRA members, police officers, and military officers.

In its World Wide Web site, the organization explains its goals.

DOCUMENT 66: The American Firearms Association (1996)

The American Firearms Association ("AFA") is a non-profit nationwide gun-owners and sportsmen's organization dedicated to safeguarding and promoting the shooting sports while seeking to reconcile the Second Amendment and gun owners rights with fair and reasonable gun control legislation. We dispute the notion that gun owners rights must be in opposition to the majority of public opinion with regards to gun control. We believe that the Second Amendment guarantees Americans an individual right to own guns, but that it does not preclude fair gun control measures which seek to safeguard society. We believe that it is unwise and shortsighted for gun owners to continually stonewall public opinion on gun control issues, as this allows anti-gun organizations to portray us in a negative light. It is our conviction that it is wiser to implement a compromise strategy which seeks to enact legislative guarantees for gun owners within future legislation. We have endorsed both the Brady Bill and the Assault Weapons Freeze; we are especially pleased that the Assault Weapons bill excludes an extensive list of sporting firearms. We reject the "Armed Populace" doctrine of the NRA as misguided and unrealistic. We believe that Americans have the right to obtain firearms for self-defense against criminal behavior. We promote the acquisition and use of sporting firearms for sporting purposes.

Source: American Firearms Association.

ADDITIONAL READING

Anderson, Jack. *Inside the NRA: Armed and Dangerous, an Expose*. Beverly Hills, Calif.: Dove Books, 1996.
LaPierre, Wayne. *Guns, Crime and Freedom*. Washington, D.C.: Regnery, 1994.
National Rifle Association material, including monthly magazines and Web site: http://www.nra.org.
Simon, Jonathan. "The NRA under Fire." *Public Citizen* (July/August 1989): 9.
Sugarmann, Josh. *National Rifle Association: Money, Firepower & Fear*. Washington, D.C.: National Press Books, 1992.

Part V

Legislative Responses to Gun Violence

EARLY LEGISLATIVE ACTION

The National Firearms Act of 1934 (26 USC 5801) was passed on June 26 of that year and prohibited the transfer and possession of machine guns and sawed-off shotguns. It also taxed the manufacture and distribution of these guns and required registration for those owning these guns.

Four years later, Congress passed the Federal Firearms Act of 1938 (52 State 1250), which prohibited unlicensed dealers from selling guns across state lines. Only manufacturers and federally licensed dealers could send and accept guns mailed across state borders. The act also banned the sale of firearms to convicted felons and fugitives and made it illegal to transport stolen guns if the manufacturer's mark had been tampered with. (For a summary of federal gun regulations, see Appendix III.)

In 1939, the U.S. Supreme Court heard arguments in a case in which defendants Jack Miller and Frank Layton were indicted for transporting a 12-gauge shotgun with a barrel less than 18 inches long from Caremore, Oklahoma, to Salem Springs, Arkansas. The firearm was not registered, nor did the men have in their possession the stamps that represented the transfer tax fee. A district court upheld that the National Firearms Act violated the Second Amendment. The Supreme Court disagreed.

DOCUMENT 67: *U.S. v. Miller* (1939)

In the absence of any evidence tending to show that possession or use of a "shotgun having a barrel of less than eighteen inches in length" at this time has some reasonable relationship to the preservation or efficiency of a well regulated militia, we cannot say that the Second Amendment guarantees the right to keep and bear such an instrument. Certainly it is not within judicial notice that this weapon is any part of the ordinary military equipment or that its use could contribute to the common defense.

The Constitution as originally adopted granted to the Congress power—"to provide for calling for the Militia to execute the Laws of the Union, suppress Insurrections and repel Invasions; To provide for organizing, arming and disciplining, the Militia, and for governing such Part of them as may be employed in the Service of the United States, reserving to the States respectively, the Appointment of the Officers, and the Authority of training the Militia according to the discipline prescribed by Congress." With obvious purpose to assure the continuation and render possible the effectiveness of such forces the declaration and guarantee of the Second Amendment were made. It must be interpreted and applied with that end in view.

The Militia which the States were expected to maintain and train is set in contrast with Troops which they were forbidden to keep without the consent of Congress. The sentiment of the time strongly disfavored standing armies; the common view was that adequate defense of country and laws could be secured through the Militia—civilians, primarily, soldiers on occasion.

The signification attributed to the term Militia appears from the debates in the Convention, the history and legislation of Colonies and States, and the writing of approved commentators. These show plainly enough that the Militia comprised all males physically capable of acting in concert for the common defense. "A body of citizens enrolled for military discipline." And further, that ordinarily when called for service these men were expected to appear bearing arms supplied by themselves and of the kind in common use at the time . . .

Most if not all of the States have adopted provisions touching the right to keep and bear arms. Differences in the language employed in these have naturally led to somewhat variant conclusions concerning the scope of the right guaranteed. But none of them seem to afford any material support for the challenged ruling of the court below. . . . We are unable to accept the conclusion of the court below and the challenged judgment must be reversed.

Source: U.S. v. Miller, 307 U.S. 174 (1939).

The following represents some of the recent scholarly debate on this court decision.

DOCUMENT 68: "To Preserve Liberty—A Look at the Right to Keep and Bear Arms," Richard Gardiner (1982)

In *United States v. Miller*, the only case in which the Supreme Court has had the opportunity to apply the Second Amendment to a federal firearms statute, the Court carefully avoided making an unconditional finding of the statute's constitutionality; it instead devised a test by which to measure the constitutionality of statutes relating to firearms. The holding of the Court in *Miller*, however, should be viewed as only a partial guide to the meaning of the Second Amendment, primarily because neither defense counsel nor defendants appeared before the Supreme Court, and no brief was filed on their behalf giving the Court the benefit of argument supporting the trial court's holding that Section 11 of the National Firearms Act was unconstitutional . . .

[The court's] conclusion, that for the keeping and bearing of a firearm to be constitutionally protect[ed], the firearm's possession or use must have some reasonable relationship to the preservation of a well-regulated militia, is however, an unjustified limitation upon the rights guaranteed by the Second Amendment and is based upon the Court's failure to consider fully the common law and the history of the Second Amendment as well as its misinterpretation of cited authorities. As the discussions of the common law and the history of the Second Amendment demonstrate, the Second Amendment was also intended to guarantee the right of each individual to have arms for his own defense.

Source: "Second Amendment Symposium: Rights in Conflict in the 1980s," *Northern Kentucky Law Review* 10, no. 1 (1982).

DOCUMENT 69: "Handgun Control by Local Government," Martin C. Ashman, J.D. (1982)

Arguments have been made by pro-handgun forces contending that . . . under *Miller*, if a weapon is proved to be reasonably related to the preservation of the militia, there is a Second Amendment violation in limiting access to that weapon.

There is no such holding in the case. The lack of relationship between regulated weapons and the militia is only one ground for finding that a regulation does not impair the efficiency of the militia and hence, under *Miller*, is not in violation of the Second Amendment. Certain persons subject to a firearms regulation, minors and incompetents for example, might not be fit for service in the militia; presumably even a total prohibition of all firearms possession by such persons would comport with the Second Amendment.

Similarly, a restriction of access to military weapons even by persons qualified to serve in the military would not impair the effectiveness of the militia—or violate the Second Amendment—so long as the restriction did not prevent participation in military training or performance of military duties . . .

Arguments have been made that the Second Amendment protects a right to arms not dependent on the militia but on the need to provide self-defense or to allow citizens to take up arms against an oppressive government. These arguments, however, are really stating that *Miller* was wrongly decided by the Supreme Court. *Miller* declares that the second amendment must be interpreted and applied to "assure the continuation and render possible the effectiveness" of states militias, not to assure the continuations (or creation) of a nation armed with military weapons for personal protection or for revolution.

Source: "Second Amendment Symposium: Rights in Conflict in the 1980s," *Northern Kentucky Law Review* 10, no. 1 (1982).

DOCUMENT 70: "The Embarrassing Second Amendment," Sanford Levinson (1989)

The Supreme Court reversed (a lower court's decision) unanimously, with the arch-conservative Justice McReynolds writing the opinion. Interestingly enough, he emphasized that there was no evidence showing that a sawed-off shotgun "at this time has some reasonable relationship to the preservation or efficiency of a well regulated militia." And "certainly it is not within judicial notice that this weapon is any part of the ordinary military equipment or that its use could contribute to the common defense." *Miller* might have had a tenable argument had he been able to show that he was keeping or bearing a weapon that clearly had a potential military use . . .

It is difficult to read *Miller* as rendering the Second Amendment meaningless as a control on Congress. Ironically, *Miller* can be read to support some of the most extreme anti-gun control arguments, e.g., that the individual citizen has a right to keep and bear bazookas, rocket launchers, and other armaments that are clearly relevant to modern warfare, including of course, assault weapons. Arguments about the constitutional legitimacy of a prohibition by Congress of private ownership of handguns, or what is much more likely, assault rifles, might turn on the usefulness of such guns in military settings.

Source: Yale Law Journal 99, no. 637 (1989): 654–55.

DOCUMENT 71: "The Second Amendment in the Twentieth Century: Have You Seen Your Militia Lately?" Keith A. Ehrman, J.D., and Dennis A. Henigan, J.D. (1989)

Does *Miller* mean that weapons which can be shown to have a military use are protected by the Second Amendment? One commentator has interpreted *Miller* as holding that "the Constitution protects the right to possession or use of arms having a militia utility, e.g., shotguns, rifles, and pistols." This argument seems absurd on its face, because it would accord constitutional protection to machine guns, bazookas, hand grenades, and other military hardware of staggering destructive potential.

The proposition that *Miller* recognizes the protected status of any weapon that could have a military use has been rejected by every court which has addressed it. . . . In fact, the courts consistently have read *Miller* to mean that federal statutes regulating firearms do not offend the Second Amendment unless the statutes are shown to interfere with the maintenance of an organized state militia. Because privately-owned firearms are no longer used for militia purposes, this analytical framework has meant that, since *Miller*, no federal gun law has been held to violate the second amendment.

Source: University of Dayton Law Review 15 (1989): 5–58.

In response to Sanford Levinson's comments that, ironically, *Miller* can be "read to support some of the most extreme anti-gun control augments [Document 70]," Dennis Henigan noted the following.

DOCUMENT 72: "Arms, Anarchy and the Second Amendment," Dennis A. Henigan, J.D. (1991)

Thus, instead of concluding that a right to keep and bear bazookas is the reduction ad absurdum of the insurrectionist interpretation of *Miller*,

Levinson appears to be comfortable with the possibility that this is exactly what the Court meant. If such a bizarre view of the Second Amendment seems divorced from real courts and real cases, consider the fact that the National Rifle Association and its lawyers have made the identical argument, invoking *Miller*, to urge courts to strike down the 1986 federal machine gun ban, and the California law banning possession and sale of semi-automatic military assault weapons.

Source: Valparaiso University Law Review 26 (1991): 127.

To date, those bans stand.

GUN CONTROL ACT OF 1968

The 1968 shootings of civil rights leader Martin Luther King, Jr., and Sen. Robert F. Kennedy prompted Congress to enact the next major piece of gun control legislation: the Gun Control Act of 1968 (18 USC 921 et *seq.*). The law was passed in October of that year. (See Appendix III for text of the law.)

The act required that a federal license be obtained by anyone dealing in firearms and ammunition, prohibited the interstate mail order sales of all guns and ammunition, and essentially prohibited the interstate sale of handguns. It also established special penalties for the use of a firearm while committing a federal felony.

Among its key provisions, the Gun Control Act of 1968 banned the importation of nonsporting firearms—"Saturday Night Specials," generally defined as cheaply made, easily concealed small handguns. For handgun manufacturers to import these weapons, they would have to meet a certain qualifying score on a criteria test set up by the Internal Revenue Service. A gun is assigned points based on its overall length, construction, weight, caliber, and safety features. The criteria are different for pistols and revolvers.

However, the act did not specifically ban the importation of parts to make these guns. Three years later, the Senate held hearings on a bill to try to close the loophole that allowed foreign gun manufacturers to import parts to American affiliate companies so that the guns could be completed here and sold. The expansion of such a prohibition for U.S. manufacturers and closing the loophole so that parts cannot be imported and assembled here have been debated regularly—and the arguments have not changed much since 1971. Such a law has not yet been passed.

At that time, Sen. Birch Bayh from Indiana introduced legislation that would amend the Gun Control Act on this point.

DOCUMENT 73: Remarks of Sen. Birch Bayh (September 13, 1971)

The [Gun Control Act of 1968] prohibited the importation into the United States of foreign manufactured small caliber, inexpensive, pot metal pistols and revolvers. In the decade of the 1960s these "Saturday night specials" were being shipped into the United States in the millions, and substantial numbers are being used in crimes of violence.

Because of the prohibition in the 1968 act, we witnessed the ingenuity of gun manufacturers and former importers, who began to make the basic frame of the gun here, import parts for that frame and then assemble the finished product in the United States. In addition, other entrepreneurs began to manufacture these very guns in their entirety in this country.

Thus, both of these operations clearly circumvented the intent of Congress necessitating these hearings, and the legislation that I propose today.

Source: Hearings before the Subcommittee to Investigate Juvenile Delinquency of the Committee on the Judiciary, U.S. Senate, 92d Cong., pursuant to S. Res. 32 (Washington D.C.: Government Printing Office, 1972), 26.

DOCUMENT 74: Remarks of Sen. Roman L. Hruska (September 13, 1971)

Imported firearms should be subjected to the same restrictions, regulations and requirements as all other firearms. If properly enforced, those provisions will do much to prevent misuse of all firearms without resorting to protectionist practices.

[A] gun is not evil per se because it was manufactured abroad or in some cases it is cheaper than a gun of similar quality manufactured in the United States. Therefore, an attempt is being considered to eliminate these discriminatory provisions when the bill comes up for consideration on the Senate floor.

When is a firearm, in the words of the 1968 Act, "particularly suitable for sporting purposes"? Is there a way to bring objectivity into such a standard? Are the present factoring criteria employed by the Internal Revenue Service sound? Are we overemphasizing the question of price or "cheapness"?

The proposed Amendment seeks to apply to firearms (other than rifles and shotguns), the same regulations promulgated by the Secretary and applied by him to imports of such firearms. These regulations are based solely on the "sporting purposes" test.

The "sporting purpose" test is entirely subjective. No standards, limits, or requirements are prescribed or indicated, except a showing "to the satisfaction of the Secretary." So the following questions present themselves:

Is such a subjective test desirable?

Is it practicable, since any Secretary may have his own ideas of satisfaction in this regard? Or he may change even his own ideas in this regard.

Are the present regulations satisfactory, useful or effective?

How have they worked?

What progress has been made to develop more objective, scientific, and effective methods of meeting the special problem at hand?

. . . Is there not a better test basis? One which would bear upon safety and reliability of the weapon.

Source: Hearings before the Subcommittee to Investigate Juvenile Delinquency of the Committee on the Judiciary, U.S. Senate, 92d Cong., pursuant to S. Res. 32 (Washington, D.C.: Government Printing Office, 1972), 40.

It is interesting to note that the arguments over sporting use and difficulty of definition have arisen again nearly 20 years later in the assault weapons debate.

ADDITIONAL READING

Hearings before the Subcommittee to Investigate Juvenile Delinquency of the Committee on the Judiciary, U.S. Senate, 92d Cong., pursuant to S. Res. 32. Washington, D.C.: Government Printing Office, 1972.

TOWNS TAKE ACTION

Some gun control laws go further than others. Among the most restrictive laws in the country is legislation passed in Morton Grove,

Illinois, in 1981. The village passed an ordinance banning the sale and private possession of handguns.

DOCUMENT 75: Morton Grove Ordinance No. 81–11, an Ordinance Regulating the Possession of Firearms and Other Dangerous Weapons (1981)

Whereas, it has been determined that in order to promote and protect the health and safety and welfare of the public it is necessary to regulate the possession of firearms and other dangerous weapons, and

Whereas, the Corporate Authorities of the Village of Morton Grove have found and determined that the easy and convenient availability of certain types of firearms and weapons have increased the potentiality of firearm related deaths and injuries, and

Whereas, handguns play a major role in the commission of homicide, aggravated assault, and armed robbery, and accidental injury and death.

Now, therefore, be it ordained by the President and Board of Trustees of the Village of Morton Grove, Cook County, Illinois, as follows . . .

No person shall possess, in the Village of Morton Grove, the following:

(1) Any bludgeon, black-jack, slug, shot, sand bag, metal knuckles or any knife, commonly referred to as a switchblade knife, which has a blade that opens automatically by hand pressure applied to a button, spring, or other device in the handle of the knife, or

(2) Any weapons from which 8 or more shots of bullets may be discharged by a single function of the firing device, any shotgun having one or more barrels less than 18 inches in length, sometimes called a sawed off shotgun or any weapons made from a shotgun, whether by alteration, modification or otherwise, if such weapon, as modified or altered has an overall length of less than 26 inches, or a barrel length of less than 18 inches or any bomb, bomb-shell, grenade, bottle or other container containing an explosive substance of over one-quarter ounce for like purposes, such as, but not limited to black powder bombs and molotov cocktails or artillery projectiles; or

(3) Any handgun, unless the same has been rendered permanently inoperative.

(C) Subsection B(1) shall not apply to or affect any peace officer.

(D) Subsection B(2) shall not apply to or affect the following:

(1) Peace officers;

(2) Wardens, superintendents and keepers of prisons, penitentiaries,

jails and other institutions for the detention of persons accused or convicted of an offense;

(3) Members of the Armed Services or Reserve Forces of the United States or the Illinois National Guard, while in the performance of their official duties; and

(4) Transportation of machine guns to those persons authorized under Subparagraphs (1) and (2) of this subsection to possess machine guns, if the machine guns are broken down in non-functioning state or not immediately accessible.

(E) Subsection B(3) does not apply to or affect the following:

(1) Peace officers or any person summoned by any peace officer to assist in making arrests or preserving the peace while he is actually engaged in assisting such officer and if such handgun was provided by such peace officer.

(2) Wardens, superintendents and keepers of prisons, penitentiaries, jails and other institutions for the detention of persons accused or convicted of an offense;

(3) Members of the Armed Services or Reserve Forces of the United States or the Illinois National Guard or the Reserve Officers Training Corps while in the performance of their official duties.

(4) Special Agents employed by a railroad or a public utility to perform police functions; guards of armored car companies; watchmen and security guards actually and regularly employed in the commercial or industrial operation for the protection of persons employed and private property related to such commercial or industrial operation;

(5) Agents and investigators of the Illinois legislative Investigating Commission authorized by the commission to carry such weapons;

(6) Licensed gun collectors;

(7) Licensed gun clubs provided the gun club has premises from which it operates and maintains possession and control of handguns used by its members, and has procedures and facilities for keeping such handguns in a safe place, under the control of the club's chief officers, at all times when they are not being used for target shooting or other sporting or recreational purposes at the premises of the gun club; and gun club members while such members are using their handguns at the gun club premises.

(8) A possession of an antique firearm;

(9) Transportation of handguns to those persons authorized under Subparagraphs 1 through 8 of this subsection to possess handguns, if the handguns are broken down in a non-functioning state or not immediately accessible.

(10) Transportation of handguns by persons from a licensed gun club to another licensed gun club or transportation from a licensed gun club to a gun club outside the limits of Morton Grove; provided however that

the transportation is for the purpose of engaging in competitive target shooting or for the purpose of permanently keeping said handgun at such new gun club; and provided further that at all times during such transportation said handgun shall have trigger locks securely fastened to the handgun.

Source: Village of Morton Grove, Ill., Ordinance No. 81–11, 1981.

Victor D. Quilici challenged the ordinance in state court, but it was moved to federal court and consolidated with two similar challenges. In the first case, *Quilici v. Village of Morton Grove*, 532 F. Supp. 1169 (N.D.Ill. 1981), the district court upheld the handgun ban's validity under the state and federal constitutions, in part because it banned only certain kinds of arms.

DOCUMENT 76: *Quilici v. Village of Morton Grove* (1983)

We consider the state constitutional issue first. The Illinois Constitution provides;

Subject only to the police power, the right of the individual citizen to keep and bear arms shall not be infringed.

Ill. Const. art. I, section 22. The parties agree that the meaning of this section is controlled by the terms "arms" and "police power" but disagree as to the scope of these terms . . .

We agree that the state may not exercise its police power to violate a positive constitutional mandate, but we reiterate that section 22 simply prohibits an absolute ban on all firearms. Since Ordinance No. 81–11 does not prohibit all firearms, it does not prohibit a constitutionally protected right. There is no right under the Illinois Constitution to possess a handgun, nor does the state have an overriding state interest in gun control which requires it to retain exclusive control in order to prevent home rule units from adopting conflicting enactments. Accordingly, Morton Grove may exercise its police power to prohibit handguns even though this prohibition interferes with an individual's liberty of property . . .

The Illinois Constitution establishes a presumption in favor of municipal home rule. Once a local government identifies a problem and enacts legislation to mitigate or eliminate it, that enactment is presumed valid and may be overturned only if it is unreasonable, clearly arbitrary, and has no foundation in the police power. Thus, it is not the province of this court to pass judgment on the merits of Ordinance No. 81–11; our task is simply to determine whether Ordinance No. 81–11's restrictions are rationally related to its stated goals. As the district court noted, there is at least some empirical evidence that gun control legislation may reduce the number of deaths and accidents caused by handguns. This evidence is sufficient to sustain the conclusion that Ordinance No. 81–11 is neither wholly arbitrary nor completely unsupported by any set of facts. Accordingly, we decline to consider plaintiffs' arguments that Ordinance No. 81–11 will not make Morton Grove a safer, more peaceful place.

We agree with the district court that Ordinance No. 81–11: (1) is properly directed at protecting the safety and health of Morton Grove citizens; (2) is a valid exercise of Morton Grove's police power; and (3) does not violate any of appellants' rights guaranteed by the Illinois constitution.

We next consider whether Ordinance No. 81–11 violates the second amendment to the United States Constitution. [Appellants argue] that the second amendment applies to state and local governments and that the second amendment guarantee of the right to keep and bear arms exists, not only to assist in the common defense, but also to protect the individual. While reluctantly conceding that *Presser v. Illinois*, 116 U.S. 252, 6S.Ct. 580, 29 L.ed. 615 (1886) held that the second amendment applied only to action by the federal government, they nevertheless assert that *Presser* also held that the right to keep and bear arms is an attribute of national citizenship which is not subject to state restriction . . .

As we have noted, the parties agree that *Presser* is controlling, but disagree as to what *Presser* held. It is difficult to understand how appellants can assert that *Presser* supports the theory that the second amendment right to keep and bear arms is a fundamental right which the state cannot regulate when the *Presser* decision plainly states that "[t]he Second Amendment declares that it shall not be infringed, but this . . . means no more than that it shall not be infringed by Congress. This is one of the amendments that has no other effect than to restrict the powers of the National government." As the district court explained in detail, appellants' claim that *Presser* supports the proposition that the second amendment guarantee of the right to keep and bear arms is not subject to state restriction is based on dicta quoted out of context. This argument borders on the frivolous and does not warrant any further consideration.

Apparently recognizing the inherent weakness of their reliance on *Presser*, appellants urge three additional arguments to buttress their claim that the second amendment applies to the states. They contend that: (1) *Presser* is no longer good law because later Supreme Court cases incorporating other amendments into the fourteenth amendment have effectively overruled *Presser*; (2) *Presser* is illogical; and (3) the entire Bill of Rights has been implicitly incorporated into the fourteenth amendment to apply to the states.

None of these arguments has merit. First, appellants offer no authority, other than their own opinions, to support their arguments that *Presser* is no longer good law or would have been decided differently today. Indeed, the fact that the Supreme Court continues to cite *Presser*, leads to the opposite conclusion. Second, regardless of whether appellants agree with the *Presser* analysis, it is the law of the land and we are bound by it. Their assertion that *Presser* is illogical is a policy matter for the Supreme Court to address. Finally, their theory of implicit incorporation is wholly unsupported. The Supreme Court has specifically rejected the proposition that the entire Bill of Rights applies to the states through the fourteenth amendment.

Since we hold that the second amendment does not apply to the state, we need not consider the scope of its guarantee of the right to bear arms. For the sake of completeness, however, and because appellants devote a large portion of their briefs to this issue, we briefly comment on what we believe to be the scope of the second amendment.

The second amendment provides that "A well regulated Militia, being necessary to the security of a free State, the right of the people to keep and bear Arms shall not be infringed."

Construing this language according to its plain meaning, it seems clear that the right to bear arms is inextricably connected to the preservation of a militia. This is precisely the manner in which the Supreme Court interpreted the second amendment in *United States v. Miller*, 307 U.S. 174, 59 S.Ct. 816, 83 L.Ed. 1206 (1939), the only Supreme Court case specifically addressing that amendment's scope. There the court held that the right to keep and bear arms extends only to those arms which are necessary to maintain a well regulated militia . . .

[Appellants] argue that handguns are military weapons. Our reading of *Miller* convinces us that it does not support either of these theories. As the Village correctly notes, appellants are essentially arguing that *Miller* was wrongly decided and should be overruled. Such arguments have no place before this court. Under the controlling authority of *Miller* we conclude that the right to keep and bear handguns is not guaranteed by the second amendment.

Because the second amendment is not applicable to Morton Grove and because possession of handguns by individuals is not part of the right to keep and bear arms, Ordinance No. 81–11 does not violate the second amendment . . .

Reasonable people may differ about the wisdom of ordinance No. 81-11. History may prove that the Ordinance cannot effectively promote peace and security for Morton Grove's citizens. Such issues, however, are not before the court. We simply hold that Ordinance No. 81–11 is a proper exercise of Morton Grove's police power and does not violate art. 1, section 22 of the Illinois Constitution or the second, ninth, or fourteenth Amendments of the United States Constitution.

Source: Quilici v. Morton Grove, 695 F.2d 261 (Thea Cur. 1983).

The U.S. Supreme Court declined to review the circuit court's decision.

While Morton Grove leaders made a symbolic stand against handgun ownership, leaders in Kennesaw, Georgia, passed an ordinance in 1982 requiring every head of household in the city limits to maintain a firearm and ammunition. There are exemptions: those prohibited by law from doing so, those with moral or religious objections, and those who are unable physically or mentally to do so.

DOCUMENT 77: City of Kennesaw Code (1981)

In order to provide for the civil defense of the City of Kennesaw, and further in order to provide for and protect the safety, security and general welfare of the City and its inhabitants, pursuant to the Charter of the City of Kennesaw, the following ordinance is adopted, to wit:

(1) Every head of household residing in the City Limits of the City of Kennesaw is required to maintain a firearm, together with ammunition therefore.

(2) Exempt from the effect of said ordinance are those ... heads of households who suffer a physical disability which would prohibit them from using such a firearm. Further exempt from the effect of said ordinance are those heads of households who conscientiously oppose firearms as a result of religious doctrine or belief, or persons convicted of a felony.

Source: City of Kennesaw Code, Chapter 8, Civil Defense, sections 8–10, 1982.

THE EFFECTIVENESS OF GUN CONTROL LEGISLATION

Have the Morton Grove and Kennesaw laws worked? There are shortcomings in trying to extrapolate the relative success or failure of either of these laws for national policy purposes. The laws were mostly symbolic, and the communities are small. But other gun laws that encompass larger areas are continually under scrutiny by both opponents and supporters.

There are more than 20,000 gun laws on the books in this country. Most deal with such undebated safety precautions as prohibitions on minors buying guns and discharging weapons in urban areas. But others aim to address core issues of gun violence and self-protection.

Along with Morton Grove, the cities of Washington, D.C., Chicago, and San Francisco and several other Chicago suburbs have banned or placed significant restrictions on handguns. Both sides have used results from these experiences to draw conclusions about the effectiveness of gun control debate.

DOCUMENT 78: "Handgun Bans: A History of Failure," National Rifle Association Institute for Legislative Action (February 1995)

Firearm ownership rates were not expected to change in Kennesaw after passage of the ordinance; most households were presumed to have firearms. Instead, it was expected that publicity surrounding the ordinance would warn criminals that residents were capable of protecting themselves and their community and would do so with the government's blessing.

Between 1981–1985 violent crimes in Kennesaw dropped 71%; burglaries dropped 65%. Between 1981–1993, though Kennesaw's population doubled, burglaries dropped 16% . . .

The District of Columbia has required police approval to buy a handgun, and handgun registration, since the 1960s. A law prohibiting the possession of handguns not previously registered with the police took effect in February 1977. Firearms ownership opponents claim that homicide declined thereafter, deceptively counting annual homicide numbers, at a time during which the city's population was rapidly falling, and ignoring the fact that homicides were declining before the law took effect. Per capita homicide rates, however, increased gradually after the law, dropped sharply after enactment (1982) of an NRA-backed mandatory penalty for use of a firearm during a violent crime, rose gradually as the penalty fell into disuse, and then skyrocketed with the advent of the "crack" cocaine trade.

Washington Homicide Numbers/Per Capita Rates, 20-Year Trend

1973	1974	1975	1976	1977	1978	1979	1980	1981	1982
268	277	234	188	192	189	180	200	223	194
35.9	38.3	32.8	26.8*	27.8	28.9	27.4	30.5	36.9	30.8

1983	1984	1985	1986	1987	1988	1989	1990	1991	1992
183	178	147	194	225	369	434	472	482	443**
29.6	28.1	23.6	30.9	35.8	49.5	70.0	79.6	80.6	75.2

*From 1974 to 1976, before the law took effect, the homicide rate dropped 30%.
**Each of the city's 368 firearm-related homicides was committed with a handgun.
***D.C.'s homicide rate tripled, 1976–1991.

Source: Fact Sheet, National Rifle Association Institute for Legislative Action, February 1995.

Proponents of gun control argue that since the borders of cities like Washington, D.C., cannot be closed off, restrictive measures can have little effect. The argument was often brought up in efforts to tighten handgun purchasing restrictions in neighboring Virginia, which is one of several states to have passed legislation that limits the number of guns an individual may purchase in a certain amount of time. These laws were designed to stop "straw purchases," sales of guns to people who would buy many guns at a time, then resell them illegally in a nearby state or locality that more tightly regulates its gun sales.

Other states have passed right-to-carry laws that allow a gun owner to carry his or her gun, openly or concealed.

The following documents show some of the views on the success or failure of gun control laws.

DOCUMENT 79: "Views on Gun Control Legislation," B. Bruce-Briggs (1976)

The most important national measure is the Gun Control Act of 1968, the immediate result of the disturbances in the 1960s and the assassinations of Robert Kennedy and Martin Luther King, Jr. The Act raised taxes on firearms dealers, added cannon to the list of weapons subject to punitive taxes, prohibited the importation of surplus military firearms and "Saturday Night Specials," and prohibited the interstate retailing of all firearms. The last provision is the most important. The purpose was to prevent individuals like Lee Harvey Oswald from ordering weapons by mail under phony names. But it also has more annoying side effects. For example, if you live in Kansas City, Kansas, and wish to give your brother, who lives in Kansas City, Missouri, a .22 caliber rifle for his birthday, it is illegal for you to do so. If you are traveling in another state and see a weapon you wish to buy, you must go through the rigamarole of having it sent to a dealer in your own state. So far as one can determine, the law has had no perceptible effect in slowing down the interstate sale of arms.

Source: The Public Interest 45 (Fall 1976): 37–62.

In the following entry, Arizona attorney and former Department of Interior staffer David T. Hardy explains why he feels handgun restrictions have little or no impact on violent crime. He begins with the subject of registering guns, noting that those who purchased their guns with criminal intent are extremely unlikely to follow the rule.

DOCUMENT 80: "Legal Restriction of Firearm Ownership as an Answer to Violent Crime: What Was the Question?" David T. Hardy, J.D. (1983)

A comparison of patterns of firearm ownership with rates of violent crime demonstrates that firearm regulation is inherently incapable of controlling criminal violence . . .

Further, the argument of gun control proponents that regulation would prevent homicides involving persons who know each other is flawed. The argument requires a dubious logical leap that the perpetrators are otherwise law-abiding citizens. The fact that the victims and assailant knew each other, however, proves nothing of itself. In fact, such violence between acquaintances or family members is highly concentrated in a violent subculture atypical of society as a whole. A study of domestic homicide in Kansas City found, for example, that in 85% of domestic homicides the police had previously been summoned to the household to stop violence, and in over half they had been summoned five times or more. A recent medical study of *victims* of such attacks found that 78% volunteered a history of hard drug use and 16% specifically admitted heroin usage on the day of the attack. Presumably, the perpetrators' background was even less respectable. Such individuals are unlikely either to heed regulatory measures or be deterred by prosecutions of shopkeepers and the elderly . . .

Source: Hamline Law Review 6 (July 1983): 391–408.

In the following excerpt of a research report compiled for the *Hamline Law Review*, author Mary K. Mills explains the difficulty inherent in trying to correlate restrictive firearms laws to declines or increases in gun violence.

DOCUMENT 81: "Research Report, Licensing and Registration Statutes," Mary K. Mills (1983)

A major part of the handgun controversy has centered on whether regulation of handguns has made any appreciable impact on crime rates. Part of the problem is that there are numerous difficulties with any attempt to correlate handgun regulation with crime rates. Significant demographic and cultural differences as well as differences in enforcement techniques make valid comparisons both doubtful and problematic. One of the most serious flaws in attempting to correlate state crime statistics with state handgun regulations is the failure to account for local regulations which impose more stringent requirements than the state laws. Thus it is impossible to assess the impact of handgun regulation on crime rates with anything approaching scientific precision, simply because there is no way to establish a control group. For example, New York may experience a high crime rate despite comparatively stringent handgun regulation, but it is impossible to determine what the crime rate would be under a different regulatory system.

Some commentators have attempted to imply a cause and effect relationship between handgun regulation and crime rates. While no one has suggested that more lenient handgun regulation would reduce crime rates, it is often asserted that handgun regulation has no discernible impact on crime rates, thus making regulation irrelevant. However, while it is true that there is no clear statistical support for the notion that handgun regulation actually reduces the rate of violent crime, there is some support for the conclusion that deaths resulting from violent crime are lower in states with stricter regulation of handguns.

One of the biggest obstacles to assessing the effectiveness of handgun regulation is the lack of nationwide uniformity. For example, Washington, D.C., has what appears to be a strict handgun registration law, but it is easily circumvented by traveling a few miles to neighboring Virginia or Maryland. The paradox of handgun regulation is that nothing less than nationwide regulation can possibly be effective, yet federal legislation similar to the more stringent local regulations is perceived as impermissibly intrusive.

Source: Hamline Law Review 6 (July 1983): 419–30.

The NRA's Wayne LaPierre also weighs in on the "Saturday Night Special" ban.

DOCUMENT 82: *Guns, Crime and Freedom*, Wayne LaPierre (1994)

A ban on any firearm is a vehicle for banning all firearms. The "Saturday Night Special" ban revives the 1970s' concept that was exposed years ago as a scam designed to ban all handguns.

Calling these guns "small, cheap handguns—the weapons of choice of criminals," gun banners claimed that "Saturday Night Specials" were handguns that "had no sporting use, no hunting use, were not suitable for self-defense, and that their only purpose is for killing people." Such broad definitions could apply to almost all handguns.

Suppose the government were to declare that some item in your home was contraband—that its mere possession was a felony. That's what a ban on "Saturday Night Specials" amounts to.

Source: Wayne LaPierre, *Guns, Crime and Freedom* (Washington, D.C.: Regnery, 1994), p. 91.

Right-to-carry laws have been passed in at least 31 states (see Appendix II for a summary of state laws). Under these laws, applicants for a gun license need to meet only fixed statewide standards, leaving local law enforcement no subjective reason for denying carrying permits. Proponents say permits are being granted arbitrarily; opponents say police should have some input into who gets to carry guns. These laws are sometimes also referred to as "shall issue," meaning that if an applicant meets a series of objective criteria, he or she shall be issued a permit.

Although Florida was not the first state to pass such a law in 1987, it quickly became the most watched.

DOCUMENT 83: "The Right to Carry Firearms," NRA ILA Fact Sheet

Right-to-carry is the law in Florida today, and the anti-gunners' doomsday prophecies have been proven false. The state's homicide rate has decreased 22%, and its handgun-related homicide rate has decreased 29% since the law took effect. At the same time, U.S. rates have risen 15% and 50% respectively. On March 15, 1995, James T. Moore, Commissioner of the Florida Department of Law Enforcement, in an official correspondence to the governor and other state officials, stated that, "From a law enforcement perspective, the licensing process has not resulted in problems in the community from people arming themselves with concealed weapons. The strict provisions . . . preclude the licensing of convicted felons, etc., thus allowing the permitting of law abiding citizens who do not routinely commit crimes or otherwise violate the law. . . . Of 295,220 carry licenses issued in Florida through July 31, 1995, only 48—0.016%—have been revoked because of crimes committed with firearms after issuance of a carry license.

Source: National Rifle Association, Institute for Legislative Action Fact Sheet, undated.

In Oregon, the right-to-carry law was passed around the same time as a law requiring a 15-day waiting period for handgun purchases. The state code outlines when physical force can be used and appropriate conduct.

DOCUMENT 84: Highlights of the Oregon Statutes of the Criminal Code (February 11, 1990)

• When physical force can be used to defend a premises. A person is justified in using physical force (force that is not capable of causing death or serious physical injury) to prevent criminal trespass. He may use deadly force (capable of causing death or serious physical injury) only to defend himself or another person or to prevent arson or a felony by force and violence.

• When physical force can be used to defend property. Physical force may be used to prevent theft or criminal mischief of property. Deadly force may not be used.

• Negligently wounding another person. A person who carelessly shoots another person may be imprisoned for up to six months or fined up to $500, or both. He also forfeits any hunting license and the right to a hunting license for 10 years after conviction.

• Pointing a firearm at another person. Anyone over the age of 12 who is convicted of pointing a loaded or empty firearm at another person within shooting range, except in self-defense, can be fined up to $500 and imprisoned for up to six months.

• Unlawful possession of firearms. A person cannot possess an unregistered machine gun or carry or transport without a permit a firearm capable of being concealed.

• Who may keep a firearm that is capable of being concealed, and where. Any U.S. citizen over the age of 18 (except for certain ex-convicts) may own, possess or keep within his residence (including a recreational vehicle or vessel being used as a residence) or place of business a firearm that is capable of being concealed [without a permit] . . .

• Where a firearm is not permitted. An ordinary citizen without a concealed-handgun permit may not take a loaded or unloaded firearm onto public property.

Source: Oregonian, Portland, Ore., 11 February 1990.

In their paper on concealed handgun permit laws, Clayton E. Cramer and David B. Kopel, research director of a Colorado think tank, The Independence Institute, analyze the effect of such laws in 14 states. Since Florida's 1987 law set the stage for most of the "shall issue" today, and because the state has gathered significant data since the law's inception, analysis of Florida's experience is the most in-depth. Other state statutes analyzed in the report are: Alaska, Arizona, Georgia, Idaho, Mississippi, Montana, Oregon, Pennsylvania, Tennessee, Virginia, Washington, West Virginia, and Wyoming.

DOCUMENT 85: " 'Shall Issue': The New Wave of Concealed Handgun Permit Laws," Clayton E. Cramer and David B. Kopel (1995)

In most of the United States, laws prohibiting concealed carrying of handguns without a permit are relatively recent. Recognizing that at least some civilians would have a legitimate need for concealed carry of a handgun, most states adopted provisions allowing a sheriff, police chief, or judge to issue concealed handgun permits. Significantly, such statutes were broadly discretionary; while the law might specify certain minimum standards for obtaining a permit, the decision whether a permit should be issued was not regulated by express statutory standards.

Concealed handgun permit statutes were passed in some parts of the United States as a method of prohibiting blacks from carrying arms. In the words of a Florida Supreme Court justice, "The statute was never intended to be applied to the white population and in practice has never been so applied." [*Watson v. Stone*, 4 So. 2d 700, 703 (Fla. 1941)] . . .

Florida's 1987 reform law set off the modern wave of carry reform that has now been copied in many other states. Among all the states, Florida has collected the most detailed information about the impact of the carry laws. Florida also provides a good test case for the possible negative impacts of carry reform.

A state such as Vermont, which has never required a license for open or concealed carry, might be expected to suffer few consequences from widespread handgun carrying; Vermont already has a low crime rate, is relatively homogeneous, and is mostly rural. Florida, however, has all the ingredients for concealed carry disaster: a high-crime state with heavy urbanization, a massively overcrowded prison system, and an extremely diverse (and often tense) ethnic population mix . . .

In 1987, Florida adopted a nondiscretionary concealed weapon permit law guaranteeing issuance of a concealed weapon permit to any Floridian who is (1) at least twenty-one years old, (2) "Does not suffer from a physical infirmity which prevents the safe handling of a weapon or firearm," (3) has not been convicted of a felony, (4) has not been convicted of a drug charge within the preceding three years, (5) has not been confined for alcohol problems within the preceding three years, (6) has completed any of a number of firearms safety classes, and (7) has not been committed to a mental hospital within the preceding five years. A 1993 revision allows American citizens who are not Florida residents to obtain a permit that can be used when visiting Florida . . .

How many permits were actually issued? From October 1, 1987, when the new law went into effect, to April 30, 1994, there were 233,870 applications received. A total of 1019 applications were denied (585 for criminal history, 434 for incomplete application). A total of 221,443 licenses were issued, of which 124,405 were valid as of April 30, 1994. Many licensees did not renew; several thousand applications were either in process, denied and under appeal, suspended, or withdrawn by the applicant.

A total of 362 licenses have been revoked. The revocations were for: clemency rule change or legislative change (66), illegible prints (10), crime prior to licensure (78, of which 4 involved a firearm), crime after licensure (193, of which 18 involved a firearm), and "other" (15). Thus, of the 221,443 licensees, approximately 1 in 10,000 (1/100th of 1%) had a license revoked for a crime involving a firearm . . .

The very fact that negative incidents involving permit holders were so rare . . . is evidence of the lack of negative effects of carry reform. Representative Ron Silver, the leading opponent of Florida's carry reform, graciously admitted in November 1990: "There are a lot of people, including myself, who thought things would be a lot worse as far as that particular situation [carry reform] is concerned. I'm happy to say they're not." John Fuller, general counsel for the Florida Sheriffs Association, stated, "I haven't seen any instances of persons with permits causing violent crimes, and I'm constantly on the lookout." . . .

Of all the states that enacted concealed carry reform, Florida shows the most dramatic change. Florida's murder rate from 1975 to 1986 was between 118 and 157% of the murder rate elsewhere in the United States. After the passage of Florida's law, the state's murder rate began declining rapidly and consistently. The decline provided dramatic contrast to the increase in murder rates experienced in the rest of the United States.

By 1991, Floridians were less likely to be murdered than people else-where in America . . .

[An] important benefit to be derived from properly licensed, trained and armed citizens is peace of mind. By the way of analogy, many people choose to buy automobiles with passenger-side air bags or other safety features. Many people also choose to use the seat belts in a car. Of course, the odds are small that on any given automobile trip there will be an accident in which the safety belt or other safety device will serve its ultimate purpose. Similarly, the odds are small that a person who goes out in public will be attacked by a criminal on any given day. But even on days when drivers are not struck by other cars, the car's safety devices confer a genuine benefit because the drivers feel safer. Likewise, if people feel safer because they carry a gun and in turn lead happier lives because they feel safer and more secure, then the carrying of guns makes a direct and nontrivial contribution to their overall quality of life . . .

Source: Tennessee Law Review 62 (Spring 1995): 679, 680, 681, 690, 691, 692, 721, 722.

Another group of researchers, however, found that firearm homicides increased in several study areas after "shall issue" laws went into effect, while the number of nonfirearm homicides remained stable. The study looked at the impact of shall issue laws in large urban areas of Florida, Mississippi, and Oregon. The authors concluded, "The analysis provides no support for the idea that the laws reduced homicides; instead, it finds evidence of an increase in firearm murders."

DOCUMENT 86: "Easing Concealed Firearms Laws: Effects on Homicide in Three States," David McDowall, Colin Loftin, and Brian Wiersema (1995)

Prior to the passage of the Florida shall issue law [in 1987], county officials set their own standards for concealed carrying. Throughout the state, about 17,000 persons held permits. . . . The number of licenses rose steadily after the passage of the new law, reaching 141,000 in September 1994.

Mississippi adopted a shall issue law on July 1, 1990. The Mississippi law was similar to the Florida law, except that it did not require firearms safety training. Mississippi's earlier law was highly restrictive, generally allowing only security guards to have concealed weapons. In contrast, the new law is more lenient; by November 1992, the state had issued 5,136 new licenses.

Oregon adopted a shall issue law on January 1, 1990, in a compromise between supporters and opponents of stricter gun control measures. Oregon's new law required county sheriffs to provide a concealed handgun license to any qualified adult who had taken a firearms safety course. People who could not obtain a license included: those with outstanding arrest warrants, those on pretrial release, those with a history of mental illness, or those with a felony or recent misdemeanor conviction.

In addition to easing laws on concealed carrying, Oregon's new law also tightened standards for buying a gun. While the old law barred convicted felons from owning handguns, the new law prohibited convicted felons from owning any type of firearm. Oregon's new law also lengthened the waiting period for handgun purchases and required more detailed background checks. It further prohibited most persons ineligible for a concealed handgun license from obtaining any firearm . . .

The results . . . show that firearms homicides increased in four of the five areas in the post-law period. Except the increase in Miami and the decrease in Portland, these changes were statistically significant. Expressed as percentages, the changes varied from a decrease of 12% (Portland) to an increase of 75% (Jacksonville). Considering each area as a replication of the same experiment, gun homicides increased by an average of 26% . . .

In contrast to gun homicides, homicides by other means did not show a consistent pattern of effects. Homicides without firearms increased in Tampa and Jacksonville, but they fell in the other three areas. Across all five areas, the average change in homicides without guns was an increase of less than 1% . . .

The pattern of results leads us to two conclusions, one stronger than the other. The stronger conclusion is that shall issue laws do not reduce homicides, at least in large urban areas. If there were such a decrease, other events would have to push murders up strongly enough to mask it in all five areas that we studied. Such events are possible, of course, but we believe that they are extremely unlikely.

The weaker conclusion is that shall issue laws raise levels of firearms murders. Coupled with lack of influence on murders by other means, the laws thus increase the frequency of homicide. This interpretation is consistent with other work showing that policies to *discourage* firearms in public may help prevent violence . . .

Despite this evidence, we do not firmly conclude that shall issue licensing leads to more firearms murders. This is so because the effects varied over the study areas. Firearms homicides significantly increased in only three areas, and one area witnessed an insignificant decrease. In combination, the increase in gun homicides was large and statistically significant. Yet we have only five replications, and two of these do not clearly fit the pattern . . .

While our analysis does not allow a firm conclusion that shall issue licensing increases firearms homicides, it does suggest caution about these laws. Some observers consider strict limits on firearms outside the home to be among the most effective forms of gun control. Beyond any influence on violence, the policies are easy to enforce and they do not inconvenience most gun owners. When states weaken limits on concealed weapons, they may be giving up a simple and effective method of preventing firearm deaths.

Source: Northwestern University School of Law, *The Journal of Criminal Law and Criminology* 86 (Fall 1995): 193–206.

More recently, David B. Kopel outlined his findings in *Policy Review*, the magazine of the Heritage Foundation. He called the trend to concealed carry permits "a quiet revolution in gun policy," noting the effects of this wave "will be far more significant than either the Brady waiting period or the ban on certain semiautomatics." Kopel also commented on the study included above.

DOCUMENT 87: "The Untold Triumph of Concealed-Carry Permits," David B. Kopel (July/August 1996)

This movement began in the early 1980s, when gun-rights activists in Florida joined with law-enforcement lobbies such as the Florida Chiefs of Police Association to reform the state's handgun law. They proposed legislation that entitled any citizen who clears a fingerprint-based background check and passes gun-safety classes to receive a permit to carry a concealed handgun for protection. . . . Republican governor Bob Martinez signed the bill in 1987 . . .

Whenever a state legislature first considers a concealed-carry bill, opponents typically warn of horrible consequences: Permit holders will slaughter each other in traffic disputes, while would-be Rambos shoot bystanders in incompetent attempts to thwart crime. But within a year of passage, the issue usually drops off the news media's radar screen, while gun-control advocates in the legislature conclude that the law wasn't so bad after all . . .

Has this movement toward concealed-carry laws made America safer or more dangerous? In an article for the *Tennessee Law Review* [Document

85], historian Clayton Cramer and I examined homicide rates in states that had adopted concealed-carry laws, adjusted for the effects of national homicide trends. In all but one state we examined, homicide rates did not appear to change as a result of the laws. We saw fluctuations, of course, but nothing out of the ordinary.

The lone exception was Florida, where the murder rate started an immediate, steady decline. Before the law, Floridians were about 36 percent more likely to be murdered than other Americans; after a few years, the Florida rate was equal to or slightly less than the national rate. As for other violent crimes, Florida was the worst state in the nation both before and after the new law. Florida's overall violent-crime rate, however, rose much more slowly since 1987 than did the national violent-crime rate.

Advocates of gun-control sometimes cite a 1995 study of concealed-carry policies by three researchers from the University of Maryland [Document 86]. The study looked at five urban areas and found that in four of them, the handgun homicide rate rose after a concealed-carry law had been enacted. But David McDowall, one of the authors, says that the small set of data limits the conclusions to be drawn from the study. He also states that there is no evidence permit holders commit crimes. The study is a classic illustration of how changing the parameters of a "before-and-after" analysis can change the results. For each city, McDowall and his colleagues averaged the yearly crime rates from 1973 until the year before the law went into effect, and compared that figure to the average rate of all subsequent years. If, instead, we compare the year before the law went into effect with the most recent year for which we have complete data (1994), then the homicide rate declined in three of the five cities. . . .

Of course, data alone cannot measure the benefits of concealed-carry reform. If a gun permit helps a woman feel safe enough to go jogging, her increased sense of security is an important social benefit—even if she never has to draw a gun. If she does encounter a criminal, the chances are small that she will actually have to fire, and less than 1 percent that he will take the gun away. In the most thorough study ever done on this subject, Florida State University criminologist Gary Kleck found that most instances of a citizen drawing a gun in self-defense end with the assailant simply retreating.

Although solid proof of the effect of concealed-carry laws in reducing violent crime is relatively recent, it has long been clear that they do not threaten public safety. . . . In Florida as a whole, 315,000 permits had been issued by December 31, 1995. Only five had been revoked because the permit holder committed a violent crime with a gun.

Permit holders are not angels, but they are an unusually law-abiding collection of citizens. In Florida, for example, permit holders are about 300 times less likely to perpetrate a gun crime than Floridians without permits. Florida's experience has been copied nationwide. This should not be at all surprising: A person could carry a concealed handgun without a permit and, unless he gives himself away by committing some other offense, he would never be caught. Hence permit applicants tend to be those citizens willing to pay a large fee (usually more than $100) to comply with a law they could probably break with impunity.

Although 1 to 4 percent of the adult population exercises the freedom to carry a handgun for protection, a much larger group believes they should have such a choice. Polls usually show that one-half to two-thirds of the population supports concealed-carry laws. Higher rates are reported when respondents are informed about the various restrictions—such as training requirements—typically included in concealed-carry laws. These laws appeal to citizens who object neither to gun ownership nor to the use of force in self-defense, yet welcome moderate regulation to screen out undesirables.

Similarly, law-enforcement organizations in many states have supported concealed-carry laws. . . .

Of course, everyone is a potential beneficiary of concealed-carry reform. Since criminals do not know which of their potential victims may be armed, even persons without carry permits would enjoy increased safety from any deterrent effect. Moreover, a Psychology Today study of "good Samaritans" who came to the aid of violent-crime victims found that 81 percent were gun owners, and many of them carried guns in their cars or on their persons.

Source: Policy Review: The Journal of American Citizenship, no. 78 (July–August 1996).

In a study that exceeded earlier entries in terms of scope and conclusions, two University of Chicago researchers concluded that concealed weapons do indeed prevent crimes and save lives—to a significant degree. Their research determined that if those states without right-to-carry laws "had adopted them in 1992, approximately 1,570 murders; 4,177 rapes; and over 60,000 aggravated assaults would have been avoided yearly."

To reach those conclusions, the researchers studied crime data for the United States from 1977 to 1992. They also relied on county level data, rather than state level figures because of the disparity within states on how readily concealed weapons permits are granted. In general, county level data provide more reliable results on that as well as on arrest and crime rates. However, in counties with a low incidence of crime, small numbers can skew result.

DOCUMENT 88: "Crime, Deterrence, and Right-to-Carry Concealed Handguns," John R. Lott, Jr., and David B. Mustard (July 26, 1996)

This aggregation of crime categories [in FBI data] makes it difficult to separate out which crimes might be deterred from increased handgun ownership, and which crimes might be increasing as a result of a substitution effect. Generally, we expect that the crimes most likely to be deterred by concealed handgun laws are those involving direct contact between the victim and the criminal, especially those occurring in a place where victims otherwise would not be allowed to carry firearms. For example, aggravated assault, murder, robbery, and rape seem most likely to fit both conditions, though obviously some of all these crimes can occur in places like residences where the victims could already possess firearms to protect themselves.

By contrast, crimes like auto theft seem unlikely to be deterred by gun ownership. While larceny is more debatable, in general—to the extent that these crimes actually involve "stealth"—the probability that victims will notice the crime being committed seems low and thus the opportunities to use a gun are relatively rare. The effect on burglary is ambiguous from a theoretical standpoint. It is true that if "shall issue" laws cause more people to own a gun, the chance of a burglar breaking into a house with an armed resident goes up. However, if some of those who already owned guns now obtain right-to-carry permits, the relative cost of crimes like armed street robbery and certain other types of robberies (where an armed patron may be present) should rise relative to that for burglary . . .

The results are large empirically. When state concealed handgun laws went into effect in a county, murders fell by 8.5 percent, and rapes and aggravated assaults fell by 5 and 7 percent. In 1992, there were 18,469 murders; 79,272 rapes; 538,368 robberies; and 861,103 aggravated assaults in counties without "shall issue" laws. The coefficients imply that if these counties had been subject to state concealed handgun laws, murders in the United States would have declined by 1,570. Given the concern that has been raised about increased accidental deaths from concealed weapons, it is interesting to note that the entire number of accidental gun deaths in the United States in 1992 was 1,409. Of this total, 546 accidental deaths were in states with concealed handgun laws and 863 were in those without these laws. The reduction in murders is as much as three times greater than the total number of accidental deaths in concealed handgun states. Thus, if our results are accurate, the net effect of allowing concealed handguns is clearly to save lives. Similarly, the results indicate that the number of rapes in states without "shall issue" laws would have declined by 4,177; aggravated assaults by 60,363; and robberies by 11,898.

On the other hand, property crime rates definitely increased after "shall issue" laws were implemented. The results are equally dramatic. If states without concealed handgun laws had passed such laws, there would have been 247,165 more property crimes in 1992 (a 2.7 percent increase). Thus, criminals respond substantially to the threat of being shot by . . . substituting . . . less risky crimes.

A recent National Institute of Justice study provides estimates [of] the costs of different types of crime based upon lost productivity; out-of-pocket expenses such as medical bills and property losses; and losses for fear, pain, suffering, and lost quality of life. While there are questions about using jury awards to measure losses such as fear, pain, suffering, and lost quality of life, the estimates provide us one method of comparing the reduction in violent crimes with the increase in property crimes. . . . The estimated gain from allowing concealed handguns is over $6.214 billion in 1992 dollars. The reduction in violent crimes represents a gain of $6.6 billion ($4.75 billion from murder, $1.4 billion from aggravated assault, $374 million from rape, and $98 million from robbery), while the increase in property crimes represents a loss of $417 million ($342 million from auto theft, $73 million from larceny, and $1.5 million from burglary). However, while $6.2 billion is substantial, to put it into perspective, it equals only about 1.33 percent of the total aggregate losses from these crime categories. . . . Higher estimated values of life will increase the net gains from concealed handgun use, while lower values of life will reduce the gains. To the extent that people are taking greater risks towards crime because of any increased safety produced by concealed handgun laws, these numbers will underestimate the total savings from concealed handguns.

The arrest rate produces the most consistent effect on crime. Higher arrest rates imply lower crime rates for all categories of crime. A one standard deviation change in the probability of arrest accounts for 3 to 17 percent of a one standard deviation change in the various crime rates. The crime most responsive to arrest rates is burglary (11 percent), followed by property crimes (10 percent); aggravated assault and violent crimes more generally (9 percent); murder (7 percent); rape, robbery, and larceny (4 percent); and auto theft (both [sic] 3 percent) . . .

Do concealed handgun laws cause a substitution in the methods of committing murders? For example, it is possible that the number of gun murders rises after these laws are passed even though the total number of murders falls. While concealed handgun laws raise the cost of committing murders, murderers may also find it relatively more dangerous to kill people using nongun methods once people start carrying concealed handguns and substitute into guns to put themselves on a more even basis with their potential prey . . .

There is also the question of what effect does conceal[ed] handgun laws have on determining which types of people are more likely to be murdered? Using the Uniform Crime Reports Supplementary Homicide Reports we were able to obtain annual state level data from 1977 to 1992 on the percent of victims by sex and race as well as information on whether the victim and the offender knew each other (whether they were members of the same family, knew each other but were not members of the same family, strangers, or the relationship is unknown). . . . However . . . two of the point estimates appear economically important and imply that in states with concealed handgun laws victims know their nonfamily offenders 2.6 percentage points more frequently and that the percent of victims where it was not possible to determine whether a relationship existed declined by 2.9 percentage points. This raises the question of whether concealed handguns cause criminals to substitute into crimes against those whom they know and presumably are also more likely to know whether they carry concealed handguns.

The arrest rate for murder variable produces more interesting results. The percent of white victims and the percent of victims killed by family members both declined when states passed concealed handgun laws, while the percent of black victims and the percent that [were] killed by nonfamily members that they know both increased. The results imply that higher arrest rates have a much greater deterrence effect on murders involving whites and family members. One explanation is that whites with higher incomes face a greater increase in expected penalties for any given increase in the probability of arrest . . .

Even if "shall issue" handgun permits lower murder rates, the question of what happens to accidental deaths still remains. Possibly, with more people carrying handguns, accidents may be more likely to happen . . .

While there is some evidence that the racial composition of the population and the level of income maintenance payments affect accident rates, the coefficient of the shall issue dummy is both quite small economically and insignificant. The point estimates for the first specification implies that accidental handgun deaths rose by about .5 percent when concealed handgun laws were passed. With only 156 accidental handgun deaths occurring in counties over 100,000 population (27 accidental handgun deaths occurred in states with "shall issue" laws), this point estimate implies that implementing a concealed handgun law in those states which currently do not have it would produce less than one more death (.645 deaths) . . .

Allowing citizens without criminal records or histories of significant mental illness to carry concealed handguns deters violent crimes and appears to produce an extremely small and statistically insignificant change in accidental deaths. If the rest [of the] country had adopted right-to-carry concealed handgun provisions in 1992, at least 1,570 murders and over 4,177 rapes would have been avoided. On the other hand, consistent with the notion that criminals respond to incentives, county level data provides evidence that concealed handgun laws are associated with increases in property crimes involving stealth and where the probability of contact between the criminal and the victim are minimal. The largest population counties where the deterrence effect on violent crimes is the greatest . . . [are] also where the substitution effect into these property crimes is the highest. The estimated annual gain in 1992 from allowing concealed handguns was over $6.21 billion.

The data also supply dramatic evidence supporting the economic notion of deterrence. Higher arrest and conviction rates consistently and dramatically reduce the crime rate. Consistent with other recent work, the results imply that increasing the arrest rate, independent of the probability of eventual conviction, imposes a significant penalty on criminals. Perhaps the most surprising result is that the deterrence effect of a one percentage point increase in arrest rates is much larger than the same increase in the probability of conviction. Also surprising was that while longer prison lengths usually implied lower crime rates, the results were normally not statistically significant.

Source: *Journal of Legal Studies* 26 (1) (January 1997). John Lott at University of Chicago Law School, David B. Mustard at University of Chicago Department of Economics, http://www.lib.uchicago.edu/~llou/guns.html

As with most studies, this one, too, is likely to draw praise and criticism. The day after it was released, Reuter news service reported that The Center to Prevent Handgun Violence argued that the study did not take factors such as gun control laws and other crime prevention measures into account.

On the other hand, the research was immediately lauded by the National Rifle Association, which issued this press release.

DOCUMENT 89: "New Study Shows: Concealed Carry Laws Save Lives . . . ," National Rifle Association (August 8, 1996)

"Rather than standing in the way of public safety, the NRA has been promoting it. With the release of Professor John Lott's study, which shows that the passage of concealed carry laws has reduced violent crime including homicide, aggravated assault and rape, our efforts have been validated," said Mrs. Tanya K. Metaksa, Chief Lobbyist for the 3 million member National Rifle Association. "In state after state, the NRA has made life saving right-to-carry laws a reality. Not only has gun control failed in reducing criminal access to firearms, it has actually facilitated violent crime. Right-to-carry marks the triumph of victims over criminals. Today, 31 states have acted on the principle that honest citizens can and should be trusted to defend themselves and families against criminal attack."

Source: NRA Press Release, 8 August 1996.

The debate over right-to-carry laws may move beyond state boundaries. In July 1996, for example, Rep. Cliff Stearns (R-Fla.) introduced a bill to allow those persons with permits to carry concealed weapons in their home state to do so in other states, regardless of whether those other states issue concealed firearms permits.

Beyond right-to-carry law, in an article printed in the *Atlantic Monthly*, writer Daniel D. Polsby argued that not only does gun control not work, but it also diverts attention away from more effective crime control measures.

DOCUMENT 90: "The False Promise of Gun Control," Daniel D. Polsby (March 1994)

Gun-control laws don't work. What is worse, they act perversely. While legitimate users of firearms encounter intense regulation, scrutiny, and bureaucratic control, illicit markets easily adapt to whatever difficulties a free society throws in their way. . . .

The thousands of gun-control laws in the United States are of two general types. The older kind sought to regulate how, where, and by whom firearms could be carried. More recent laws have sought to make it more costly to buy, sell, or use firearms (or certain classes of firearms, such as assault rifles, Saturday-night specials, and so on) by imposing fees, special taxes, or surtaxes on them. The Brady bill is of both types: it has a background-check provision, and its five-day waiting period amounts to a "time tax" on acquiring handguns. All such laws can be called scarcity-inducing, because they seek to raise the cost of buying firearms, as figured in terms of money, time, nuisance, or stigmatization.

Despite the mounting number of scarcity-inducing laws, no one is very satisfied with them. Hobbyists want to get rid of them, and gun-control proponents don't think they go nearly far enough. Everyone seems to agree that gun-control laws have some effect on the distribution of firearms. But it has not been the dramatic and measure effect their proponents desired . . .

. . . Over the long run, however, there is no substitute for addressing the root causes of crime—bad education and lack of job opportunities and the disintegration of families. Root causes are much out of fashion nowadays as explanations of criminal behavior, but fashionable or not, they are fundamental. *The root cause of crime is that for certain people, predation is a rational occupational choice.* Conventional crime-control measures, which by stiffening punishments or raising the probability of arrest aim to make crime pay less, cannot consistently affect the behavior of people who believe that their alternatives to crime will pay virtually nothing. . . .

The solution to the problem of crime lies in improving the chances of young men. Easier said than done, to be sure. No one has yet proposed a convincing program for checking all the dislocating forces that government assistance can set in motion. One relatively straightforward change would be reform of the educational system. Nothing guarantees prudent behavior like a sense of the future, and with average skills in reading, writing, and math, young people can realistically look forward to constructive employment and the straight life that steady work makes possible.

But firearms are nowhere near the root of the problem of violence. As long as people come in unlike sizes, shapes, ages, and temperaments, as long as they diverge in their taste for risk and their willingness and capacity to prey on other people or to defend themselves from predation, and above all as long as some people have little or nothing to lose by spending their lives in crime, disposition to violence will persist.

This is what makes the case for the right to bear arms, not the Second Amendment. It is foolish to let anything ride on hopes for effective gun control. As long as crime pays as well as it does, we will have plenty of it, and honest folk must choose between being victims and defending themselves.

Source: Atlantic Monthly, March 1994.

DOCUMENT 91: "Ten Essential Observations on Guns in America," James D. Wright (1995)*

[M]any efforts at gun control pertain to the initial retail sale of weapons, for example, the prohibition against gun purchases by people with felony records or alcohol or drug histories contained in the Gun Control Act of 1968, the national five-day waiting period, or various state and local permit and registration laws. Since felons rarely obtain guns through retail channels, controls imposed at the point of retail sale necessarily miss the vast majority of criminal firearms transactions . . .

Having learned (now more than a decade ago) that the criminal acquisition of guns involves informal and intrinsically difficult-to-regulate transfers that are entirely independent of laws concerning registration and permits, average gun owners often conclude (whether rightly or wrongly) that such measures must therefore be intended primarily to keep tabs on them, that registration or permit requirements are "just the first step" toward outright confiscation of all privately held firearms, and that mandated registration of new gun purchases is thus an unwarranted "police state" intrusion on law-abiding citizens' constitutional rights. Reasoning in this vein often seems bizarre or even psychotic to proponents of registration or permit laws, but it is exactly this reasoning that accounts for the white-hot ferocity of the debate over guns in America today . . .

Hardly any of the 50 million or so American families that own guns have ever harmed anyone with their guns, and virtually none ever intend to. Nearly everything these families will ever do with their firearms is both legal and largely innocuous. When, in the interests of fighting crime, we advocate restrictions on their rights to own guns, we are casting aspersions on their decency, as though we somehow hold them responsible for the crime and violence that plague this nation. Is it any wonder they object, often vociferously, to such slander?

Source: Society 32, no. 3 (March/April 1995).

Even though a majority of Congress or a state legislature may agree on a bill and pass it into law, that rarely stops the debate. For years after its passage, parties along the spectrum analyze statistics to see what can be determined about the effectiveness or ineffectiveness of such legislation.

The Brady Handgun Violence Prevention Act is certainly one such law. Passed into law on November 30, 1993, as Public Law 103–159, the battle to make the bill law lasted seven years. The main provisions require that a handgun purchaser wait five business days between applying for a handgun and actually purchasing it. During that time, the chief local law enforcement officer is required to conduct a background check on the applicant.

The Violent Crime Control and Law Enforcement Act of 1994 (P.L. 103–322) added to the prohibited persons list those who are under court order to stay away from a family member or who are otherwise engaging in stalking or threatening behavior.

The Brady law goes on to state that the information from the statement cannot be used for any other purpose than to approve or deny a handgun purchase and that the chief law enforcement officer to whom the statement was provided will destroy it and any records created as a result of that statement within 20 business days. The law also calls for the establishment of a national system that federally licensed dealers can reach by telephone or other electronic means to check an applicant's criminal background.

The bill contains a "sunset clause," meaning that at the end of five years, it will cease to be. By then, a national instant background check should be in place. States that already have a system by which to check a purchaser's background (an instant check or permit system, for example) are exempt from the provisions of Brady. However, states wishing to maintain their waiting periods after the law elapses will be allowed to do so. (See Appendix III.)

For now, however, in any state that does not have an acceptable alternative to the requirements detailed in Brady, a five-day waiting period exists during which time the licensed dealer, manufacturer, or importer must try to ensure the person purchasing the handgun is not prohibited from doing so. Purchasers must submit a statement containing name, address, date of birth, and the following data.

DOCUMENT 92: Brady Handgun Violence Prevention Act (1993)

(B) a statement that the transferee—

(i) is not under indictment for, and has not been convicted in any court of, a crime punishable by imprisonment for a term exceeding 1 year;

(ii) is not a fugitive from justice;

(iii) is not an unlawful user of or addicted to any controlled substance . . . ;

(iv) has not been adjudicated as a mental defective or been committed to a mental institution;

(v) is not an alien who is illegally or unlawfully in the United States;

(vi) is not a person who, having been a citizen of the United States, has renounced such citizenship; . . .

Source: Brady Law, Public Law 103–159, 30 November 1993.

One year after the enactment of Brady, the research arm of the U.S. Congress, the General Accounting Office, decided to look at the law's impact. Some of the criticisms and limitations of the Brady law are that it applies only to primary gun sales—those handguns sold by a federally licensed firearms dealer—and that there are no federal funds to back up this federal mandate.

DOCUMENT 93: *Gun Control: Implementation of the Brady Handgun Violence Prevention Act*, General Accounting Office (January 25, 1996)

To be implemented effectively, Brady depends on the cooperation of local law enforcement officials and gun dealers. However, Brady provides no federal funds to local law enforcement agencies to conduct the background checks, and, according to the Department of Justice (DOJ), these agencies cannot be penalized for refusing to conduct them. In addition, several local law enforcement officials have challenged in court the phase I background check provision. Gun dealers are heavily relied on to stop prohibited persons from buying guns, but ATF lacks the resources to inspect all gun dealers to ensure compliance with Brady. . . .

In July 1995, the Department of Justice issued a report on guns and crime in the United States. Among other information, the report noted that:

Over 40 million handguns have been produced in the United States since 1973. Most guns are not used to commit crimes. Further, most crime is not committed with guns. However, most gun crime is committed with handguns.

During 1993, there were 4.4 million murders, rapes, robberies, and aggravated assaults in the United States, and more than one-fourth of these violent crimes involved the use of a gun. From 1985 through 1994, the FBI received an annual average of over 274,000 reports of stolen guns. By definition, all stolen guns are available to criminals.

At the request of police agencies, ATF's National Tracing Center will trace firearms back to their original point of sale. More than three-quarters of the 83,000 guns used in crime that ATF traced for law enforcement agencies in 1994 were handguns.

Policymakers recognize that even a perfect felon identification system may not keep felons from obtaining firearms and that Brady may not directly result in measurable reductions of gun-related crimes.

For example, Brady does not apply to transactions between nonlicensed individuals. Tens of millions of handguns are already in private hands. Thus, the apparently sizable numbers of handgun transactions that take place between private individuals, such as at gun shows and even "on the street," are not subject to Brady's requirements. In fact, the purpose of Brady is to prevent convicted felons and other ineligible persons from purchasing firearms from licensed dealers.

Opponents of Brady point to a 1991 survey of state prison inmates, which showed that 73 percent of those who had ever possessed a handgun did not purchase it from a gun dealer. Generally, opponents contend that it is a mistake to claim Brady prevents criminals from obtaining handguns since anyone denied a purchase from a licensed dealer can easily obtain a gun from another source and will almost certainly do so. Also, denied applicants may have friends or spouses without a criminal record make the purchases from dealers for them.

On the other hand, Brady proponents use the same study to counter that 27 percent of those inmates surveyed obtained their firearms from licensed gun dealers and argue that no criminals should be able to buy guns from licensed dealers. Proponents acknowledge that criminal records checks alone will not prevent felons from obtaining firearms but could reduce dealer sales to disqualified persons; complement other crime control measures, such as stiffer mandatory sentences for firearms offenses; and clamp down on illegal gun trafficking.

Source: General Accounting Office *Gun Control: Implementation of the Brady Handgun Violence Prevention Act* (Washington, D.C.: Government Printing Office, 25 January 1996).

In the following entry, two professors from the Center for Research in Crime and Justice at New York University evaluate the Brady law.

DOCUMENT 94: "Keeping Guns out of the 'Wrong' Hands: The Brady Law and the Limits of Regulation," James B. Jacobs, J.D., and Kimberly A. Potter, J.D. (1995)

Gun control advocates hailed Brady as the most important federal gun control legislation of this generation. Its passage was greeted with predictions of a safer, more secure society . . .

Before the Brady law officially went into effect on February 28, 1994, gun control advocates predicted that 100,000 handgun purchases, out of 3.5 million, would be prevented annually. For supporters of Brady, every rejection of a handgun sale to an ineligible person constitutes one less armed and potentially dangerous person to threaten others. One year after Brady became effective, the law was declared a success. According to a survey by BATF, Brady prevented 41,000 people from purchasing handguns. BATF examined a random sample of 441,545 applications for handgun purchases from February 1994 to February 1995. It found 15,506 denials, for the following reasons: 4,365 felony records; 945 fugitives from justice; 97 people under indictment; 649 drug users; 152 illegal aliens; 63 people subject to restraining orders; 36 dishonorable discharges; 23 mental defectives; 2 juveniles; and 1 person who renounced U.S. citizens . . .

Assuming that under the Brady regulatory machinery up to 41,000 would-be handgun sales have been rejected, must we conclude that an equal number of presumptively dangerous persons have been prevented from obtaining handguns? Obviously not. Some percentage of the rejected purchasers already possessed a handgun and were merely attempting to add to their arsenal. More importantly, some unknown percentage of rejected purchasers subsequently may have obtained a handgun by submitting a false application to another FFL, by having a "straw man"—an eligible friend or relative—purchase the handgun for him, or by purchasing a handgun on the secondary market . . .

Brady supporters may have underestimated the ease with which this regulatory system can be circumvented and they may have overestimated the ability of government agencies to enforce these regulations . . .

It is hard to see the Brady law, heralded by many politicians, the media, and Handgun Control, Inc. as an important step toward keeping handguns out of the hands of dangerous and irresponsible persons, as anything more than a sop to the widespread fear of crime and to the feeling that "something has to be done" about guns. The Brady bill apparently plays into a strong American faith in the capacity of law and regulation to shape behavior. On its face, this faith is curious given the extent of law and regulatory evasion, especially in the area of gun control . . .

It is likely that, as time passes, Brady, although once heralded as a significant step toward curbing violent crime, will be demoted to a "small step" and more regulation will be demanded. . . . Extending Brady to the secondary market would be complex, expensive, and ineffective. Many different types of evasion would still be quite simple.

Thus, it is likely that the regulatory mind will turn to other strategies to create a thickened web of regulation that will make it difficult for irresponsible and dangerous persons to obtain handguns. But no such plausible system has, at least to our knowledge, yet been proposed. There is no reason why a federal licensing system would be any more successful than existing state and local licensing systems. Likewise, a registration system offers little promise in terms of crime control . . .

Unlike the matter of gun possession, on which the society is sharply divided, there is a unanimity in condemning the use of firearms to commit crimes. Thus, there is no political or practical obstacle to ensuring severe sentences for gun offenders. This should be the top priority for American law enforcement. At a minimum, it should be recognized that the premise underlying federal gun control policy—strong gun laws keep guns out of the wrong hands—has little, if any effect, in disarming ex-felons and other ineligibles.

Source: The Journal of Criminal Law and Criminology 86 (Fall 1995): 93–120.

One emotional moment at the Democratic National Convention came on August 26, 1996, during an address by Sarah Brady, chairman of Handgun Control, Inc., and her husband James—still disabled from a handgun injury suffered during an assassination attempt on President Reagan in 1981. James Brady was the Republican president's press secretary. The law is named for him.

She spoke about the difficulty of getting this piece of legislation passed and thanked President Clinton for keeping his promise to sign the law. She said the law has been tremendously effective. "Since the Brady law went into effect on February 28, 1994, the Brady law has stopped more than 100,000 convicted felons and other prohibited purchasers from buying a handgun. One hundred thousand. Today, and every day, the Brady law is stopping an estimated 85 felons from buying a handgun," she fold a supportive crowd.

As the entry above mentioned, gun control laws such as Brady are limited because they affect only primary gun markets—ones where guns are sold by licensed dealers. In the following entry, the authors discuss the secondary gun markets—ones where guns are sold by someone without a license.

DOCUMENT 95: "Regulating Gun Markets," Philip J. Cook, Ph.D., Stephanie Molliconi, M.P.H., and Thomas B. Cole, M.D., M.P.H. (1995)

[Licensed firearms] dealers are not well-regulated and used guns can be readily purchased from other sources. Both of these issues undercut the discrimination strategy for reducing gun violence . . .

In trying to understand gun markets and how they relate to criminal activity, it is useful to consider that guns have value in exchange as well as in use. For someone living a chaotic life without a regular address or source of income, a gun may serve as an important store of value that can be readily exchanged for other goods and services. A youth who purchases or steals a gun may hold on to it for a few weeks and then decide that he needs money—or drugs—more than a gun, at which point he will find a ready market among his peers . . .

Regulating gun transfers appears to be a promising method of keeping guns from the hands of youths and criminals or, at least, of limiting the time that they are armed. When guns are relatively scarce and expensive, youths may be slower to acquire a gun and quicker to sell it . . .

Youths and criminals tend to obtain their guns outside the regulated sector of licensed dealers. When asked in a recent survey how and where they got their last handgun, 43% of adult prisoners reported purchasing the gun. Of those who had purchased their handguns, only one-third purchased them in the primary market, a gun store or pawnshop. About 15% of their most recent handguns were acquired in primary transactions . . .

Youth are less likely than adult felons to obtain guns in the primary market since federal law prohibits FFLs from selling handguns to those under twenty-one and prohibits the sale of long guns to those under eighteen. In a survey of delinquents and inner-city youths, only 7% of inmates and 11% of students who owned handguns had purchased the gun from a gun or pawn shop . . .

Theft is an important source of guns for youths and criminals. . . . The average number of guns owned by gun-owning households is about four and one-half, so when a gun-owning household is successfully burglarized, several guns are likely to be included in the loot.

The 150–200 million firearms in private hands, one-third of which are handguns, provide an enormous pool of potential weapons for the illicit market. While no precise estimates are available, it is safe to say that more than a half million guns are stolen each year . . .

Police data understate the true number of guns lost to theft because not all gun thefts are reported to law enforcement agencies. One reason for non-report is that the victim himself is on the wrong side of the law . . .

Stolen guns differ from other stolen goods: the thief may be able to use the gun himself, he can easily transport it to the buyer, and he is likely to know individuals who are interested in buying a gun. Therefore, in the redistribution of stolen guns there is less need for a middleman than would be true for jewelry, silver, or collectors items. Professional fences and pawn shops do not appear to be critical links in this illegal market . . .

There are a variety of measures that would help reduce availability of guns to youths and criminals:

1. Both federal and state government can adopt reforms to increase the licensing fee for FFLs and regulate them more closely.

2. Local law enforcement agencies should give higher priority to burglaries and other crimes where guns are stolen.

3. Gun shows should be regulated or abolished.

4. The state or federal government could require all transactions to be channeled through FFLs or a government office.

Source: The Journal of Criminal Law and Criminology 86 (Fall 1995): 59–92.

ADDITIONAL READING

Department of the Treasury. *The Brady Law: The First 100 Days*, 27 July 1994.

———. *One-Year Progress Report: Brady Handgun Violence Prevention Act*, 28 February 1995.

Lacayo, Richard. "Gun Control: A Small-Bore Success." *Time*, 20 February 1995, 47–48.

McDowall, David, Colin Loftin, and Brian Wiersema. "Additional Discussion about Easing Concealed Firearms Laws." *The Journal of Criminal Law and Criminology* 86 (Fall 1995): 221–226.

McNichol, Tom. "Secret Weapons." *USA Weekend*, 29–31 December 1995, 4–5.

Polsby, Daniel D. "Firearms Costs, Firearms Benefits and the Limits of Knowledge." *The Journal of Criminal Law and Criminology* 86 (Fall 1995): 207–20.

———. "Daniel D. Polsby Replies." *The Journal of Criminal Law and Criminology* 86 (Fall 1995): 227–30.

Snyder, Jeffrey R. "A Nation of Cowards." *The Public Interest* 113 (Fall 1993): 40–55.

Violence Policy Center. "More Gun Dealers Than Gas Stations." Washington, D.C., 1992.

Witkin, Gordon, and Ted Gest. "Gun Control's Limits." *U.S. News and World Report*, 6 December 1993, 24–26.

Part VI

A Nation Divided

How we view the crime issue—and the gun control issue—depends somewhat on where we live. Rural residents often believe that they need to protect themselves and their neighbors because they cannot count on a small or distant police force to do it for them. Rural Americans often have a more pronounced connection to gun ownership. Target shooting and hunting are rites of passage for some rural youths. They are hardly urban pastimes.

While urban residents split on gun control, urban areas are generally the areas of strictest controls. The higher crime rate and residents' perceptions of their own safety play a role. Some say guns are an essential self-defense tool in a violent society. Others argue that the presence of guns further escalates the violence and believe that stricter controls would ultimately benefit the majority.

PUBLIC OPINION

Public opinion polls reflect these views. Generally, public opinion polls show that Americans do not favor lessening gun control regulations. In fact, there is usually a majority that wants stronger laws. However, results of opinion polls depend somewhat on the precise nature of what is being asked—and the timing. Some say that in polls taken shortly after a high profile shooting, the numbers favoring gun control are slightly higher.

DOCUMENT 96: Bureau of Justice Statistics Poll (1982)

Would you favor or oppose a law that would require a person to obtain a police permit before he or she could buy a gun?

	% Favor	% Oppose	% Don't Know
1972	70	27	3
1973	74	25	2
1974	75	24	1
1975	74	24	1
1976	72	27	1
1977	72	26	2
1980	69	29	2

Source: Bureau of Justice Statistics, U.S. Department of Justice, sourcebook 215 (1982).

The following entry shows some fluctuation in public opinion about stricter gun control. The May 1995 Gallup poll was taken just after the bombing of a federal office building in Oklahoma. That event involved no gun violence, but was linked to antigovernment sentiment. The poll included a question on stricter gun laws with other questions on Americans' views of paramilitary groups, distrust of the government, and citizens' rights to arm themselves against the government.

DOCUMENT 97: Gallup Poll Trend (May 1995)

In general, do you feel that the laws covering the sale of firearms should be made more strict, less strict or kept as they are now?

	Stricter Gun Laws—Trend			
	More strict	Less strict	Kept as are now	No opinion
1995 Apr 23–24	62%	12%	24%	2%
1993	67	7	25	1
1991	68	5	25	2
1990	78	2	17	3

Source: The Gallup Organization, May '95 Newsletter, Vol. 60, No. 2, Saturday, 13 May 1995.

The National Rifle Association provided the following summary findings of two national surveys commissioned by the NRA Institute for Legislative Action. In general, the surveys showed that Americans do not equate gun control with crime control; it noted that 20% of respondents thought the best thing the government could do to help reduce crime was to provide greater punishment for convicts and mandatory sentences. Reducing unemployment and bolstering the economy ranked second. The following relates some of the questions and answers from that report.

DOCUMENT 98: "Attitudes of the American Electorate toward Gun Control, 1978," Decision/Making/Information (1979)

The Perceived Efficacy of, and Need for, Gun Control Measures

"Anyone using a gun while committing a violent crime should receive a severe and mandatory prison sentence."   December 1978: 93% agree

"In general, would you say there are: already too many laws governing the present use of firearms, the present laws are about right, or that we need more such laws?"   May/June 1978: 13%—"already too many"; 41%—"about right"; 44%—"need more."

"And if there were to be more firearm laws, would you expect the crime rate to increase or increase? And would you expect that decrease/increase to be large or small?"   6%—large increase; 10%—small increase; 41%—stay the same; 33%—small decrease; 10%—large decrease.

"Occasional domestic shootings are tragic, but do not justify taking away the right of everyone to own a handgun."   May/June 1978: 72% agree.

". . . It has been estimated that a national gun registration program would cost about $4 billion per year, or about 20% of all dollars now spent on crime control. Would you favor or oppose the Federal government's spending $4 billion to enact a gun registration program?"   December 1978: 61% oppose.

"Have you yourself or a member of your household ever used a gun, even if it wasn't fired, for self-protection or for protection of property at home, at work, or elsewhere (except in military and police work)?"   14% answered yes, 86% answered no.

"Of those who used a gun for self-protection: Was this to protect against an animal or a person?"   44% said animal; 42% said person. 14% said both, bringing the total up to 58% animals and 56% persons.

"And, have you, yourself, ever been in a situation where you needed a gun to protect yourself or your family or property but there was no gun available?"   90% said have never needed and not had, 9% said needed to protect against person and 1% said needed to protect against animal.

Source: Decision/Making/Information, "Attitudes of the American Electorate toward Gun Control 1978," Commissioned by the Institute for Legislative Action of the National Rifle Association, 1979.

As already stated, the way questions are asked and the timing of the polls can sometimes influence the results. In the following entry, the NRA explains why.

DOCUMENT 99: "10 Myths of Gun Control," National Rifle Association (1994)

MYTH: "The majority of Americans favor strict new additional federal gun controls."

Polls can be slanted by carefully worded questions to achieve any desired outcome. It is a fact that most people do not know what laws currently exist; thus, it is meaningless to assert that people favor "stricter" laws when they do not know how "strict" the laws are in the first place. Asking about a waiting period for a police background check presumes, incorrectly, that police can and will actually conduct a check during the wait.

Similarly, it is meaningless to infer anything from support of a 7- or 5-day waiting period when respondents live in a state with a 15-day wait or a 1–6 month permit scheme in place. Asked whether they favor making any particular law "stricter," however, most people do not. Unbiased, scientific polls have consistently shown that most people:

• Oppose costly registration of firearms.
• Oppose giving police power to decide who should own guns.
• Do not believe that stricter gun laws would prevent criminals from illegally obtaining guns.

In 1993, Luntz Weber Research and Strategic Services found that only 9% of the American people believe "gun control" to be the most important thing that could be done to reduce crime. By a margin of almost 3–1, respondents said mandatory prison would reduce crime more than "gun control." This poll, unlike many others, allowed respondents to answer more honestly by using open ended questions without leading introductions. The result was an honest appraisal of the attitude of the American people: "gun control" is not crime control . . .

A more direct measure of the public's attitude on "gun control" comes when the electorate has a chance to speak on the issue. Public opinion polls do not form public policy, but individual actions by hundreds of thousands of citizens do . . .

In 1993, the Southern States Police Benevolent Association [SSPBA] conducted a scientific poll of its members. Sixty-five percent of the respondents identified "gun control" as the least effective method of combating violent crime. Only 1% identified guns as a cause of violent crime, while 48% selected drug abuse, and 21% said the failure of the criminal justice system was the most pressing cause. The officers also revealed that 97% support the right of the people to own firearms, and 90% said they believed the Constitution guarantees that right.

The SSPBA findings affirmed a series of polls conducted by the National Association of Chiefs of Police of every chief and sheriff in the country, representing over 15,000 departments. In 1991 the poll discovered for the third year in a row that law enforcement officers overwhelmingly agree that "gun control" measures have no effect on crime. A clear majority of 93% of the respondents said that banning firearms would not reduce a criminal's ability to get firearms, while 89% said that the banning of semi-automatic firearms would not reduce criminal access to such firearms. Ninety-two percent felt that criminals obtain their firearms from illegal sources; 90% agreed that the banning of private ownership of firearms would not result in fewer crimes. Seventy-three percent felt that a national waiting period would have no effect on criminals getting firearms. An overwhelming 90% felt that such a scheme would instead make agencies less effective against crime by reducing their manpower and [would] only serve to open them up to liability lawsuits.

These are the only national polls of law enforcement officers in the country, with the leadership of most other major groups adamantly refusing to poll their membership on firearms issues.

Source: National Rifle Association.

The following two entries demonstrate the divide that exists. Representatives from the National Rifle Association and Handgun Control, Inc. faced off in a January 29, 1990, issue of *Time* magazine.

DOCUMENT 100: "The Case for Firearms . . . The N.R.A.'s Executive Vice President Says Guns Will Keep America Free," J. Warren Cassidy (1990)

Scholars who have devoted careers to the study of the Second Amendment agree in principle that the right to keep and bear arms is fundamental to our concept of democracy. No high-court decision has yet found grounds to challenge this basic freedom. Yet some who oppose this freedom want to waive the constitutionality of the "gun control" question for the sake of their particular—and sometimes peculiar—brand of social reform.

In doing so they seem ready, even eager, to disregard a constitutional right exercised by at least 70 million Americans who own firearms. Contrary to current antigun evangelism, these gun owners are not bad people. They are hard working, law abiding, tax paying. They are safe, sane and courteous in their use of guns. They have never been, nor will they ever be, a threat to law-and-order.

History repeatedly warns us that human character cannot be scrubbed free of its defects through vain attempts to regulate inanimate objects such as guns. What has worked in the past, and what we see working now, are tough, N.R.A.-supported measures that punish the incorrigible minority who place themselves outside the law.

As a result of such measures, violent crimes with firearms, like assault and robbery, have stabilized or are actually declining. We see proof that levels of firearm ownership cannot be associated with levels of criminal violence, except for their deterrent value. On the other hand, tough laws designed to incarcerate violent offenders offer something gun control cannot: swift, sure justice meted out with no accompanying erosion of individual liberty.

Violent crime continues to rise in cities like New York and Washington even after severe firearm-control statutes were rushed into place. Criminals, understandably, have illegal ways of obtaining guns. Antigun laws—the waiting periods, background checks, handgun bans, et al.—only harass those who obey them. Why should an honest citizen be deprived of a firearm for sport or self-defense when, for a gangster, obtaining a gun is just a matter of showing up on the right street corner with enough money?

Antigun opinion steadfastly ignores these realities known to rank-and-file police officers—men and women who face crime firsthand, not police administrators who face mayors and editors. These law-enforcement professionals tell us that expecting firearm restrictions to act as crime-prevention measures is wishful thinking. They point out that proposed gun laws would not have stopped heinous crimes committed by the likes of John Hinckley Jr., Patrick Purdy, Laurie Dann or mentally disturbed, usually addicted killers. How can such crimes be used as examples of what gun control could prevent?

Source: Time, 29 January 1990, 22.

DOCUMENT 101: ". . . And the Case against Them . . . The Head of Handgun Control Says Weapons Are Killing the Future," Sarah Brady (1990)

[W]e are killing our future. Every day a child in this country loses his or her life to a handgun. Hundreds more are permanently injured, often because a careless adult left within easy reach a loaded handgun purchased for self-defense.

Despite the carnage, America stands poised to face an even greater escalation of bloodshed. The growing popularity of military-style assault weapons could turn our streets into combat zones. Assault weapons, designed solely to mow down human beings, are turning up at an alarming rate in the hands of those most prone to violence—drug dealers, gang members, hate groups and the mentally ill. . . .

. . . The only cooling-off period the N.R.A. favors is a postponement of legislative action. It counts on public anger to fade before such outrage can be directed at legislators. The N.R.A. runs feel-good ads saying guns are not the problem and there is nothing we can do to prevent criminals from getting guns. In fact, it has said that guns in the wrong hands are the "price we pay for freedom." I guess I'm just not willing to hand the next John Hinckley a deadly handgun. Neither is the nation's law-enforcement community, the men and women who put their lives on the line for the rest of us every day.

Two pieces of federal legislation can make a difference right now. First, we must require a national waiting period before the purchase of a handgun, to allow for a criminal-records check. Police know that waiting periods work. In the 20 years that New Jersey has required a background check, authorities have stopped more than 10,000 convicted felons from purchasing handguns.

We must also stop the sale and domestic production of semiautomatic assault weapons. These killing machines clearly have no legitimate sporting purpose, as President Bush recognized when he permanently banned their importation.

These public-safety measures are supported by the vast majority of Americans—including gun owners. In fact, these measures are so sensible that I never realized the campaign to pass them into law would be such an uphill battle. But it can be done.

Jim Brady knows the importance of a waiting period. He knows the living hell of a gunshot wound. Jim and I are not afraid to take on the N.R.A. leaders, and we will fight them everywhere we can. As Jim said in his congressional testimony, "I don't question the rights of responsible gun owners. That's not the issue. The issue is whether the John Hinckleys of the world should be able to walk into gun stores and purchase handguns instantly. Are you willing and ready to cast a vote for a common sense public-safety bill endorsed by experts—law enforcement?"

Source: Time, 29 January 1990, 23.

ADDITIONAL READING

Jeffe, Sherry Bebitch. "Gun Control: A Shift in Attitudes." *State Legislatures* 15, no. 5 (May/June 1989): 12–15.
Kleck, Gary. "Reasons for Skepticism on the Results from a New Poll on: The Incidence of Gun Violence among Young People." *The Public Perspective* (September/October 1993).

NATIONAL STATISTICS

The Federal Bureau of Investigation gathers annual data on homicide and other crimes. These data are printed in its annual Uniform Crime Reports. The following document is a compilation of more than 20 years of firearm homicide statistics. Notice that the number of homicides doubled in about the first 10 years of these statistics and, despite small decreases for several years at a time, remains at high levels. That can help explain why gun control has become an increasingly debated issue. We can also see that handguns regularly account for 70 to 80 percent of the firearms specified as the murder weapon. This shows why the focus of the gun control debate often centers on handguns.

DOCUMENT 102: Firearms Homicides in the United States since 1962, FBI Uniform Crime Reports

Year	Murders	Firearms	Handguns	Rifles	Shotguns	Other Guns*	Percent Firearms
1962	8,430	5,058					
1963	8,530	5,118					
1964	9,250	5,550					
1965	9,850	5,910					
1966	10,920	6,552					
1967	12,090	7,254					60%
1968	13,650	8,873	6,825	819	1,229		65%
1969	14,590	9,483	7,441	875	1,167		65%
1970	15,691	10,199	8,002	942	1,255		65%
1971	17,630	11,459	8,991	1,058	1,410		65%
1972	18,520	12,223	10,001	926	1,296		66%
1973	19,510	13,072	10,340	1,171	1,561		67%
1974	20,600	14,008	11,124	1,030	1,854		68%
1975	20,510	13,537	10,460	1,231	1,846		66%
1976	18,780	12,019	9,202	1,127	1,690		64%
1977	19,120	12,046	9,178	1,147	1,721		63%
1978	19,555	12,319	9,582	1,173	1,564		63%
1979	21,456	13,517	10,728	1,073	1,716		63%
1980	23,044	14,287	11,522	1,152	1,613		62%
1981	22,516	14,185	11,258	1,126	1,801		63%
1982	21,012	12,397	9,035	1,051	1,471	840	59%
1983	19,308	11,199	8,496	772	1,352	579	58%
1984	18,692	11,215	8,225	934	1,308	748	60%
1985	18,976	11,196	8,160	949	1,328	759	58%
1986	20,613	12,162	9,070	825	1,443	825	59%
1987	20,096	11,857	8,842	804	1,206	1,005	59%
1988	20,675	12,405	9,304	827	1,240	1,034	60%
1989	21,500	13,545	10,320	1,075	1,290	860	63%
1990	23,438	15,234	11,719	937	1,406	1,172	65%
1991	24,703	17,046	13,102	988	1,235	1,236	69%
1992	23,760	16,157	13,165	713	1,164	1,115	69%
1993	24,526	17,167	13,980	736	1,226	1,225	70%
1994	23,310	16,320	13,483	763	1,006	957	70%

*and guns not specified

Source: Annual Uniform Crime Reports from the Federal Bureau of Investigation, compiled by the Coalition to Stop Gun Violence.

The following entries examine one specific year (1994) of statistics in greater detail. In its Uniform Crime Report, the FBI details similar statistics for each year. Murder circumstances by weapon in 1994 is the category looked at. A felony type killing is one in which the victim was killed during the commission of a felony. There were a total of 22,076 murder victims in 1994.

DOCUMENT 103: Murder Circumstances by Weapon, United States (1994)

	Total Firearms	Handguns	Rifles	Shotguns	Other Guns
Victims:	15,456	12,769	723	953	1,011
Felony type total	3,003	2,602	105	159	137
Rape	15	12		3	
Robbery	1,632	1,148	56	75	83
Burglary	76	56	6	7	7
Larceny-theft	14	11	1		2
Motor vehicle theft	40	28	4	7	1
Arson	2	2			
Prostitution and commercialized vice	2	1	1		
Other sex offense	7	5	1	1	
Narcotic drug laws	1,081	962	27	51	41
Gambling	10	10			
Other—not specified	124	97	9	15	3
Suspected felony type	78	61	6	5	6
Other than felony type total	8,081	6,535	512	628	406
Romantic triangle	267	213	21	25	8
Brawl due to influence of alcohol	196	151	21	18	6
Brawl due to influence of narcotics	162	121	4	16	21
Argument over money or property	280	237	15	21	7
Other arguments	3,989	3,326	240	328	95
Gangland killings	99	89	5	2	3
Juvenile gang killings	1,096	950	59	49	38
Institutional killings	2	1	1		
Sniper attack	2	1			1
Other—not specified	1,988	1,446	146	169	227
Unknown	4,294	3,571	100	161	462

Source: FBI Uniform Crime Report, 1994.

There does seem to be a shift in the relationships between offenders and victims. Whether this turns out to be a turning point or an aberration remains to be seen. For example, for several years the FBI in its annual Uniform Crime Report ran a section similar to this one.

DOCUMENT 104: FBI Uniform Crime Report (1986)

Supporting the philosophy that murder is primarily a societal problem over which law enforcement has little or no control is the fact that nearly 3 of every 5 murder victims in 1986 were related to (16%) or acquainted with (42%) their assailant. Among all female murder victims in 1986, 30% were slain by a husband or boyfriend. 6% of the male victims were slain by a wife or girlfriend.

Source: FBI Uniform Crime Report, 1986.

But the entry in the 1994 Uniform Crime Report reads differently.

DOCUMENT 105: FBI Uniform Crime Report (1994)

Historical statistics on relationships of victims to offenders showed that the majority of murder victims knew their killer. However, in the last few years (1991 through 1994) the relationship percentages have changed. In 1994, less than half of the murder victims were related to (12%) or acquainted with (35%) their assailants. 13% of the victims were murdered by strangers, while the relationship[s] among victims and offender were unknown for 40% of the murders. Among all female murder victims in 1994, 28% were slain by husbands or boyfriends. 3% of the male victims were killed by wives or girlfriends.

Source: FBI Uniform Crime Report, 1994.

Gun control opponents argue that claiming that "crimes of passion" make up a large portion of homicides is disingenuous.

DOCUMENT 106: "10 Myths of Gun Control," National Rifle Association (1994)

The vast majority of murders are committed by persons with long established patterns of violent criminal behavior. According to analyses by the U.S. Senate Subcommittee on Juvenile Delinquency, the FBI, and Chicago, New York City, and other police departments, about 70% of suspected murderers have criminal careers of long standing—as do nearly half their victims. FBI data show that roughly 47% of murderers are known to their victims.

The waiting period, or "cooling-off" period, as some in the "gun control" community call it, is the most often cited solution to "crimes of passion." However, state crime records show that in 1992, states with waiting periods and other laws delaying or denying gun purchases had an overall violent crime rate more than 47% higher and a homicide rate 19% higher than other states. In the five states that have some jurisdictions with waiting periods (Georgia, Kansas, Nevada, Ohio and Virginia), the non-waiting period portions of all five states have far lower violent crime and homicide rates.

Recent studies by the Justice Department suggest that persons who live violent lives exhibit those violent tendencies "both within their home and among their family and friends and outside their home among strangers in society." A National Institute of Justice study reveals that the victims of family violence often suffer repeated problems from the same person for months or even years, and if not successfully resolved, such incidents can eventually result in serious injury or death. A study conducted by the Police Foundation showed that 90% of all homicides, by whatever means committed, involving family members, had been preceded by some other violent incident serious enough that the police were summoned, with five or more such calls in half the cases.

Circumstances which might suggest "crimes of passion" or "spontaneous" arguments, such as a lover's triangle, arguments over money or property, and alcohol-related brawls, comprise 29% of criminal homicides, according to FBI data. Professor James Wright of the University of Massachusetts describes the typical incident of family violence as "that mythical crime of passion" and rejects the notion that it is an isolated incident by otherwise normally placid and loving individuals. His research shows that it is in fact "the culminating event in a long history of interpersonal violence between the parties."

Wright also speaks to the protective use of handguns. "Firearms equalize the means of physical terror between men and women. In denying the wife of an abusive man the right to have a firearm, we may only be guaranteeing her husband the right to beat her at his pleasure," says Wright.

Source: National Rifle Association, "10 Myths of Gun Control," 1994.

The following entry represents a study that shows that most guns used in crime are relatively new. Over half of the recovered guns used in crimes were five years old or less.

DOCUMENT 107: Street Age of Recovered Handguns Traceable to First Retail Sale: Composite for 18 Selected Greater Metro Areas, January 1–September 30, 1979

Total handguns: 14,429 (100%)

1 year or less: 2,525 (18%)

2 years: 1,405 (10%)

3 years: 1,187 (8%)

4 years: 1,206 (8%)

5 years: 1,184 (8%)

6 years: 984 (7%)

7 years: 932 (7%)

8 years: 770 (5%)

9 years: 595 (4%)

10 years or more: 3,641 (25%)

Source: Hearing before the Subcommittee on the Constitution, Committee on the Judiciary, U.S. Senate, 96th Cong., 15 September 1980.

INTERNATIONAL COMPARISONS

In contrast to many other countries, the United States has less restrictive gun control laws. Just how that impacts the U.S. violence rates is under debate. Some say U.S. laws and attitudes are too dissimilar to those of other countries to come to any conclusions; others say the numbers speak for themselves.

DOCUMENT 108: "The Allure of Foreign Gun Laws," David B. Kopel, J.D. (1994)

To many advocates of restrictive firearms laws, the necessity of imitating foreign-style gun control laws is painfully obvious. But surprisingly, there has been little research into how these foreign gun laws work, if they work at all . . .

In Japan, violent crime and homicide are virtually unknown (except for crimes perpetrated by the *yakuza* gangsters, and the murder of children by suicidal parents). Japan prohibits handguns and rifles. Shotguns may be obtained only after a rigorous licensing process that even includes a short psychiatric examination. The almost complete prohibition on guns in Japan has been strictly enforced ever since 1588 [by a military dictator] . . .

Only one other country examined . . . has a murder rate as low as Japan. That country is Switzerland, where gun control laws are also strict, but in a rather different way.

Every Swiss male aged 20 to 50 is strictly required to spend several weeks a year in militia training. Switzerland has no professional standing army and has always relied for defense on having its entire male population trained in warfare and ready to mobilize. As part of the militia duty, every militiaman (that is, every male aged 20–50) is given a fully automatic assault rifle, required to keep it in his home, and obliged to periodically demonstrate his marksmanship proficiency.

Swiss policy makes the acquisition of other weapons simple for everyone, including women and men who are too old for militia service. Ammunition sales are subsidized; 3,000 shooting ranges flourish in a nation two-thirds the size of West Virginia. Many long guns may be bought with no restrictions at all (whereas federal U.S. law requires all gun purchases to be registered at the point of sale). Most handguns and some rifles require a simple permit to purchase, which is given freely to any adult who is not a criminal, alcoholic, or otherwise disqualified . . .

What Japan and Switzerland have in common (and what is conspicuously absent in most of the metropolitan United States) is a very strong family structure, tightly-knit communities, stable residential patterns, and good relationships across generational lines. The crucial variable is not the presence of firearms, but the degree to which young people are successfully socialized into non-criminal, responsible behavior patterns . . .

Finally, the "public health" campaign to outlaw guns because of the allegedly successful gun control polices of other nations ignores the potential crimiogenic effect of those controls. American rates for crimes that usually involve guns (such as murder) and crimes that rarely involve guns (such as rape) are both far higher than the rates in most democratic nations. Curiously, the American residential burglary rate is below that of other nations. Perhaps this is because in the United States, an American burglar who breaks into an occupied home faces a risk of being shot that equals his risk of going to prison. In contrast, burglars in other nations do not face such risks . . .

Given the poor record of restrictive firearms laws in other English-speaking countries, the simplistic, reflexive insistence of the gun prohibition lobby and its medical allies that the United States immediately import foreign gun control laws may imperil, rather than protect, public health.

Source: The Journal of the Medical Association of Georgia 83 (March 1994): 153–55.

DOCUMENT 109: Basic Facts . . . International Comparisons, Coalition to Stop Gun Violence (1996)

The murder rate in the United States surpasses that of every other industrialized country in the world.

The murder rate in Washington, D.C. is fifteen times greater than that in Northern Ireland, a nation plagued by terrorism. This level of handgun violence does not occur in other developed nations. In 1990, handguns were used to murder 22 people in Great Britain, 68 in Canada, 87 in Japan, and 11,719 in the U.S.

The number of young men killed in the U.S. versus the rest of the world also is staggering. In 1990, the homicide rate per 100,000 population for males ages 15–24 was as follows:

Country	Rate
United States	37.2
Italy	4.3
Germany	1.1
Canada	0.9
United Kingdom	0.6
Japan	0.5

Why is there such a large discrepancy between these nations? One reason is that in Germany, France, Canada, Britain, and Japan, handguns and assault weapons are virtually banned from the general public.

A study by Arthur Kellermann comparing the rates of firearm violence in Seattle, Washington, and Vancouver, Canada, demonstrates how a ban on handguns in the United States would decrease violence. These two cities are less than three hours apart by car and are culturally similar in many ways. However, Vancouver regulates handguns strictly. The two cities have similar rates of burglary, robbery, and assault, but in Seattle there is an almost five times greater risk of being murdered with a handgun than in Vancouver.

Source: Coalition to Stop Gun Violence.

DOCUMENT 110: "10 Myths of Gun Control," National Rifle Association (1994)

MYTH: "Stiff 'gun control' laws work as shown by the low crime rates in England and Japan, while U.S. crime rates continue to soar."

All criminologists studying the firearms issue reject simple comparisons of violent crime among foreign countries. It is impossible to draw valid conclusions without taking into account differences in each nation's collection of crime data, and their political, cultural, racial, religious, and economic disparities. Such factors are not only hard to compare, they are rarely, if ever, taken into account by "gun control" proponents.

Only one scholar, attorney David Kopel, has attempted to evaluate the impact of "gun control" on crime in several foreign countries. In his book The Samurai, The Mountie and The Cowboy: Should America adopt the gun controls of other democracies?, named a 1992 Book of the Year by the American Society of Criminology, Kopel examined numerous nations with varying gun laws, and concluded: "Contrary to the claims of the American gun control movement, gun control does not deserve credit for the low crime rates in Britain, Japan, or other nations." He noted that Israel and Switzerland, with more widespread rates of gun ownership, have crime rates comparable to or lower than the usual foreign examples. And he stated: "Foreign style gun control is doomed to failure in America. Foreign gun control comes along with searches and seizures, and with many other restrictions on civil liberties too intrusive for America. Foreign gun control . . . postulates an authoritarian philosophy of government fundamentally at odds with the individualist and egalitarian American ethos."

America's high crime rates can be attributed to revolving-door justice. In a typical year in the U.S., there are 8.1 million serious crimes like homicide, assault, and burglary. Only 724,000 adults are arrested and fewer still (193,000) are convicted . . .

Foreign countries are two to six times more effective in solving crimes and punishing criminals than the U.S. In London, about 20% of reported robberies end in conviction; in New York City, less than 5% result in conviction, and in those cases imprisonment is frequently not imposed. Nonetheless, England annually has twice as many homicides with firearms as it did before adopting its tough laws. Despite tight licensing procedures, the handgun-related robbery rate in Britain rose about 200% during the past dozen years, five times as fast as in the U.S.

Part of Japan's low crime rate is explained by the efficiency of its criminal justice system, fewer protections of the right to privacy, and fewer rights for criminal suspects than exist in the United States. Japanese police routinely search citizens at will and twice a year pay "home visits" to citizens' residences. Suspect confession rate is 95% and trial conviction rate is over 99.9%. The Tokyo Bar Association has said that the Japanese police routinely "engage in torture or illegal treatment. Even in cases where suspects claimed to have been tortured and their bodies bore the physical traces to back their claims, courts have still accepted their confessions." Neither the powers and secrecy of the police nor the docility of defense counsel would be acceptable to most Americans. In addition, the Japanese police understate the amount of crime, particularly covering up the problem of organized crime, in order to appear more efficient and worthy of the respect the citizens have for the police. Widespread respect for law and order is deeply ingrained in the Japanese citizenry. This cultural trait has been passed along to their descendants in the United States where the murder rate for Japanese-Americans (who have access to firearms) is similar to that in Japan itself.

If gun availability were a factor in crime rates, one would expect European crime rates to be related to firearms availability in those countries, but crime rates are similar in European countries with high or relatively high gun ownership, such as Switzerland, Israel, and Norway, and in low availability countries like England and Germany. Furthermore, one would expect American violent crime rates to be more similar to European rates in crime where guns are rarely used, such as rape, than in crimes where guns are often used, such as homicide. But the reverse is true: American non-gun violent crime rates exceed those of European countries.

Source: National Rifle Association, "10 Myths of Gun Control," 1994.

ADDITIONAL READING

"Advance Data from Vital and Health Statistics," no. 242. Hyattsville, Md.: National Center for Health Statistics (NCHS), 1994.
Calathes, W. "Criminal Justice and Underdevelopment: A Case Study of the Jamaican Gun Court Act." *Journal of Caribbean Studies* 6 (1988): 323–58.

Federal Bureau of Investigation. Annual Uniform Crime Reports.
Kopel, David. *The Samurai, the Mountie, and the Cowboy: Should America Adopt the Gun Controls of Other Democracies?* Buffalo, N.Y.: Prometheus Books, 1992.
Wright, James, et al. *Under the Gun: Weapons, Crime and Violence in America.* Hawthorne, N.Y.: Aldine de Gruyther, 1983.

Part VII

Law Enforcement's Role

Police have always played a big role in the gun control debate. The views of law enforcement representatives have been eagerly sought and championed by legislators and lobbyists on both sides of the issue. Just as there is disagreement within the general population over whether gun control will curb violence, the debate is ongoing within the police community as well. The following are some representative samples of testimony or statements by leading police organizations.

DOCUMENT 111: Concluding Observations—New Approaches to Firearm Abuse, Police Foundation (1977)

1. The theft of firearms is a significant national problem that should be given careful attention by Congress and the Executive Branch. The apparent high volume of theft suggests that enough firearms are now stolen each year from law-abiding citizens to fill most criminal needs. Despite any dispute over legislative proposals to register firearms or otherwise regulate sale or possession, there should be general agreement on the urgent need to address the problem of firearm thefts. At a minimum ATF [the federal Bureau of Alcohol, Tobacco and Firearms] should be required to collect basic data on thefts from its licensees, including volume and circumstances. This step is essential to planning future action that might include requirements that licensees take special security precautions to prevent thefts.

2. ATF should centralize, monitor, and use data available from its licensees having to do with the distribution, sale and disposition of fire-

arms. ATF should also require standardization of serial numbers. These steps are essential for evaluating the effectiveness of the 1968 act, and for planning future enforcement strategies. Again this is a law enforcement need that transcends any debate about firearm registration or other new restrictions.

3. Higher priority oversight and funding from Congress and the Executive Branch are necessary to give ATF the resources and direction it needs to enforce the law effectively. As currently funded and supervised, ATF is not doing the job that the 1968 act envisioned, and is not at all prepared to enforce any new laws that might be enacted.

4. Illegal interstate commerce in firearms found in cities that have strong state restrictions on firearm purchases provides evidence that the 1968 act has not fulfilled its goal of helping states combat firearms abuse with their own laws. Isolate[d] state and local laws have not worked in keeping firearms from criminals. The 1968 act's provision that firearm purchasers need only swear that they are not felons, fugitives, narcotics abusers, or mental defectives—with no verification of the claim—has not been a realistic enforcement tool. Thus, we found firearms flowing from states with weak laws into states with strict laws in much the same way heroin and other illegal drugs enter the United States from places that have few or no restrictions on their production or sale. The most realistic enforcement efforts, therefore, require federal law or federally mandated uniform state laws.

5. The variation in confiscation rates found in the participating cities [referring to Document 107] suggests that police policies and procedures in this regard should be examined further with a view toward developing the best method of confiscating firearms from persons possessing them illegally. . . .

6. The relatively young age of firearms in the sample of confiscated firearms that were traced suggests that new federal firearm legislation might have a faster impact than had previously been thought. It seems that the older weapons are proportionately less often involved in crimes than their share of the firearm stockpiles suggests they would be, and that the firearm involved in a crime usually has been manufactured no more than four years previous to its confiscation. The relative "newness" of the firearms in those samples raises the further question of where all the old firearms are.

7. The analysis of brands of firearms seized, and the finding that the same manufacturers were represented in similar proportions in cities in every region of the country, suggests that firearm commerce flows in a national market and that regulating such commerce is appropriately a federal responsibility. We found a small number of manufacturers dominating the market in all cities, with no city showing a local manufacturer in a dominant position.

8. The analysis of types of firearms confiscated suggests that price is not a significant factor in the handguns used for the commission of crimes. The data indicate that expensive handguns are used as often as inexpensive ones. This finding bears directly on the potential of legislative proposals to ban certain types of handguns based on their quality. It also casts doubt on the potential of other proposals to tax firearms to . . . people prone to crime will not be able to afford them.

9. The data on firearm commerce reported by ATF, although not recorded precisely, suggest that the volume of commerce is so high that any registration or licensing effort requiring prescreening of firearm purchasers would require a massive paperwork and clerical effort. With millions of new firearms manufactured and sold each year and millions more transferred second hand, any system interned to keep track of them and screen their owners—without limiting the volume of such manufacture and sale to drastically smaller absolute numbers—would involve a cumbersome and expensive government effort. Such a system may be worthwhile, but the difficulty of implementing it should be acknowledged and planned for realistically.

10. The analysis of current local police efforts suggests a need for new approaches to the job of enforcing firearm possessing laws. Attention should be focused on the sellers of illegal firearms, with possession violations used as a way of reaching higher up in the chain of illegal commerce. Any new firearm legislation, whether on the national, state, or local level, should reflect this enforcement strategy by making the sale of a firearm to someone not authorized to own one a distinct and far more serious crime than simple possession.

Source: Steven Brill, *Firearm Abuse: A Research and Policy Report*, Police Foundation, 1977.

The following article was written by attorney and former Chicago police superintendent Richard J. Brzeczek.

DOCUMENT 112: "Law Enforcement Perspective on Utility of Handguns," Richard J. Brzeczek (1983)

One of the arguments I get from discussions and meetings and even debates on television with NRA people is that they try to persuade me that they know how to use a gun. . . . I can talk about my 12,575 police officers and how well they know how to use a gun, because we do spend a lot of time, a lot of money, and a lot of effort training police officers in the use of a gun, how to point it, cock the hammer, and how to pull the trigger and fire under different circumstances.

I . . . will agree that "how to use a gun" is not the problem that we have in law enforcement agencies. The problem is whether the officers know when to use the gun, and when not to use the gun, and that is the real issue with most of the people who own guns either legally or otherwise. Do they really know when to use a gun? Can they differentiate among the myriad offenses? Are they sufficiently acquainted with the intrinsic elements of different offenses so they can decide whether, in the face of that specific type of offense, a citizen can use deadly force to protect his home or protect his own life?. . . .

Source: Hamline Law Review 6 (July 1983): 333–40.

One of the first major breaches between law enforcement and the National Rifle Association, traditionally a close alliance, came over the armor-piercing bullet debate. The NRA opposed the bill banning armor-piercing ammunition, noting that the ban could affect rounds of ammunition used by hunters. Indeed, the bill was drafted using broad language that could well have banned sporting rifle cartridges. But the debate had a serious public relations fallout.

Osha Gray Davidson details the difficulties the organization had in taking what was seen as a stand against friends.

DOCUMENT 113: "The Bullet and the Badge," *Under Fire: The NRA and the Battle for Gun Control*, Osha Gray Davidson (1993)

"The NRA and the police were tight," says one twenty-seven-year police veteran and firearms instructor. "If you asked someone, 'Where do I go to learn first aid?' they'd send you to the Red Cross. There's no place else. If you asked somebody, 'Where do I go to learn how to shoot?' there was just no other place: It was the NRA."

In addition to training the police, the NRA also sponsored hundreds of shooting matches for law enforcement officers each year. Their shared affinity for guns of all kinds provided a solid foundation on which to build their relationship. The NRA emphasized this alliance in publications with titles such as *NRA and Law Enforcement: America's Anticrime Team. . . .*

The bill was overly broad, but had the legislative restrictions been more narrowly defined, the NRA would have still likely opposed it on the grounds that the bill opened the door to other gun-control measures. The group's concern about definitional problems was both a reason and an excuse.

The NRA took a drubbing for its opposition, especially after the pro-gun-control group Handgun control, Inc. ran an advertisement in police trade magazines with the headline HELP STOP THE COPKILLERS.

The strategy was effective. Across the country police groups reacted in outrage. Newspaper editorials and television commentators asked how the National Rifle Association could be defending "cop-killers.". . . .

The NRA realized that it now had a major problem on its hands. . . . Jerry Kenney of the New York Daily News—an NRA supporter—expressed the views of many people both inside the organization and out when he condemned the NRA's opposition to the bill.

"Hunters and target shooters have traditionally been known as sportsmen and most of them are members of the NRA," he wrote. "They stand by the organization in most of its decisions, particularly in the campaign against gun control. But the stand the NRA is taking in the name of its many millions of members to allow the production and sale of ammunition that has no logical use except to penetrate armor and bulletproof vests is an outrage."

The NRA sought to dampen the outcry by mailing the membership an informational call to arms:

Mark my words the so-called "cop-killer" bullet issue is a Trojan Horse waiting outside gun owners' doors. If the anti-gunners have their way, this highly publicized and emotionalized issue will be used to enact a backdoor, national gun control scheme. . . . Never has an issue been more distorted or downright lied about than the armor-piercing bullet issue. The anti-gun forces will go to any lengths to void your right to keep and bear arms. It's time we set them straight! Anti-gun groups are well aware of our activities with law enforcement and have been looking for an issue to drive a wedge between America's gun owners and our nation's law enforcement.

A variety of police groups issued formal denunciations of the NRA for opposing the legislation. There were, however, a few muted voices of dissent. For example, the chairman of the Firearms and Explosives Subcommittee of the International Association of Chiefs of Police sent a letter to the organization's director complaining about what appeared to him to be a rush to judgment on the matter:

Partial information, faulty logic and emotionalism were found to exist in public discussion, in statements with the law enforcement community, and in congressional deliberations. We urge you as president of the International Association of Chiefs of Police to suspend any official Association activities and withhold all public statements regarding "cop-killer bullets" until a rational and informed study of the problem has been conducted. This subcommittee believes that this is necessary to avoid potentially damaging legislative overreactions.

Source: Osha Gray Davidson, *Under Fire: The NRA and the Battle for Gun Control* (New York: Henry Holt, 1993), 89–92.

A compromise bill was introduced in June 1984, but support crumbled and with upcoming elections, additional hearings and a vote were shelved. In late 1985, a bill similar to the one the NRA had originally opposed was passed by a 400 to 21 vote in the House. The Senate overwhelmingly passed the bill in August 1996 and President Reagan signed it into law on August 28, 1986. In his book, Davidson explains that one of the reasons the bill passed "with little fanfare" was because the gun control debate had now shifted to the McClure-Volkmer bill, or the Firearms Owners Protection Act.

The Firearms Owners Protection Act [PL 99–308, PL 99–360], which passed in 1986 after about 10 years of congressional debate, eased some of the restrictions on interstate transport of guns and some other provisions of the 1968 Gun Control Act. By the time it passed, most of the more objectionable aspects to gun control advocates and law enforcement had been removed.

In a version of the bill being debated in 1986, the Law Enforcement Steering Committee Against S. 49 objected to provisions of the bill. The Steering Committee was comprised of the Federal Law Enforcement Officers Association, Fraternal Order of Police, International Association of Chiefs of Police, International Brotherhood of Police Officers, Major Cities Police Chiefs, National Association of Police Organizations, National Organization of Black Law Enforcement Executives, National Sheriffs' Association, National Troopers' Coalition, Police Executive Research Forum, Police Foundation, and Police Management Association.

DOCUMENT 114: Law Enforcement Steering Committee Letter (April 21, 1986)

At a time when our nation is fighting terrorists overseas, Congress soon may greatly increase the opportunities at home for terrorists and other criminals to obtain untraceable firearms, including concealable handguns, and transport them across state lines.

But the Senate can prevent the potential escalation in gun violence and thus help to safeguard the lives of law enforcement officers and the citizens they are sworn to protect.

This is because you will be able to vote with law enforcement on several key amendments to S. 49, gun legislation that is pending in the Senate after having been modified and passed by the House of Representatives.

The Law Enforcement Steering Committee Against S. 49, made up of the nation's 12 principal law enforcement organizations, urges you to support amendments to the pending legislations that will:

Maintain the right of states to control the transport of firearms within their borders, without interfering with the ability of individuals to transport across state lines unloaded, inaccessible firearm[s] for sporting purposes;

Close a loophole in House-passed legislation that would facilitate unrecorded distribution of weapons by and to terrorists and other criminals;

Retain current law that requires gun dealers to keep records on all firearms sales, thus preserving law enforcement's ability to trace firearm[s] used in crime.

These amendments represent bottom-line needs of law enforcement in its fight to forestall gun crimes and deal with violent offenders.

I. The gun lobby says that current federal gun legislation needlessly obstructs the legitimate interests of sportsmen by keeping them from transporting firearm[s] across state lines for hunting, shooting competitions and other sporting events. The Law Enforcement Steering Committee proposes to respond to that problem while retaining the rights of the states to regulate the transport of firearms across their lines. The Steering Committee's amendment would permit a resident of a state who lawfully possesses and carries a firearm in his home state to transport that firearm to another state where he may lawfully possess and carry it if:

The transport of the firearm is for a lawful sporting purpose;

The firearm is consistently transported in a way that it is not readily accessible (handguns must be in locked containers); and

Ammunition being transported for the firearm is kept in locked compartment.

In sum, the Steering Committee's amendment would keep intact the states' ability to enforce concealed weapons laws with respect to their own residents and to control the flow of firearms within their borders, except when those firearms were transported interstate for clearly defined, legitimate sporting purposes.

II. The second LESC amendment would close a loophole in the House bill that would facilitate unrecorded distribution of weapons by terrorists. According to a February 10, 1986 memo prepared by the director of the Bureau of Alcohol, Tobacco and Firearms, S.49 contains too narrow a definition of persons "engaged in the business" of dealing in firearms. "Consequently," according to the BATF memo, "some criminal activity that may be prosecuted under existing law for engaging in firearms business without a license may not be prosecutable under S.49. For example, an individual who on several occasions disposed of firearms at cost to terrorists for the purpose of facilitating their crimes may not be held to be 'engaging in the business.' "

The Steering Committee amendment makes clarifying changes in the House bill's definition of a dealer to make certain that the definition of a dealer covers individuals who dispose of firearms to terrorist groups.

III. A final LESC amendment would retain current law that requires that dealers keep records of all sales. Without such requirements, law enforcement would face a flood of untraceable firearms used in crimes. The amendment simply assures that firearms dealers continue to be required to take a few minutes to record sales of firearms.

Source: Congressional Record, Senate, 6 May 1986, p. S5356.

However, the law enforcement community cannot be pigeonholed into either a supporting or objecting role in every gun control debate. Depending on the survey and the particulars of the bills being discussed, there is room for a range of opinions. Clayton E. Cramer and David B. Kopel, research director for the Colorado think tank Independence Institute, cite surveys that show that police tend to be in favor of citizens carrying concealed weapons.

DOCUMENT 115: " 'Shall Issue': The New Wave of Concealed Handgun Permit Laws," Clayton E. Cramer and David B. Kopel (1995)

Virtually all United States citizens agree that the police may lawfully use force to protect crime victims. Accordingly, the question is not whether force per se is legitimate, but who may legitimately use force. As a moral matter, the creature of government should not have powers greater than its creator, the people. An individual police officer, acting under the best judgment and reasonable understanding of the facts of a particular encounter, has the individual moral authority to fire a weapon for protection of self or another person. How then can the same act, performed by a crime victim, suddenly become immoral? Many police officers would agree that citizen self-defense is legitimate.

The first survey of police attitudes toward concealed carry was a 1976 poll conducted by Boston Police Commissioner Robert diGrazia. Ironically, the poll was part of an effort to find national police support for an initiative to ban handgun ownership in Massachusetts. In the national survey, fifty-one percent of police chiefs agreed with the statement, "Persons who have a general need to protect their own life and property, like those who regularly carry large sums of money to the bank late at night, should be allowed to possess and carry handguns on their person." Fifty-seven percent of chiefs expected their subordinates to be more supportive of such carrying.

Rank-and-file police officers are even more supportive of citizens carrying guns. In 1991, *Law Enforcement Technology* conducted a poll of all ranks of police officers. Seventy-six percent of street officers believed that all trained, responsible adults should be allowed to obtain handgun carry permits; fifty-nine percent of managers agreed. [In their note, the authors wrote that the poll was based on readers sending in a survey form to the magazine. Because the polling was not conducted by random sample, the poll arguably may not reflect a true cross-section of all police opinion. Of course, a cadre of police chiefs who show up at a state capitol to testify against a concealed carry bill may also not be representative of police opinion, especially the opinion of street patrol officers.]

Source: Tennessee Law Review 62 (Spring 1995): 738–39.

Part VIII

The Public Health Community Enters the Debate

The debate over gun control takes on a new dimension with the entry of the public health community, which produced studies, some of which categorize the costs to society of handgun injuries and try to show how handguns are used more often to harm friends, acquaintances, and family members than for self-defense. Gun rights advocates strongly question the methodology of these studies and point to other studies that result in different conclusions.

Indeed, this is one area in which gun rights supporters say many of the documents included herein are so faulty that they object to their inclusion in this volume. However, since a computerized search of medical journals will hit on many of these studies, to omit them because one side in the debate disagrees with them would leave this volume incomplete. Instead, in many cases, the original article will be followed by responses from critics of the study. Also, some room has been devoted in this section to broader criticisms of the majority of these public health studies.

What plays out on the public health level is an interesting view on the larger gun control debate. Many physicians and researchers have come to the conclusion that restricting access to guns can reduce violence, suicide, and health care costs related to gunshot wounds. Their argument is similar to that of those who once said that mandating seat belt use would reduce the seriousness of car accident injuries or that public health campaigns that showed the hazards of smoking, coupled with increased restrictions or taxes on cigarettes, could reduce lung

Thanks to Julene Scinta for her help on Part VIII.

cancer and other smoking-related illnesses. To these researchers, gun violence is a disease and guns are the pathogens.

The other camp says these arguments are ridiculous because the studies completely leave out or skirt some issues of self-defense. Some studies count self-defense as successful only when a burglar has been killed, for example. They do not take into consideration the number of crimes averted—where the perpetrator was not shot and killed. These physicians and researchers say studies of this type are better left to criminologists and law enforcement officials than physicians.

For example, the Research Coordinator at the National Rifle Association's Institute for Legislative Action, Paul H. Blackman, Ph.D., has compiled a paper entitled *The Federal Factoid Factory on Firearms and Violence: A Review of CDC Research and Politics.* He argues that the Centers for Disease Control and Prevention (CDC), a branch of the U.S. Department of Health and Human Services, has staked out an antigun position and is avoiding or ignoring studies to the contrary. His paper also includes comments on studies that were not sponsored by the CDC, noting that in some cases, these authors established a gun control position that ensured future CDC funding for them. Some of Dr. Blackman's comments on specific documents follow the original entry. It will help show that there are very few areas of common ground in the gun control debate.

The NRA is by no means alone in its opposition to the conclusions of some of these studies. The following two documents oppose gun control.

DOCUMENT 116: "Guns in the Medical Literature—A Failure of Peer Review," Edgar A. Suter, M.D. (March 1994)

Errors of fact, design and interpretation abound in the medical literature on guns and violence. Many have credulously restated the opinions of partisan CDC researchers, but given short shrift to the refuting data and criticisms. For matters of "fact," it is not unusual to find third-hand citations of editorials rather than citations of primary data . . .

The responsible use and safe storage of any kind of firearm causes no social ill and leaves no victims. In act, guns offer positive social benefit in protecting good citizens from vicious predators. The overwhelming preponderance of data we have examined shows that between 25 to 75 lives may be saved by a gun for every life lost to a gun. Guns also prevent injuries to good people, prevent medical costs from such injuries, and protect billions of dollars of property every year. In view of the overwhelming benefits, it is ludicrous to punitively tax gun or ammunition ownership. Guns save far more lives than they cost.

The peer review process has failed in the medical literature. In the field of guns, crime, and violence, the medical literature—and medical politicians—have much to learn conceptually and methodologically from the criminologic, legal, and social science literature. Gross politicization of research will only increase the present disrespect in which medical journals and peer review are held by physicians.

To further an honest public debate, organized medicine and CDC researchers should adopt scientific objectivity and integrity and improve the peer review process. Since it has demonstrated it is unable to police itself, stringent oversight must be placed over the CDC's grant award process. Taxpayers must demand meaningful oversight of scientific integrity and competence.

If devotees of the "true faith" of gun prohibition and pacifists who deny we have a right to self-defense wish to eschew the safest and most effective tools of self-protection, they are welcome to do so. In this imperfect world their harmful philosophy must not be imposed upon an entire society. In essence, society should adopt a "Pro-Choice" approach to self-defense and gun ownership.

Source: Journal of the American Medical Association of Georgia 83 (March 1994): 133–47.

Some criminologists also view these public health studies as erroneous. The following entry relays some of their skepticism.

DOCUMENT 117: "Guns and Public Health: Epidemic of Violence or Pandemic of Propaganda?" Don B. Kates et al. (1995)

Predictably, gun violence, particularly homicide, is a major study topic for social scientists, particularly criminologists. Less predictably, gun crime, accidents, and suicide are also a topic of study among medical and public health professionals. Our focus is the remarkable difference between the way medical and public health writers treat firearms issues and the way social scientists treat those issues. Examination of the literature produced by medical and health writers reveals why their conclusions on firearms diverge so radically from those of criminological scholarship . . .

The abysmal quality of the anti-gun health advocacy literature may be explained by six conceptually discrete factors: intellectual and locutional sloppiness; intellectual confusion, ignorance of criminological or other facts; fraudulent omission of material fact, or statement of part of the fact calculated to deceive by the suppression of the whole; overt misrepresentation of facts; and what we call gun-aversive dyslexia—a reading disability engendered by a fear and loathing of guns so profound that health advocate sages who encounter adverse facts may be honestly unable to comprehend them . . .

. . . While the anti-gun editorials and articles discussed [several of them are included in the following documents] had the superficial form of academic discourse, the basic tenets of science and scholarship have too often been lacking. We call them "anti-gun health advocacy literature" because they are so biased and contain so many errors of fact, logic, and procedure that we cannot regard them as having a legitimate claim to be treated as scholarly or scientific literature.

Criminological and sociological analysis provides important, even crucial information as to the role of firearms in violence and the utility and viability of potential gun control strategies. Virtually all of this information is ignored or affirmatively suppressed in the health advocacy literature. That literature also shows consistent patterns of making misleading international comparisons, mistaking the differences between handguns and long guns, and exaggerating the number of children injured or killed, thereby building up the emotional content. Other distortions include presenting gun ownership in such a manner as to ignore or minimize the benefits, and measure defensive benefits purely in terms of attackers killed, rather than considering attacks deterred or attackers repelled. To the contrary, the criminological and sociological research literature demonstrates the existence of high risk groups for firearms misuse, and of the "career" criminals who commit many of the serious crimes in our society. Yet the anti-gun health advocacy literature consistently overlooks these data and attributes equal propensity to commit violent crime to all people.

The health advocacy literature exists in a vacuum of lock-step orthodoxy almost hermetically sealed from the existence of contrary data or scholarship. Such data and scholarship routinely goes unmentioned and the adverse emotional reaction of the gatekeepers of the health journals assures the elimination of contrary views from their pages.

Source: Don B. Kates, Henry E. Schaffer, Ph.D., John K. Lattimer, M.D., George B. Murray, M.D., and Edwin H. Cassem, M.D. *Tennessee Law Review* 62 (Spring 1995): 513, 531, 595–96.

The following public health studies aim to expand the debate beyond the core issue of individual rights by emphasizing the cost to the community. Several studies note that firearms, particularly handguns, are used disproportionately in suicides. Gun rights advocates claim this is an unfair conclusion, noting the higher suicide rate in some countries with stricter gun control laws than the United States. Proponents of stricter laws argue that gun access is one societal factor that can be controlled.

DOCUMENT 118: "Death and Injury by Firearms: Who Cares?" Janine Jagger, M.P.H., and Park Elliott, M.D., M.P.H., Ph.D. (1986)

Firearms are a major source of death and injury in the United States. The most recent available figures from the National Center for Health Statistics show that in 1982, firearms killed 33,000 people in the United States. Firearms are second only to motor vehicles as the most important cause of injury deaths.

Source: Journal of the American Medical Association 255, no. 22 (June 13, 1986): 3143–3144.

In the following study, researchers examined all gunshot deaths that occurred in King County, Washington, from 1978 to 1993. During this time, there were 743 firearm-related deaths; 398 of them (54%) occurred in the home where the gun was kept. In two instances (0.5%), the gun was used to shoot an intruder during attempted robbery. Seven persons (1.8%) were killed in self-defense.

DOCUMENT 119: "Protection or Peril?" Arthur L. Kellermann, M.D., M.P.H., and Donald T. Reay, M.D. (1986)

There are approximately 120 million guns in private hands in the United States. About half of all the homes in America contain one or more firearms. Although most persons who own guns keep them primarily for hunting or sport, three quarters of gun owners keep them at least partly for protection. One fifth of gun owners identify "self-defense at home" as their most important reason for having a gun.

Keeping firearms in the home carries associated risks. These include injury or death from unintentional gunshot wounds, homicide during domestic quarrels, and the ready availability of an immediate, highly lethal means of suicide . . .

Guns kept in King County homes were involved in the deaths of friends or acquaintances 12 times as often as in those of strangers. Even after the exclusion of firearm-related suicides, guns kept at home were involved in the death of a member of the household 18 times more often than in the death of a stranger...

Over 80 percent of the homicides noted during our study occurred during arguments or altercations. Baker has observed that in cases of assault, people tend to reach for the most lethal weapon readily available. Easy access to firearms may therefore be particularly dangerous in households prone to domestic violence...

The home can be a dangerous place. We noted 43 suicides, criminal homicides, or accidental gunshot deaths involving a gun kept in the home for every case of homicide for self-protection.

Source: The New England Journal of Medicine 314, no. 24 (June 12, 1986): 1557–560.

The NRA's Dr. Blackman points out what he sees as misleading about this study.

DOCUMENT 120: *The Federal Factoid Factory on Firearms and Violence* (1994)

The most egregious flaw in the study is that it ignores non-fatal protective uses of guns, which number over two million per year and thus exceed criminal misuses (plus suicides and accidents) by a 2.5- or 3-to-one margin. Although the authors originally warned that the study was of a single non-representative county, and noted that non-fatal protective uses were ignored, they have freely used the 43 as if it were definitive and national. As has been noted by others, their key approach was that, since the data which would test the hypothesis about the net risk-benefit of firearms for protection were not available, they would use data which was available. Of course, that meant ignoring the fact that some protective-use data were available, but were dismissed as irrelevant or imprecise.

Source: Paul H. Blackman, Ph.D., Research Coordinator, NRA Institute for Legislative Action, *The Federal Factoid Factory on Firearms and Violence: A Review of CDC Research and Politics,* presented at the annual meeting of the Academy of Criminal Justice Sciences, March 8–12, 1994.

DOCUMENT 121: "When Children Shoot Children: 88 Unintended Deaths in California," Garen J. Wintemute, M.D., M.P.H., et al. (1987)

Between 1977 and 1983, eight-eight California children 0–14 years of age were unintentionally shot and killed either by other children or by themselves. The majority of cases occurred while children were playing with guns they had found. Easy accessibility to guns, the resemblance of guns to toys, and gun malfunctions were all contributing factors. Handguns, particularly those of .22 caliber, were frequently involved.

Firearms rank among the United States' ten leading causes of death, accounting for more than 30,000 deaths annually. Unintentional firearm deaths are most common among children and young adults . . .

The belief that, on balance, firearms provide personal or household protection was directly involved in a number of deaths. Previous studies have established that this belief may be incorrect; unintentional fatal shootings of friends and family members in the home are as much as six times as common as fatal shootings of criminals.

Defects in current firearm design are important. It should be possible, for example to design firearms so that users can easily determine whether they are loaded . . .

Likewise, firearm safety catches should be designed so that they are automatically and always engaged unless held in a disengaged position by the user.

Source: Garen J. Wintemute, M.D., M.P.H., Stephen P. Teret, J.D., M.P.H., Jess F. Kraus, M.P.H., Ph.D., Mona A. Wright, and Gretchen Bradfield, M.S. *Journal of the American Medical Association* 257, no. 22 (June 12, 1987): 3107–109.

The following study was designed to extrapolate the cost of firearm injuries, based on the 133 persons admitted to San Francisco General Hospital during 1984 for firearm injuries. Handguns accounted for 81.3 percent of the injuries in which a weapon was specified; the circumstance behind nearly 70 percent of admissions was an assault.

DOCUMENT 122: "The Cost of Hospitalization for Firearm Injuries," Michael J. Martin, M.D., M.P.H., M.B.A., Thomas K. Hunt, M.D., and Stephen B. Hulley, M.D., M.P.H. (1988)

The hospital records for all patients . . . admitted during 1984 to San Francisco General Hospital because of firearm injuries were studied to determine the hospital costs and sources of payment for these injuries. . . . Only hospital costs (excluding professional fees) for the first hospitalization were studied. The total costs for the year were $905,809, an average cost per patient of $6915. Public sources paid 85.6% of this cost, while private sources paid only 14.4% . . .

Hospital costs ranged from $559 to $64,470, with an average of $6915 and a median of $4599. The total cost for all patients was $905,809. Government sources paid 85.7% of the costs. . . . Patients themselves paid only 1.4% of the costs.

Most patients were young and male and a disproportionate number were blacks. Most injuries occurred during assaults and handguns were by far the most common weapon.

Although suicides account for approximately half of all firearm deaths in the United States, they were an uncommon cause of hospitalization for firearm injury. This is not surprising, since those who attempt suicide by firearms are successful 92% of the time . . .

It is clear . . . that public sources bear the greatest burden of the cost of hospitalizations for firearm injuries. . . . The percentage of cost paid for by public sources is substantially greater for hospitalizations for firearm injuries than for all hospitalizations considered together . . .

The extrapolation of San Francisco's cost for hospitalizations for firearm injuries ($90,809/y) to the nation as a whole ($429 million/y) must be taken as a rough approximation.

The costs discussed herein substantially underestimate the total medical costs for firearm injuries, which probably total more than $1 billion per year for the United States. The costs do not include such costs as ambulance services, physicians' fees, readmissions, ambulatory care, follow-up visits, physical therapy, rehabilitation services, and long-term care. In addition, indirect costs such as lost work time, disability payments, and legal fees are not included. These indirect costs are generally twice as great as the direct costs and it is likely that they too are paid primarily by public sources.

Source: Journal of the American Medical Association 260, no. 20 (November 25, 1988): 3048–3050.

DOCUMENT 123: "Handgun Regulations, Crime, Assaults, and Homicide: A Tale of Two Cities," John Henry Sloan, M.D., M.P.H., et al. (1988)

Approximately 20,000 persons are murdered in the United States each year, making homicide the 11th leading cause of death and the 6th leading cause of the loss of potential years of life before age 65 . . .

Although similar in many ways, Seattle and Vancouver differ markedly in their approaches to the regulation of firearms.... In Seattle, handguns may be purchased legally for self-defense in the street or at home. After a 30-day waiting period, a permit can be obtained to carry a handgun as a concealed weapon. The recreational use of handguns is minimally restricted.

In Vancouver, self-defense is not considered a valid or legal reason to purchase a handgun. Concealed weapons are not permitted. Recreational uses of handguns (such as target shooting and collecting) are regulated by the province, and the purchase of a handgun requires a restricted-weapons permit. A permit to carry a weapon must also be obtained in order to transport a handgun, and these weapons can be discharged only at a licensed shooting club. Handguns can be transported by car, but only if they are stored in the trunk in a locked box.

... both cities enforce existing gun laws and regulations and convictions for gun-related offenses carry similar penalties.

Source: John Henry Sloan, M.D., M.P.H., Arthur L. Kellermann, M.D., M.P.H., Donald T. Reay, M.D., James A. Ferris, M.D., Thomas Koepsell, M.D., M.P.H., Frederick P. Rivaram, M.D., M.P.H., Charles Rice, M.D., Laurel Gray, M.D., and James Lo Gerfo, M.D., M.P.H. *The New England Journal of Medicine* 319, no. 19 (Nov. 10, 1988): 1256–261.

The following editorial accompanied the above study.

DOCUMENT 124: "Firearm Injuries: A Call for Science," Editorial, James A. Mercy, Ph.D., and Vernon N. Houk, M.D. (1988)

During 1984 and 1985 ... the number of people who died of injuries inflicted by firearms in the United States (62,897) exceeded the number of casualties during the entire 8½-year Vietnam conflict. In 1985 alone, 31,566 persons died as a result of firearm injuries—17,363 from suicide, 11,836 from homicide, 1,649 from injuries inflicted unintentionally, 242 during altercations with police, and 476 from undetermined causes. Mortality rates from firearms for women, for teenage boys, and for young men have been higher during the 1980's than at any time previously ...

... in the U.S. population 12 years of age or older, there was an annual average of 83,000 violent victimizations (i.e., assaults, rapes, and robberies) in which the offender used a gun. These victimizations resulted in at least 26,000 nonfatal firearm injuries per year. The victims had an average hospital stay of 16.3 days, more than twice as long as victims who received injuries from other weapons or unarmed offenders.

In their study, Sloan et al. analyzed data from Seattle, Washington, and Vancouver, British Columbia. These cities are fairly comparable with respect to demographic makeup, rates of criminal activity, and enforcement of firearm regulations, but Vancouver has more restrictive regulations for handgun ownership and use and a lower prevalence of firearm ownership than Seattle. During the study period, Seattle had the higher homicide rate of the two cities. This difference was accounted for by a 4.8-fold greater risk of being killed with a firearm in Seattle than in Vancouver. On the basis of these findings, the authors conclude that restricting access to handguns may reduce a community's homicide rate.

. . . Four steps can be taken to improve the base of information needed for further research and the development of effective strategies to prevent firearm injuries.

First, the magnitude, characteristics, and costs of the morbidity and disability caused by firearms should be determined, as well as the types of firearms that inflict these injuries. . . . Second, the number, type, and distribution of firearms in the United States should be determined . . .

Third, high priority should be given to epidemiologic investigations that move beyond comparisons of geopolitical units to focus on quantifying the risks of injury associated with the possession of firearms by individuals . . .

Fourth, regulations and other interventions that affect the risk of firearm injury should be evaluated rigorously.

Source: New England Journal of Medicine 319, no. 19 (November 10, 1988): 1283–1284.

However, the following study concludes that despite the difference in gun ownership rates between the two countries, the criminal homicide rate along the U.S.-Canadian border is similar.

**DOCUMENT 125: "Homicide and the Prevalence of Handguns: Canada and the United States, 1976 to 1980,"
Brandon S. Centerwall (1991)**

For the years 1976 to 1980, the mean annual rates of criminal homicide in Canada ranged from 1.1 per 100,000 in Newfoundland to 16.9 in the Yukon. In the United States, rates of criminal homicide ranged from a mean annual rate of 1.2 in North Dakota to 16.1 in Nevada.

Along the US-Canadian border, rates of criminal homicide were higher in the provinces of New Brunswick (2.9) and Quebec (3.0) than in the adjoining states of Maine (2.7), New Hampshire (2.6), and Vermont (2.8). Rates of criminal homicide were higher in Manitoba (3.7) than in the adjoining states of Minnesota (2.4) and North Dakota (1.2). Rates of criminal homicide were higher in the Yukon (16.9) than in the adjoining state of Alaska (11.6).

Conversely, rates of criminal homicide were higher in the states of Washington (4.7), Idaho (4.9), and Montana (4.7) than in the adjoining provinces of British Columbia (3.6), Alberta (3.4), and Saskatchewan (3.8). Rates of criminal homicide were higher in the states of New York (11.3) and Michigan (10.1) than in the adjoining province of Ontario (2.1).

The high rates of homicide in New York and Michigan represent the one noteworthy disparity between US and Canadian rates of criminal homicide along the US-Canadian border. However, the criminal homicide rate of New York State (11.3) was dominated by that of New York City (22.7). When New York City was excluded, the rate of criminal homicide for the rest of the state of New York was 3.4 per 100,000 population. Likewise, the rate of criminal homicide in Michigan (10.1) was dominated by that of Detroit (41.9). When Detroit was excluded, the rate of criminal homicide for the rest of Michigan was 5.0 per 100,000 . . .

In this study, it is observed that adjoining US states and Canadian provinces had similar rates of criminal homicide, even though the prevalence of privately owned handguns was 3 to 10 times greater in US border states than in adjoining Canadian provinces. From this, the plain conclusion might be that major differences in the prevalence of handguns are not associated with corresponding differences in rates of criminal homicide . . .

After detailed consideration of possible alternative explanations, it appears that, for the data presented in this analysis, the plain conclusion is the correct conclusion: When Canadian provinces and adjoining US states are compared, three- to tenfold differences in the prevalence of handguns have not resulted in consistently different rates of criminal homicide. In the relative absence of handguns, dangerously violent Canadians commit their assaults using other means which are, on the average, as lethal as handguns.

That Canada and the United States have the same annual rate of handgun homicides per 10,000 privately owned handguns might suggest that reducing the prevalence of handguns in the United States would lead to a reduction in the homicide rate. However, this attractive proposition is true if, and only if, equally lethal means are not substituted for the absent handguns. The completeness with which Canadians have indeed substituted such means indicates that the proposition is untenable . . .

Canadians are as assaultive as their US neighbors. Canadians fully compensate for the relative dearth of handguns in Canada by effectively utilizing other means for killing one another. It can be presumed that Americans would be no less resourceful under comparable circumstances. As regards homicide rates, it can be inferred that major efforts to reduce handgun prevalence in the United States would be of doubtful utility, even if successful.

Source: American Journal of Epidemiology 124 (December 1, 1991).

DOCUMENT 126: "Firearm Mortality among Children, Youth, and Young Adults 1–34 Years of Age, Trends and Current Status: United States, 1985–90," Lois A. Fingerhut (March 23, 1993)

It was previously reported that 1988 was the first year in which the firearm death rate for teenagers (15–19 years) exceeded the death rate associated with natural causes of death. That trend has continued; in 1990, among all teenagers 15–19 years, there were 39 percent more deaths from firearms than from natural causes of death. Driving that trend has been the rising rate for firearm mortality among white teenage males 15–19 years. . . . [T]he natural cause death rate remained relatively unchanged at 18 to 19 per 100,000 and the firearm death rate increased from 21.4 per 100,000 in 1988 to 26.5 per 100,000 in 1990. . . . Among black males, that trend has also continued. From 1988 to 1990, the natural cause death rate declined 12 percent while the firearm death rate increased 48 percent. Whereas in 1988, the firearm death rate among black teenage males was 2.8 times the natural cause death rate, by 1990 the firearm death rate was 4.7 times the rate for natural causes.

The firearm death rate among persons 20–24 years of age was 36 percent higher in 1990 than in 1985; virtually all of the increase was a result of increases in firearm homicide among black males. The firearm homicide rate more than doubled in this group reaching 140.7 per 100,000, its highest level ever. Among white males ages 20–24 years, . . . the firearm homicide rate in 1990 [was] 32 percent higher than what it was in 1985. Increases in firearm suicide were . . . minimal . . .

[Using a] new ranking, firearms are the second leading cause of death (after motor vehicle injury fatalities) for children 10–14 years of age, teenagers 15–19 years of age, and young adults 20–24 years and 25–34 years of age.

Source: Advance Data from the Center for Disease Control and Prevention, 23 March 1993.

DOCUMENT 127: "Firearm Violence and Public Health: Limiting the Availability of Guns," Karl P. Adler, M.D. (1994)

Firearm violence has reached epidemic proportions in this country and is now a public health emergency, accounting for one fifth of all injury deaths in the United States and second only to motor vehicles as a cause of fatal injury. In addition, for every fatal injury, an estimated seven nonfatal injuries occur. Further, firearm-related injuries imposed an estimated $19 billion economic burden on the United States in 1990 in addition to the direct health care costs. If firearm violence continues to increase, it is expected that by the year 2003, the number of deaths from firearms will surpass the number of deaths caused by motor vehicles and firearms will become this country's leading cause of injury-related death. . . .

Homicide is the leading cause of death for young black men aged 15 to 34 years and the second overall leading cause of death nationwide for individuals aged 15 to 24 years. Suicide rates for both children and adolescents have more than doubled in the last 30 years, due primarily to the increased use of firearms. For many adolescents, guns have become a part of life, with surveys reporting that many high school students either carry guns or have easy access to them. . . .

Studies clearly show that firearms are more likely to kill or injure a member of the owner's household than they are to successfully protect that household, and in addition they raise the risk several fold for a suicide in that household. Over half of all suicides (59%) are caused by firearms. . . .

[Aside from the Brady Bill, a seven-day waiting period proposal that was subsequently passed into law . . .]

Additional measures should be taken at the federal level if we are to succeed in restricting the availability of firearms.

Implementing a National Licensure System for Firearms Possession

. . . The licensing procedure should be designed to mandate a review of the individual's request for a firearm. . . . Comments from any professional organization in which the applicant will participate and indication of the intent of the applicant should also be solicited. . . . [Applicants] should be fingerprinted, provide proof of address, and have nationally recognized and Documented training in the use, safe storage, and handling of firearms. . . .

Limiting the Manufacture, Sale, and Distribution of Military-Style Assault Weapons

A federal ban currently exists on the importation of certain military-style assault weapons, but this ban should be expanded to domestic manufacture and sales. . . .

Increasing Tax on Firearms and Ammunition

An increased tax on the sale of firearms and ammunition for civilian use would serve two purposes. First, the added tax might discourage some sales, thus decreasing availability. Second, the moneys collected through the tax could be used to facilitate better education and training for, and control of gun distribution to, potential purchasers and owners. The moneys could also be used to implement a firearm fatality and injury reporting system.

Tightening Federal Licensing Requirements for Gun Dealers

Individuals who apply for a dealer's license should be more closely scrutinized than those who apply for a license to own a gun. . . .

Limiting the Number of Guns an Individual Can Buy

Most states have few restrictions on the number of guns individuals are allowed to purchase at any one time, but some are proposing to impose such limits. . . .

Implementing a Gun Return Program

A well-publicized gun return program with incentives for returning guns in to local police authorities should be implemented to reduce the number of guns now in circulation. . . .

Implementing a Firearm Fatality and Injury Reporting System

Data on firearm injuries and death are limited; additional information is needed. . . . A system . . . would provide vital information in regard to fatal shooting, but it should be expanded to include information on non-fatal firearm injuries as well. . . .

Educating the Public about the Dangers of Guns and the Need for National Regulation

The key element of these interventions and of any new national firearms control program depends on the successful education of American society about the dangers of guns and the need to regulate the ways in which they are bought, sold, and used. Other forms of education, such as conflict resolution and peer counseling programs, would offer adolescents and other individuals alternatives to violence. These programs should be started as early as possible in the elementary schools. . . .

Source: Journal of the American Medical Association 271, no. 16 (April 27, 1994): 1281–282.

The Centers for Disease Control and Prevention, a branch of the U.S. Department of Health and Human Services, noted in an editorial responding to the above study that motor vehicle and firearm-related injuries are viewed differently.

DOCUMENT 128: CDC Editorial Note (1994)

These trends may reflect differences in the approaches to preventing motor-vehicle- and firearm-related injuries. In particular, reductions in the occurrence of motor-vehicle-related injuries have been associated with the development of a set of comprehensive and science-based interventions and policies, in contrast, there have been limited efforts to develop a systematic framework to reduce the incidence and impact of injuries associated with firearms . . .

Based on the effectiveness of efforts to reduce motor-vehicle-related deaths, a multifaceted approach to reduce firearm-related injuries should include at least three elements. First, changes in behavior may be fostered by campaigns to educate and inform persons about the risks and benefits of firearm possession and the safe use and storage of firearms. Second, legislative efforts may be directed toward preventing access to or acquisition of firearms by specific groups . . . and toward regulating the storage, transport, and use of firearms. Third, technologic changes could be used to modify firearms and ammunition to render them less lethal . . .

Source: Centers for Disease Control, *Morbidity and Mortality Weekly Report* 43 (1994): 37–42.

Gun rights advocates take issue with the proposal that guns escalate crimes of passion.

DOCUMENT 129: *Guns, Crime and Freedom*, Wayne LaPierre (1994)

Advocates of waiting period legislation have claimed, however, that it will stop passion slaying in "matrimonial situations." Yet a Kansas City study concerning spouse slayings shows that in 90 percent of these murders, police had been called at least once for wife beating or some other disturbance, and in 50 percent of these cases police had been called at least five times. This is hardly a case of spontaneous passion. Rather it is a predictable situation in which the participants have a propensity for murder that law enforcement and the judicial system have failed or are unable to control.

If these "matrimonial situation" slayings are justifiable, self-defense homicides, then a waiting period could actually prevent a battered spouse from being able to get a firearm for protection when the abuse intensifies and the police cannot take action against the abuser. It is not uncommon for police to tell battered victims to purchase a gun for protection because the law does not always allow the police to take action. Waiting period proponents inevitably resort to the emotions: "If it will save one life, isn't one life worth saving?" While completely agreeing that one life is worth saving, we do not ignore the fact that a waiting period is far more likely to cause the loss of a life by denying a person a firearm for protection than it is to save one.

Source: Wayne LaPierre, *Guns, Crime and Freedom* (Washington, D.C.: Regnery, 1994), p. 47.

DOCUMENT 130: "A Public Approach to Making Guns Safer," Editorial, Charles Marwick (1995)

... in 1992, 13,220 people in the United States died from homicides committed with handguns. In contrast, during the same period in Australia, there were only 13 homicides caused by handguns; in the United Kingdom, 33; in Japan, 60; and in Canada, 128 ...

... In 1976, there were 23,000 deaths (including homicides, suicides, and other fatalities) from firearms. In 1993, the number had risen to 40,230. Gun deaths now outnumber motor vehicle deaths in eight states ...

... there are between 3 and 4 million handguns circulating in the United States.... Handguns are immune from regulations that apply to many other far less dangerous consumer products.... Household items from power mowers to children's teddy bears are subject to federal safety regulations. There's no reason that guns should not have features, such as load indicators and magazine safety devices, to prevent accidental firing ...

... Stephen P. Teret ... cited childproof pill containers developed to prevent children from ingesting hazardous prescription drugs. "Make guns personalized so that they can be used only by the owner," Teret said. He argued that this might reduce the chances of a stolen gun being used in a crime or by someone in a fit of passion.

"Lemon Squeezers" and Other Guns

... In 1884, Smith and Wesson, the gun manufacturers, designed a gun that could not be fired by a child. To fire the weapon the grip had to be squeezed at the same time as the trigger is pulled. It was nicknamed "the lemon squeezer." ... The idea was that a child's hand was too small and not strong enough to perform both actions at once. Smith and Wesson continued to make this type of gun until the 1930's ...

... Mark Polston ... discussed some modern versions of the "personalized gun," which cannot be fired by an unauthorized user. They include a push button locking mechanism on the gun, somewhat like a security door lock. The gun cannot be fired by someone who does not have the correct combination ...

Another variation is a magnet trigger. The gun will not fire unless the operator is wearing a ring that contains a magnetic chip that unlocks the firing mechanism ...

Other high-technology designs are being developed ... such as fingerprint and voice recognition devices ...

Source: Journal of the American Medical Association 273, no. 22 (June 14, 1995): 1743–744.

DOCUMENT 131: "Trends in Death Associated with Traumatic Brain Injury, 1979 through 1992," Daniel M. Sosin, M.D., M.P.H., Joseph E. Sniezek, M.D., M.P.H., and Richard J. Waxweiler, Ph.D. (1995)

Traumatic brain injury (TBI) accounts for one third of all injury deaths in the United States. Approximately 89,999 survivors each year will have some loss of function, residual disability, and increased medical care needs because of TBI. The direct medical costs for treatment of TBI have been estimated at more than $4 billion annually ...

... In 1992, the rate for motor vehicle-related TBI deaths was 2.4 times greater for males than females ... and the rate for firearm-related deaths was 6.0 times greater for males than for females. ... Firearms were the largest single cause of TBI-associated deaths for black males throughout the study period and surpassed motor vehicles for white males in 1986. ... In 1992, the distribution of TBI-associated deaths among persons aged 15 to 24 years was 44% due to motor vehicles, 49% due to firearms, and 1% due to falls. ... Motor vehicle-related rates declined more than 25% across all age groups. ... Firearm-related rates for persons 15 to 24 years increased 72% from 1983 . . . and surpassed rates for all other age groups since 1989 . . .

. . . Despite the success in reducing TBI-associated deaths related to motor vehicles, these data demonstrate our failure to curb the increase of firearm-related violence. Firearms have surpassed motor vehicles as a cause of death in several states and are predicted to become the leading single cause of injury death in the United States by the year 2000. However, firearms are already the leading cause of TBI-associated deaths in the United States. . . . One way to confront the problem of firearm-related violence may be to apply the public health model used to make motor vehicles travel safer (monitoring the occurrence and circumstances of crashes, altering behavior through public education, enacting laws to limit risk factors, applying new technology whenever possible, and changing environments to reduce crash frequency and injury risk in the event of a crash).

Source: Journal of the American Medical Association 273, no. 22 (June 14, 1995): 1778–780.

Several years later, another study tries to estimate firearm-related health care costs. This study involves 787 patients admitted for inpatient care at a university trauma center. This study's estimate of firearm-related costs quadruples the estimate in the earlier study (Document 122).

DOCUMENT 132: "Hospitalization Charges, Costs, and Income for Firearm-Related Injuries at a University Trauma Center," Kenneth W. Kizer, M.D., M.P.H., et al. (1995)

Men aged 15 to 44 years accounted for 77% of patients with firearm-related injuries. The overall mean and median hospital charges per admission were $52,271 and $28,033, respectively, whereas the overall mean and median hospital costs per admission were $13,794 and $7,964, respectively. The net income per patient ranged from an average loss of $6,980 for each patient having no insurance to an average profit of $28,557 for each patient with a health maintenance organization contract. The losses sustained on non-sponsored and Medicaid patients were more than offset by net income from patients having private health insurance, Medicare, or other insurance coverage such that there was an average profit of $5,809 per admission for a firearm-related injury . . .

Treatment of firearm-related injuries produces net income for this university trauma center by virtue of the cost shifting built into its pricing structure. If data from this institution are extrapolated to the nation, then the actual cost of providing medical care for firearm-related injuries in the United States in 1995 is projected to be $4.0 billion. The majority of this cost will be paid indirectly by private health insurance.

In 1991, there were 38,317 firearm-related fatalities in the United States, making firearms the second leading cause of injury death in the United States and the second most frequent cause of death from all causes for persons aged 15 to 34 years. For every firearm-related fatality, there are estimated to be seven nonfatal injuries requiring hospitalization or outpatient medical treatment . . .

The cost of health care and lost productivity resulting from firearm-related injuries has been estimated at $20 billion per year, $1.4 billion of which is direct expenditures for medical care . . .

Admissions to the UCDMC [University of California, Davis, Medical Center] for firearm-related injuries increased by 33% between 1990 and 1992 . . .

. . . Seventy-six percent . . . of all injuries were due to assaults; 52 (9%) of these patients died. Ninety-five injuries (17%) were Documented as the result of drive-by shootings; three (3%) of these patients died. Thirty-three (42%) of the 79 patients with self-inflicted injuries died . . .

. . . The total and annual mean number of hospital days for the 3 study years for all patients with firearm-related injuries was 4824 days and 1608 days respectively. . . . The mean hospital length of stay for survivors was 6.9 days vs 2.9 days for nonsurvivors . . .

. . . For $39,203,119 in charges, the hospital was reimbursed $14,701,969 (38%). Ninety-one (12%) of the patients had charges in excess of $100,000 . . .

During the 3-year study period, income losses based on the actual cost of providing care totaled nearly $2.2 million for treatment of the 495 patients (66%) with firearm-related injuries were covered by Medi-Cal (California's Medicaid program) or Sacramento County's Medically Indigent Adults program . . . or . . . were non sponsored. . . . However, these losses were more than offset by the $6.5 million in net income from the 255 patients (34%) whose care was paid for by private indemnity insurance, by Medicare, or via contracts with health maintenance organizations (HMOs) or other managed care plans and other counties . . .

Max and Rice updated the 1985 estimates of the costs of firearm-related injuries showing that total costs in 1990 exceeded $20 billion per year and that direct hospitalization costs increased 55% in the 5-year period from 1985 to 1990.

Source: Kenneth W. Kizer, M.D., M.P.H., Mary K. Vassar, R.N., M.S., Randi L. Harry, M.B.A., Kathleen D. Layton et al. *Journal of the American Medical Association* 273, no. 22 (June 14, 1995): 1768–773.

DOCUMENT 133: "National Estimates of Nonfatal Firearm-Related Injuries: Beyond the Tip of the Iceberg," Joseph L. Annest, Ph.D., James A. Mercy, Ph.D., Delinda R. Gibson, and George W. Ryan, Ph.D. (1995)

... From 1968 through 1991, the number of firearm-related deaths increased by 60% (from 23,875 to 38,317). In 1991, firearm-related injuries were the eighth leading cause of death and the fourth leading cause of years of potential life lost before 65 years of age in the United States ...

Our data were obtained from June 1, 1992, through May 31, 1993, using the National Electronic Injury Surveillance System (NEISS) of the US Consumer Product Safety Commission (CPSC).

From June 1, 1992, through May 31, 1993, 4468 nonfatal gun-related injuries were reported through NEISS. Using weighted NEISS data, we estimated that 152,373 (95% ...) persons with nonfatal gun-related injuries were treated annually in hospital emergency departments in the United States. Of these injured persons, 99,025 (95% ...) were treated for nonfatal firearm-related injuries.... The remaining nonfatal gun-related injuries resulted from penetrating wounds from discharge of a BB gun or pellet gun and from injuries associated with violent behavior (eg, pistol whippings or purposely struck with the butt of a gun) and unintentional causes (eg, weapon recoil, kickbacks, fingers bruised or lacerated while cleaning a gun, contusion from falling on a gun, or powder burns), as well as those with undetermined intent.

The annual rate of patients with nonfatal firearm-related gun GSWs [gunshot wounds] treated in hospital emergency departments in the United States exceeds the rate of firearm-related deaths in 1992 by a ratio of 2.6:1.... The ratio was approximately the same for males and females. ... Overall, for firearm-related injuries associated with assaults (including 1.8% of injuries occurring during legal intervention by a law enforcement officer), the nonfatal-to-fatal injury ratio was 3.3:1. In contrast, the rate ratio of firearm-related suicide attempts treated in emergency departments to completed suicides was 0.3:1 ...

During the study period, an estimated average of 270 (95% ...) nonfatal firearm-related GSWs occurred per day, of which 160 (95% ...) were associated with assaults ...

Our findings have several important implications. First, nonfatal firearm-related injuries treated in hospital emergency departments outnumber firearm-related fatalities by an estimated ratio of 2.6:1. . . . Moreover, firearm-related GSWs were severe enough to require hospitalization in an estimated 57% of patients. Second, in contrast to firearm-related mortality in which suicides using a firearm account for the greatest proportion of deaths, the predominant context for nonfatal firearm-related injuries are assaults. These data are a clear indication that suicide attempts involving firearms are usually fatal. Third, NEISS provides a sensitive system for describing and monitoring nonfatal firearm-related injuries treated in hospital emergency departments in the United States . . .

A national injury surveillance system that provides uniform data on firearm-related mortality and morbidity is needed to aid in risk factor research and in developing and evaluating firearm and violence-related intervention programs.

Source: Journal of the American Medical Association 273, no. 22 (June 14, 1995): 1749–754.

The following study attempts to document the types of firearms associated with gun deaths and to find out how much information on firearms is available from current data sources. The researchers studied the 175 firearm suicides and 524 firearm homicides that occurred in Milwaukee, Wisconsin, from 1990 to 1994.

DOCUMENT 134: "Characteristics of Firearms Involved in Fatalities," Stephen W. Hargarten, M.D., M.P.H., et al. (1996)

Handguns accounted for 46 (89%) of 534 firearm homicides and 124 (17%) of 175 firearm suicides. Handguns of .25 caliber accounted for 14% . . . of 438 firearm homicides and 12% . . . of all firearm suicides in which caliber was known. The Raven MP-35 was the single most commonly identified firearm and accounted for 10% . . . of 153 handgun homicide cases and 7% . . . of the 76 suicide cases in which the manufacturer was identified.

Inexpensive, short-barreled .25 caliber handguns were the most common weapon type associated with firearm homicides and suicides in Milwaukee during 1990 through 1994.

For firearm homicides, 456 (87%) of 524 victims were male. Of these 456 males, 361 (79%) were African American, of whom 271 (75%) were aged 30 years or younger. . . . For firearm suicides, 155 (89%) of 175 victims were male. Of these 155 males, 105 (68%) were white, of whom 59 (56%) were older than 40 years.

... Assault weapons were identified in five firearm homicide cases ...

Source: Stephen W. Hargarten, M.D., M.P.H., Trudy A. Karlson, Ph.D., Mallory O'Brien, M.S., Jerry Hancock, J.D., Edward Quebbeman, M.D., Ph.D., et al. *Journal of the American Medical Association* 275, no. 1 (January 3, 1996): 42–45.

The same issue of the publication printed this editorial, regarding the above study.

DOCUMENT 135: "The Firearm Injury Reporting System Revisited," Stephen P. Teret, M.P.H., J.D. (1996)

... we still need a national system that can collect uniform data from each state and provide those data to researchers, thereby enabling a better understanding of fatal and nonfatal firearms-related injuries. Such national data collection would help reveal many of the factors that are critically important to policy formulation, such as the following: what firearms are used in homicides and suicides; what is the role of alcohol and other drugs in gun-related deaths; and do changes in the design of firearms affect the involvement of those firearms in homicide, suicide, and unintended shootings? Information on these and other topics would enhance understanding of gun-related injuries and might even lead to some areas of greater agreement regarding effective gun policy ...

... Cost is a factor; the cost of such a system may approximate that of the highway fatality reporting system, which was approximately $3.5 million in 1992. But the lifetime costs for gun injuries incurred in 1990 were estimated to be $20 billion. This makes the cost of a reporting system appear to be a wise investment in prevention. The question of who pays for a national reporting system is also problematic, but there are logical answers to this question. Approximately 5 million new firearms are manufactured each year in the United States, and a relatively small tax on the manufacture and sale of these guns could easily pay the costs of a reporting system.

Source: Journal of the American Medical Association 275, no. 1 (January 3, 1996): 70.

The June 12, 1996, issue of the *Journal of the American Medical Association* focused on violence. The following are some of the abstracts (in both Documents 136 and 137) of that issue. The National

Rifle Association issued a press release entitled "All Sputter, No Science," contending that the studies and conclusions were flawed.

DOCUMENT 136: "Population Estimates of Household Firearm Storage Practices and Firearm Carrying in Oregon," David E. Nelson, M.D., M.P.H., et al. (June 12, 1996)

Ten percent of adults (197,400 persons) lived in households with firearms that were always or sometimes stored loaded and unlocked. An estimated 6.2% of households with children had firearms that were loaded and unlocked, and about 40,000 children lived in these households. Overall, 4.4% of adults carried loaded firearms in the past month. Rural residence, male sex, and less than a college education were associated with living in a household with loaded and unlocked firearms and with firearm carrying. Drinking 5 or more alcoholic beverages on 1 or more occasions in the past month or drinking 60 or more alcoholic beverages in the past month were independently associated with living in households with loaded and unlocked firearms.

Many adults and children are exposed to unsafely stored firearms in Oregon, and many adults carry loaded firearms. Improved public health surveillance of firearm storage and firearm carrying using standardized questions and definitions is needed at the national, state, and local levels.

Source: David E. Nelson, M.D., M.P.H., Joyce A. Grant-Worley, M.S., Kenneth Powell, M.D., M.P.H., James Mercy, Ph.D., and Deborah Holtzman, Ph.D. *Journal of the American Medical Association* 275 (June 12, 1996): 1744–748.

In the following study, researchers wanted to determine if the 1993 law limiting handgun purchases to one a month in Virginia had an effect on interstate transfer of guns. Most states have no such limitation, allowing, theoretically, for large purchases of guns to be made in areas with lenient guns laws and resold in areas with stricter laws.

DOCUMENT 137: "Effects of Limiting Handgun Purchases on Interstate Transfer of Firearms," Douglas S. Weil, Sc.D., and Rebecca C. Knox, M.P.H., M.S.W. (June 12, 1996)

For firearms recovered anywhere in the United States, 3201 (27%) of 11,876 acquired prior to the implementation of the [Virginia] law and

519 (19%) of 2730 purchased after the law was enacted were traced to Virginia. For traces initiated in the northeast corridor (New York, New Jersey, Connecticut, Rhode Island, and Massachusetts), 1103 (34.8%) of 3169 of the firearms acquired before the 1-gun-a-month law took effect and 142 (15.5%) of 919 firearms purchased after implementation were traced to Virginia.

Gun control policies involving licensing, registration, and restricting the number of purchases represent efforts to limit the supply of guns available in the illegal market. This study provides evidence that restricting handgun purchases to 1 per month is an effective means of disrupting the illegal interstate transfer of firearms.

Source: Journal of the American Medical Association 275 (June 12, 1996): 1759–761.

"Hogwash" said the National Rifle Association, which issued a press release coinciding with release of the journal.

DOCUMENT 138: AMA on Guns: All Sputter, No Science, National Rifle Association (June 11, 1996)

On Gun Sale Limits. The AMA release states, "Researchers cite Virginia law as evidence of effective legislation"—but the "researchers" are advocates of that law. They base their "research" on BATF trace data which the Congressional Research Service (CRS) cautions is unrepresentative of guns used in crime. Observed Mrs. [Tanya K.] Metaksa [executive director, NRA Institute for Legislative Action]: "On BATF trace data, CRS cautions, Don't draw inferences—but the AMA doesn't listen. The BATF data is silent on whether the guns traced were stolen from dealers or stolen from their law-abiding customers, rendering gun purchase limits meaningless. Plus, the AMA researchers committed still another methodological sin: they got the math wrong (paragraph 5). When it comes to doctors, you can't trust their math any more than you can read their handwriting."

Mrs. Metaksa concluded that the AMA approach to gun control is fatally flawed. "As preeminent sociologist James Wright of Tulane has observed, 'The contemporary urban environment breeds violence no less than swamps breed mosquitoes. Attempting to control the problem of violence by trying to disarm the perpetrators is as hopeless as trying to contain yellow fever through mandible control.' "

Source: National Rifle Association, press release of June 11, 1996.

While the bulk of the above studies suggests that greater restrictions on guns could reduce the rate of gun-related injuries and deaths, some doctors' publications have printed other opinions. For example, the March 1994 issue of the *Journal of the Medical Association of Georgia* focused on the gun control issue. Dr. Edgar Suter's article (Document 116) and David B. Kopel, J.D.'s, entry (Document 108) on foreign gun laws were two of the contributions in that issue.

DOCUMENT 139: "Guns: Health Destroyer or Protector?" W. W. Caruth III (1994)

How do guns cause crime? Some people actually attribute evil intentions and power to the gun, as if that inanimate object of metal and wood or plastic has a mind and will of its own. Anyone who truly believes the gun to be the problem should seek professional help. How can we explain our society's attempts to combat crime by legislating against firearm ownership without using words like totemism or witchcraft? Why do we think a person who is determined to commit a robbery or murder will be deterred by a law against buying a gun unless we believe in magic? In the real world we must realize that criminals are too affected by these laws. The only people who will obey these laws are already obeying laws against real crime, so why propose laws we know to be useless? . . .

Why shouldn't people be disarmed? . . . This question can be answered on several levels. In the first place, the burden of proof should be on those who are trying to take away our right to freely possess guns, and they have not made their case. Firearms are used in many harmless recreational activities; even if guns had no more important function, a compelling reason would have to be present to restrict their use . . .

Another point which is quite pertinent today is the use of guns to defend against criminals. We often hear that the gun kept in the home is more likely to be used against a friend or family member than against a burglar. The study used to justify that contention massaged the numbers pretty drastically. For instance, it included suicides which, though tragic, are not really criminal, and it excluded all shootings of criminals except burglars shot in the house . . .

A better picture of the utility of firearms in self-defense may be inferred from the fact that firearms are used by private citizens in defensive situations about 2.1 million times each year in the United States. About a million and a half of those folks use handguns. Most of these incidents did not involve shooting anyone; in most cases merely exhibiting the weapon or, at most, firing a warning shot into the ground was enough to stop the crime in progress . . .

I don't think I would go sc far as to require that all citizens be armed to share the burden of our common defense against tyrants and other types of criminals, but there should be no hindrance to those who are willing to take up arms. We should recognize that they make life safer for all of us.

Source: Journal of the Medical Association of Georgia 83 (March 1994): 157–59.

The following entry was written by Larry Pratt, executive director of Gun Owners of America.

DOCUMENT 140: "Health Care and Firearms," Larry Pratt (1994)

Are guns leading us to a healthcare crisis? Some would say "yes." Many doctors are concerned about the number of bullet wounds they see in the emergency rooms, and this has led them to conclude hastily that strict gun controls are desperately needed. But while any death is tragic, one wonders if these doctors are only getting part of the picture— the negative part. Are these doctors failing to see the millions of deaths and injuries which firearms *prevent* each year?

Do they ever see examples of how a gun in private hands can repel a criminal attack when the police are not there to protect them? The truth is, the police are rarely present to protect people before a crime is committed. These questions must be answered, because if they are not, then they may lead the country to make wrong policy decisions . . .

People need to have the choice to defend themselves if they so choose. . . . [F]irearms may save as many as 15 lives for every life lost to a gun. The corollary is that the medical costs saved by firearms will be 15 times greater than the costs incurred by guns. Of course, this contradicts the recent New England Journal of Medicine study which allegedly showed that keeping a gun at home nearly triples the likelihood that someone in the household will be slain there. But the study, by ignoring the tremendous number of non-lethal defensive uses of firearms, understated the positive benefits to gun ownership.

Source: Journal of the Medical Association of Georgia 83 (March 1994): 149–52.

In the following entry, the author asserts that gun violence is a cause better left to the experts for it falls outside of physicians' domain.

DOCUMENT 141: "Handgun Control, M.D.," Tucker Carlson (1996)

For a better sense of why otherwise sensible physicians would go out of their way to advise the public on subjects they know little about, it's worth taking a look at the American Academy of Pediatrics, the most radically anti-gun of the major medical associations. . . . The group's nannyish instincts really run amok when it comes to warning parents about the dangers of skateboards, pick-up trucks, snowmobiles, trampolines, bicycles, horseback riding, all-terrain vehicles, ride-on lawn mowers, and most recently, shopping carts. If there was ever an organization on the lookout for a new "national epidemic," this is it.

Why, then, does anybody listen to these self-appointed gun experts? The short answer: Because they're doctors. As a paper from the Center to Prevent Handgun Violence shrewdly points out, "Doctors are among the most asked—and trusted—sources of child safety information." And a lot more. Even to a skeptical public, a physician's judgment—on just about any subject—carries considerable weight. All doctors know it; ideological doctors use it . . .

The physicians churn out a seemingly endless series of op-eds, though it is not clear that they are adding much to the debate. The arguments that surround gun violence are complicated, the obvious conclusions often less obvious than they appear. Perhaps it is a subject that, as a doctor might say, is best left to the experts.

Source: The Weekly Standard, New York, 15 April 1996.

ADDITIONAL READING

"Emergency Department Surveillance for Weapon-Related Injuries—Massachusetts, November 1993–April 1994." Centers for Disease Control and Prevention. MMWR 44 (1995): 160–69.

Kellermann, Arthur, et al. "Gun Ownership as a Risk Factor for Homicide in the Home." *New England Journal of Medicine* 467 (1993).

Lester, David. "The Relationship between Gun Control Statutes and Homicide Rates: A Research Note." *Crime and Justice* 4 (1981): 146–48.

Linsky, Arnold S., Murray A. Strauss, and Ronet Bachman-Prehn. "Social Stress,

Legitimate Violence, and Gun Availability." Paper presented at the annual meeting of the Society for the Study of Social Problems, 1988.

GUNS IN SUICIDE

Most of the studies cited earlier deal with the role of firearms in intentional and unintentional shootings of others. Another area that has received public health attention is the role that guns play in suicide.

DOCUMENT 142: "Self-Inflicted Gunshot Wounds: Lethality of Method versus Intent," Linda G. Peterson, M.D., McKim Peterson, M.D., Gregory J. O'Shanick, M.D., and Alan Swann, M.D. (February 1985)

Traditional formulations of suicide risk have held that the most lethal suicide attempts are planned, while impulsive suicide attempts are considered to be less lethal, often only "gestures." . . .

Many patients in our sample admitted that while they had originally expected to die, they were glad to be alive and would not repeat the self-destructive behavior despite the continued presence of significant medical, psychological and social problems. To date, none of these patients have died or attempted suicide in the two years since they wounded themselves.

Source: American Journal of Psychiatry 142, no. 2 (February 1985).

In the following study, researchers found that 57 percent (235 deaths) of all suicides in the Sacramento County, California, area were firearm related.

DOCUMENT 143: "The Choice of Weapons in Firearms Suicides," Garen J. Wintemute, M.D., M.P.H., Stephen P. Teret, J.D., M.P.H., Jess F. Kraus, Ph.D., M.P.H., and Mona W. Wright, B.S. (1988)

Handguns were used in 161 (60 percent) of these 235 deaths, 65 percent of 201 firearms suicides among males, and 88 percent of 34 firearms

suicides among females. . . . What might account for a seeming prefer-
ence for handguns as a means of committing suicides? Handguns may
be more immediately available than other home firearms. Handguns are
most often kept for protection and are therefore particularly prone to be
stored loaded and within easy reach. As survivors of firearm suicide
attempts often report acting on impulse, such easy access is likely to be
a major contributing factor. The handgun's short barrel length may also
be important; it is difficult to aim a rifle or shotgun at oneself and pull
the trigger. Finally, persons living at a household where a handgun is
kept may for other reasons be at increased risk.

Source: American Journal of Public Health 78, no. 4 (July 1988).

DOCUMENT 144: "Policy Research on Firearms and Violence," Franklin Zimring (1993)

Although the rate of suicide remains highest among older white males,
rates of suicide have grown disproportionately in groups that were traditionally at low risk, and increasing rates of firearm suicide appear to
be a striking part of this dynamic transformation. Between 1960 and 1980
the total number of females committing suicide by all means other than
firearms increased 16 percent, while the number of females committing
suicide using firearms more than doubled. Suicide of young persons ages
5–19 by all means other than firearms increased 175 percent between
1960 and 1980; over the same period the percentage increase of suicide
by firearms among this age group was 299 percent. Nonwhites, typically
a low-risk group for suicide, experienced an 88 percent increase in nonfirearm suicides between 1960 and 1980, compared with a 160 percent
increase in the volume of firearm suicide.

Source: Health Affairs 12, no. 4 (Winter 1993): 114–15.

In their report on firearm suicide, two groups suggest that one aspect
of increased access to guns is that women are using guns more often
in suicide attempts than in the past.

DOCUMENT 145: "The Unspoken Tragedy: Firearm Suicide in the United States," Report of the Educational Fund to End Handgun Violence and the Coalition to Stop Gun Violence (1995)

One researcher (Weed, 1985) reported that in 1960 females completed suicides most frequently by poisoning themselves. That year only 25.3 percent of all female suicides resulted from firearms injuries. By 1982, however, females completed suicides more often by shooting themselves and guns were responsible for 40.7 percent of all female suicides. That same year guns were responsible for 64.2 percent of all male suicides. Thus, while firearms suicides still are attributed disproportionately to males, the gap between female and male suicide rates rapidly is narrowing.

The trend of increased firearm use in female suicides is particularly evident among younger age groups. In 1970, according to one study, firearms were responsible for 32.3 percent of suicides committed by females between 15- and 24-year-olds. In 1984, firearm-related deaths accounted for 51.3 percent of suicides committed by the same demographic group.

In the past, men and women in the United States favored different methods of committing suicide. Males traditionally utilize firearms, while women utilize less lethal means such as poison. While this still is true, an increasing percentage of females end their lives by fatally shooting themselves. The trend of increasing use of firearms in female suicides is particularly alarming given that females attempt suicide much more frequently than males and that firearm suicides carry a greater fatality rate than other methods traditionally used by women. Since females attempt suicide so frequently, any increase in use of firearms will result in a dramatic increase in female suicide fatalities.

Source: "The Unspoken Tragedy: Firearm Suicide in the United States." Report of the Educational Fund to End Handgun Violence and the Coalition to Stop Gun Violence, 31 May 1995, pp. 16–17.

ADDITIONAL READING

Brent, David A., M.D., Joshua A. Perper, M.D., Christopher J. Allman, Grace M. Moritz, Mary E. Wartella, and Janice P. Zelenak, Ph.D. "The Presence and Accessibility of Firearms in the Homes of Adolescent Suicides, A Case Control Study." *Journal of the American Medical Association* 266, no. 21 (December 12, 1991).

Clarke, Ronald V., and Peter R. Jones. "Suicide and Increased Availability of Handguns in the United States." *Social Science and Medicine* 28 (1989): 805–809.

Kellermann, Arthur L., M.D., M.P.H., et al. "Suicide in the Home in Relation to Gun Ownership." *New England Journal of Medicine* 327, no. 7 (August 13, 1992).

Lester, David. "The Preventive Effect of Strict Gun Control Laws on Suicide and Homicide." *Suicide and Life-Threatening Behavior* 12 (1982): 131–40.

———. "An Availability-Acceptability Theory of Suicide." *Activitas Nervosa Superior* 29 (1987): 164–66.

———. "Gun Control, Gun Ownership, and Suicide Prevention." *Suicide and Life-Threatening Behavior* 18 (1988): 176–80.

———. "Restricting the Availability of Guns as a Strategy for Preventing Suicide." *Biology and Society* 5 (1988): 127–29.

———. "Gun Ownership and Suicide in the United States." *Psychological Medicine* 19 (1989): 519–21.

Lester, David, and Mary E. Murrell. 1980. "The Influences of Gun Control Laws on Suicidal Behavior." *American Journal of Psychiatry* 137 (1980): 121–22.

Markush, Robert E., M.D., M.P.H., and Alfred A. Bartolucci, Ph.D. "Firearms and Suicide in the United States." *American Journal of Public Health* 74, no. 2 (February 1984).

Rosenberg, Mark L., M.D., James A. Mercy, Ph.D., Vernon N. Houk, M.D. "Guns and Adolescent Suicides." Editorial. *Journal of the American Medical Association* 26, no. 21 (December 4, 1991).

Part IX

Guns as Self-Defense Security

Criminologists and public health researchers alike have tried to gain a handle on whether or not guns are a deterrent to crime. As with nearly every other aspect of the debate, there are strong differences of opinion.

The following study from 1981, which uses data from 1975, was funded by the U.S. Department of Justice. In it, the researchers reviewed literature, conducted a police department survey, and gathered data from Los Angeles Superior Court. They found that information was lacking in many areas necessary to make good gun laws and measure their effectiveness. Since this time, criminologists and public health researchers have tried to grasp some of the issues brought up in the study.

DOCUMENT 146: *Weapons, Crime, and Violence in America,* **James D. Wright and Peter H. Rossi (November 1981)**

Gun ownership in the United States is claimed to be at least partially influenced by the individuals' desires to protect themselves against crime. Some observers have noted that this pattern of arming may have the effect of motivating criminals to arm themselves and to carry arms while committing crimes in which weapons are not intrinsically necessary (e.g. burglary). Others claim that widespread possession of firearms makes it easier for criminals to obtain arms through theft. On the other side, there are claims that widespread gun ownership reduces some types of crimes because criminals are not willing to risk encountering an armed potential victim.

To cast some definitive light from hard evidence on this issue would require time-series data on both crime and weapons ownership that are virtually impossible to obtain. But, it would be worthwhile encouraging researchers to investigate the utility of gun licensing information in states that have had licensing laws over a sufficient period of time, and to relate any trends therein to the crime rates . . .

Local police departments constitute the ultimate source of data on the use of firearm[s] in the commission of crimes. As our survey of police departments reveals, most departments record highly differentiated data on weapons, but because this information is not collected in a uniform way nor stored in an easily retrievable form, it is not currently available either for operational or research purposes . . .

Our recommendations to legislative bodies . . . concern steps that should be taken before *any* measure is enacted, no matter what its specific form or content. And our recommendations in this regard can be quickly summarized: *First*, be explicit about the underlying assumptions upon which the proposed measures are based; and *secondly*, to the extent possible, be sure these assumptions are plausible in light of current evidence and research.

Any attempt to control crime through controlling firearms is based on assumptions and presuppositions about how weapons are acquired, distributed, and used. At present, knowledge about these topics is highly limited, although it is transparently obvious that the existing distribution system is quite complex and multifaceted, and thus, that simple-minded interventions in the system are readily circumvented . . .

For good and obvious reasons, policy makers are concerned to develop "interventions" that somehow influence the criminal market for firearms but do not infringe on the rights of legitimate firearms owners. Again, this is a laudable goal, but it presupposes that these two parts of the market are sufficiently distinct that policy efforts can be focused, somehow, on the one but not the other. There is nothing in the literature suggesting this to be the case, with the exception that [the] proportion of handguns among "crime guns" is higher than the equivalent proportion among the general private firearms stock. Policy makers should thus be aware that any action taken to deny firearms to would-be criminals will necessarily deny them to a vastly larger group of persons who will never even contemplate, much less commit, a violent criminal act. This, of course, is *not* to argue that such actions should not be undertaken, which is an entirely separate matter. It *is* to argue that infringements on access to guns by legitimate firearms consumers is one, among many, costs of a firearms regulation policy, and one which must, therefore, be weighed against the anticipated benefits before a rational policy decision can be made.

Source: *Weapons, Crime, and Violence in America.* Executive Summary, Natic Institute of Justice, pp. 34–38. Washington, D.C.: U.S. Department of Justice, N vember 1981.

DOCUMENT 147: "Second Thoughts about Gun Control," James D. Wright (1988)

The NRA maintains that gun laws won't work because they can't work. Widely ignored (especially by criminals) and unenforceable, gun-control laws go about the problem in the wrong way. For this reason, the NRA has long supported mandatory and severe sentences for the use of firearms in felonies, contending that we should punish firearms abusers once it is proven that an abuse has occurred, and leave legitimate users alone until they have actually done something illegal with their weapon.

The pro-control forces argue that gun laws don't work because there are too many of them, because they are indifferently enforced, and because the laws vary widely from one jurisdiction to the next . . .

One of the favorite aphorisms of the pro-gun forces is that "if guns are outlawed, only outlaws will have guns." Sophisticated liberals laugh at the point, but they shouldn't. No matter what laws we enact, they will be obeyed only by the law abiding. . . . Why should we expect felons to comply with a gun law when they readily violate laws against robbery, assault, and murder? . . .

As long as there are *any* handguns around (and even "ban handgun" advocates make an exception for police or military handguns), they will obviously be available to anyone at *some price* . . . demand will always create its own supply: just as there will always be cocaine available to anyone willing to pay $200 a gram for it, so too will handguns always be available to anyone willing to pay a thousand dollars to obtain one . . .

A black market in guns, run by organized crime, would almost certainly spring up to service the demand. It is, after all, no more difficult to manufacture a serviceable firearm in one's basement than to brew up a batch of home-made gin . . .

The notorious Saturday Night Special has received a great deal of attention. The term is used loosely: it can refer to a gun of low price, inferior quality, small caliber, short barrel length, or some combination of these. The attention is typically justified on two grounds: first, these guns have no legitimate sport or recreational use, and secondly, they are the firearms preferred by criminals . . .

... It would be sophistic to claim that most Saturday Night Specials are purchased for use as trail guns; my point is only that some are. Most small, cheap handguns are probably purchased by persons of modest means to protect themselves against crime.

... It is worth stressing, however, that poor, black, central-city residents are by far the most likely potential victims of crime; if self-protection justifies owning a gun, then a ban on small, cheap handguns would effectively deny the means of self-protection to those most evidently in need of it.

... a ban on Saturday Night Specials would leave heavy-duty handguns available as substitute weapons . . . most people would just give up and not use guns for whatever they had in mind. But certainly some of them, perhaps many of them, would move to bigger and better handguns instead. . . .

The handgun used by John Hinckley in his attack on President Reagan was a .22 caliber revolver, a Saturday Night Special. Some have supported banning the Saturday Night Special so as to thwart psychopaths in search of weapons. But would a psychopath intent on assassinating a President simply give up in the absence of a cheap handgun? Or would he, in that event, naturally pick up some other gun instead? Suppose he did pick up the most commonly owned handgun available in the United States, the .38 Special. Suppose further that he got off the same six rounds and inflicted the same wounds that he inflicted with the .22. A .38 slug entering Jim Brady's head where the .22 entered would, at the range in question, probably have killed him instantly. The Washington policeman would not have had a severed artery but would have been missing the larger part of his neck. The round that deflected from its path to President Reagan's heart might have reached its target. One can readily imagine at least three deaths, including the President's, had Hinckley fired a more powerful weapon.

Source: The Public Interest, no. 91 (Spring 1988): 23–39.

Just as the public health studies in the earlier section have their critics, so do studies that conclude that guns are effective self-defense weapons. For example, in their book Franklin E. Zimring and Gordon Hawkins question the methodology and conclusions of Gary Kleck, a researcher at Florida State University's School of Criminology. Just as with critics of public health studies, such counter-arguments often blast away on the original study point by point. Indeed, some conclusions about the original authors or researchers focus on their presumed bias.

DOCUMENT 148: *The Citizen's Guide to Gun Control,* Franklin E. Zimring and Gordon Hawkins (1987)

[Kleck] argues in Firearms and Violence: Issues of Public Policy (1984) that if severe limits were imposed on the legal ownership of handguns, then the restricted availability of handguns could result in a higher death rate from attacks if more deadly weapons like rifles and shotguns were substituted.

On the question of displacement or substitution, he asserts that "long guns are eminently substitutable for handguns in virtually all felony killing situations." He treats a guess in the literature that the displacement to long guns would be no more than one-third as the equivalent of a finding that it would be a third. With regard to a differential deadliness he says that "it would be pointless to compare actual observed assault fatality rates of handguns and long guns in order to determine relative deadliness, even if adequate data were available for such an effort, since the fatality rates are not just the result of the deadliness of the weapons themselves."

In place of deadliness he employs the concept of the relative "stopping power" of guns. Although this appears to represent an acknowledgment of instrumentality effects by one of their critics, the superiority of "stopping power" over the actual death rate is difficult to discern. Indeed, when it is applied to what is known about death rates it yields quite preposterous conclusions.

Thus, the use of this method results in estimates that some guns, such as the 12-gauge shotgun with double-ought cartridges, would produce fatalities in head and chest wounds about 18 times as often as .22-caliber rifles. But the death rate from .22-caliber, single wound attacks with a head or chest injury has been found to be 16 percent. Multiplying this death rate by 18 (the difference in relative "stopping power") produces an estimated death rate of 288 percent for single-wound attacks with 12-gauge shotguns that result in head or chest wounds, or approximately three deaths for every individual attacked! The death rate from multiple-wound .22-caliber attacks has been found to be 28 percent. Multiplying this estimate by 18 produces an estimated death rate for shotgun attacks of 504 percent, or five deaths for every individual attacked!

A critique that involves a comparison of the deadliness of different guns but studiously neglects to consider the use of those guns in actual attacks, and entails death rate estimates of three per wounding, tells us nothing about the potential effectiveness of handgun controls. But its aracter demonstrates that in regard to this topic, even on the level, partisanship can engender strange aberrations. It must ꜱotent combination of wishful thinking, reciprocal noncriticism by peers, and absence of self-examination for this kind of catastrophic error to march into the public debate on guns and gun control.

Source: Franklin E. Zimring and Gordon Hawkins, *The Citizen's Guide to Gun Control* (New York: MacMillian Publishing, 1987), 97–99.

DOCUMENT 149: "The Value of Civilian Arms Possession as Deterrent to Crime or Defense against Crime," Don B. Kates, Jr., LL.B. (1991)

The only extant study specific to gun-armed civilian resisters found they suffered slightly lower rates of death or injury at the hands of criminals (17.8%) than did police (21%). These results are open to question because the study involved only a very small sample. But confirming evidence from an enormously larger data base is available in the national crime victim surveys. (These, however, provide information only as to victim injury, not death, since victims who died resisting robbers are not available to answer survey questions.)

In fact, earlier versions of the national victim surveys were cited by the one specifically anti-gun presentation which has tried to empirically validate the dangers of resistance argument. However, the survey questions in those early versions of the surveys lumped all resistance together without differentiating the injury and success rates of gun-armed resisters from those of resisters who were unarmed or armed only with less effective weapons. The more recent national victim surveys which do so differentiate have already been cited as showing that victims who resisted with guns were much less likely to lose their possessions to robbers than those who resisted with any other kind of weapon. . . . [R]ecent data finds gun-armed resisters approximately 50% less likely to be injured than victims who submitted to the criminal. In contrast, knife-armed resisters were more likely to suffer injury than non-resisters and much more likely to be injured than gun-armed resisters. Comparisons to other forms of resistance are also favorable to the effectiveness of gun-armed self-defense.

Care must be taken to avoid exaggerating the importance of these findings as support for the utility of defensive gun use. Ironically, a major factor which might lead to exaggerating their import is a basic conceptual error in anti-gun analyses of the utility of gun-armed self-defense. Implicit in many such anti-gun analyses has been the unexamined assumption that having a gun somehow compels the victim to resist with it even in circumstances that make it senseless and dangerous to do so. But the whole point of a gun, or any other precaution against emergency, is to provide an option for use if, but only if, this is wise under the circumstances.

With this point in mind it becomes evident that the survey data on victim injury do not support any suggestion that victims who have guns can safely resist no matter what the circumstances. On the contrary, though guns do maximize successful resistance, of at least equal importance in minimizing injury is that gun owners seem to eschew resistance when submission is the wiser choice. Although the number of victims in the surveys who say they resisted with a gun is not statistically insignificant, it is dwarfed by the number who tried to flee or scream or resisted forcibly without a gun . . .

. . . Anti-gun claims that "those who own handguns for self-defense are engaging in dangerous self-deception" *imply* that at least delusive peace of mind may be a benefit of the opposing faith. In fairness, even ardent anti-gun advocates ought to admit the value of this in a society so crime ridden that they themselves proclaim that crime, and the fear it creates, palpably diminishes the quality of life. More neutral observers forthrightly acknowledge that "[I]f people feel safer because they own a gun and in turn lead happier lives because they feel safer and more secure, then their guns make a direct and nontrivial contribution to their overall quality of life."

Although increased peace of mind due to gun ownership may be dismissed as a benefit only to the owners themselves and not to society as a whole, it may have wider ramifications. Two fear related problems that have received increasing attention in recent years are the reluctance of bystanders to come to the aid of victims or to bear witness against their attackers. There has been no study of any relationship that may or may not exist between witnesses' or victims' gun ownership and their likelihood of cooperating with law enforcement authorities. But studies have linked gun ownership to Good Samaritanship. Gun owners are apparently more likely than non-owners both to feel a duty to come to the aid of others in distress and to actually do so.

Of course defensive gun ownership is a dangerous self-deception if it causes gun owners to be injured or killed through involvement in otherwise avoidable situations. But the evidence reviewed in *this* section does not suggest that gun ownership produces feelings of invulnerability that encourage owners to recklessly court danger. If anything, non-owners appear less able to evaluate the danger and the opportunities of opposing criminals, and thus more inclined to unwise opposition, than are gun owners. . . .

. . . It may tentatively be concluded that handguns are used as or more often to prevent the commission of crimes than by felons attempting them. This should not be understood as suggesting that the decision to resist a felon can be made lightly or that their handguns automatically insulate resisters from injury. The unique defensive value of a handgun is not the only cause for comparatively low rates of injury among gun-armed resisters; *of equal* or more important *value* is the wisdom not to resist in circumstances in which *resistance* is unlikely to succeed. *The evidence on* the gun lobby's vaunted deterrent effect of gun ownership is even more equivocal. In general, it does support the common sense intuition that the average criminal has no more desire to face an armed citizen than the average citizen has to face an armed criminal. Widespread defensive gun ownership benefits society as a whole by deterring burglars *from entering* occupied premises and by deterring from confrontation offenses altogether an unknown proportion of criminals, who might otherwise be attracted by the immediate profitability of robbery. Even when criminals are not so deterred, widespread gun ownership may frighten them *sufficiently to reduce* the overall number of such offenses they commit. And, it does frighten them into abandoning some specific offenses, particularly in areas where special local programs have dramatized the likelihood of victim arms possession and training. Yet it must also be noted that the possibility that gun ownership reduces the activity level of confrontation offenders is only an unsubstantiated speculation; gun lobby propaganda has exaggerated the deterrent effect of gun ownership by not discounting for displacement effects that represent no net gain in overall crime reduction.

Finally some caveats may be offered on the limited import of the evidence I have reviewed for issues of firearms regulation. Clearly this evidence disposes of the claim that handguns are so lacking in social utility that courts should, in effect, eliminate their sale to the general public under the doctrine of strict liability. This evidence likewise cuts strongly against severe statutory restrictions based on the belief that handgun ownership offers few social benefits to offset the harms associated with it. Moreover, even if handguns offered no benefits whatever, neither does banning them—except as part of a policy of outlawing and confiscating guns of all kinds.

Source: American Journal of Criminal Law 18 (1991): 147–49, 151, 164–65.

Generally considered the seminal work in the crime prevention aspects of gun ownership is Gary Kleck's 1991 *Point Blank: Guns and Violence in America*. The book summarizes the literature on gun ownership and crime and reports new literature. Kleck's summary of his research follows.

DOCUMENT 150: Summary of *Point Blank: Guns and Violence in America*, Gary Kleck (1991)

Gun ownership increased from the 1960's through the 1980's, especially handgun ownership. Some of the increase was due to the formation of new households and to growing affluence enabling gun owners to acquire still more guns; however, a substantial share of the increase was also a response to rising crime rates among people who previously did not own guns. Most handguns are owned for defensive reasons, and many people get guns in response to high or rising crime rates. Therefore, part of the positive association sometimes observed between gun ownership levels and crime rates is due to the effect of the latter on the former, rather than the reverse. Nevertheless, most guns, especially long guns, are owned primarily for recreational reasons unconnected with crime.

Gun owners are not, as a group, psychologically abnormal, nor are they more racist, sexist, or pro-violent than nonowners. Most gun ownership is culturally patterned and linked with a rural hunting subculture. The culture is transmitted across generations, with recreation-related gun owners being socialized by their parents into gun ownership and use from childhood. Defensive handgun owners, on the other hand, are more likely to be disconnected from any gun subcultural roots, and their gun ownership is usually not accompanied by association with other gun owners or by training in the safe handling of guns. Defensive ownership is more likely to be an individualistic response to life circumstances perceived as dangerous. Defensive ownership is also a response to the perception that the police cannot provide adequate protection. This response to dangers, however, is not necessarily mediated by the emotion of fear, but rather may be part of a less emotional preparation for the possibility of future victimization.

The strongest and most consistent predictors of gun ownership are hunting, being male, being older, higher income, residence in rural areas or small towns, having been reared in such small places, having been reared in the South, and being Protestant . . .

Probably fewer than 2% of handguns and well under 1% of all guns will ever be involved in a violent crime. Thus, the problem of criminal gun violence is concentrated within a very small subset of gun owners, indicating that gun control aimed at the general population faces a serious needle-in-the-haystack problem. Criminal gun users most commonly get their guns by buying them from friends and other nonretail sources, or by theft. Therefore, gun regulation would be more likely to succeed in controlling gun violence if it could effectively restrict non-dealer acquisitions and possession of guns by this small high-risk subset of gun owners.

Policy analysts seeking to assess the relative costs and benefits of gun control sometimes simplify their task by assuming that gun ownership has no significant benefits, beyond the relatively minor ones of recreational enjoyment of shooting sports like hunting. Under this assumption, it is unnecessary to show that a given law produces a large reduction in violence, since even one life saved would surely outweigh the supposedly negligible benefits of gun ownership. This simplification, however, is unrealistic, because it erroneously assumes that gun ownership and use has no defensive or deterrent value, and thus no potential for preventing deaths or injuries.

Each year about 1,500–2,800 criminals are lawfully killed by gun-wielding American civilians in justifiable or excusable homicides, far more than are killed by police officers. There are perhaps 600,000–1 million defensive uses of guns each year, about the same as the number of crimes committed with guns. These astounding totals may be less surprising in light of the following facts. About a third of U.S. households keep a gun at least partially for defensive reasons; at any one time nearly a third of gun owners have a firearm in their home (usually a handgun) which is loaded; about a quarter of retail businesses have a gun on the premises; and perhaps 5% of U.S. adults regularly carry a gun for self-defense.

Keeping a gun for home defense makes most defensive gun owners feel safer, and most also believe they are safer because they have a gun. The belief is not necessarily a delusion. People who use guns for self-protection in robberies and assaults are less likely to have the crime completed against them (in a robbery, this means losing their property), and, contrary to widespread belief, are less likely to be injured, compared to either victims who use other forms of resistance or to victims who do nothing to resist. (Criminals take the gun away from the victim in less than 1% of these incidents.) The evidence does not support the idea that nonresistance is safer than resisting with a gun.

Defensive uses of guns most often occur in circumstances where the victims are likely to have access to their guns, mostly in their homes or places of business. Thus, defensive gun uses are most commonly linked with assaults in the home (presumably mostly domestic violence), commercial robberies, and residential burglaries.

The fact that armed victims can effectively disrupt crimes suggests that widespread civilian gun ownership might also deter some criminals from attempting crimes in the first place. There probably will never be definitive evidence on this deterrence question, since it revolves around the issue of how many crimes do not occur because of victim gun ownership. However, scattered evidence is consistent with a deterrence hypothesis. In prison surveys criminals report that they have refrained from committing crimes because they thought a victim might have a gun. "Natural experiments" indicate that rates of "gun deterrable" crimes have declined after various highly publicized incidents related to victim gun use, including gun training programs, incidents of defensive gun use, and passage of a law which required household gun ownership. Widespread gun ownership may also deter burglars from entering occupied homes, reducing confrontations with residents, and thereby reducing deaths and injuries. U.S. burglars are far less likely to enter occupied premises than burglars in nations with lower gun ownership.

Gun use by private citizens against violent criminals and burglars is common and about as frequent as legal actions like arrests, is a more prompt negative consequence of crime than legal punishment, and is more severe, at its most serious, than legal system punishments. On the other hand, only a small percentage of criminal victimizations transpire in a way that results in defensive gun use; guns certainly are not usable in all crime situations. Victim gun use is associated with lower rates of assault or robbery victim injury and lower rates of robbery completion than any other defensive action or doing nothing to resist. Serious predatory criminals perceive a risk from victim gun use which is roughly comparable to that of criminal justice system actions, and this perception may influence their criminal behavior in socially desirable ways.

The most parsimonious way of linking these previously unconnected and unknown or obscure facts is to tentatively conclude that civilian ownership and defensive use of guns deter violent crime and reduce burglar-linked injuries. Rates of commercial robbery, residential burglary injury, and rape might be still higher than their already high levels were it not for the dangerousness of the prospective victim population.

Gun ownership among prospective victims may well have as large a crime-inhibiting effect as any crime-generating effects of gun possession among prospective criminals. This could account for the failure of researchers to find a significant net relationship between rates of crime like homicide and robbery, and measures of general gun ownership—the two effects may roughly cancel each other out. Guns are potentially lethal weapons whether wielded by criminals or victims. They are frightening and intimidating to those they are pointed at, whether these be predators or the preyed upon. Guns thereby empower both those who would use them to victimize and those who would use them to prevent their victimization. Consequently, they are a source of both social order and disorder, depending on who uses them, just as is true of the use of force in general.

The failure to fully acknowledge this reality can lead to grave errors in devising public policy to minimize violence through gun control. While some gun laws are intended to reduce gun possession only among relatively limited "high-risk" groups such as convicted felons, through such measures as laws licensing gun owners or requiring permits to purchase guns, other laws are aimed at reducing gun possession in all segments of the civilian population, both criminal and noncriminal. Examples would be the Morton Grove, Illinois, handgun possession ban, near approximations of such bans (as in New York City and Washington, D.C.), prohibitions of handgun sales (such as those in Chicago), and restrictive variants of laws regulating the carrying of concealed weapons. By definition, laws are most likely to be obeyed by the law-abiding, and gun laws are no different. Therefore, measures applying equally to criminals and noncriminals are almost certain to reduce gun possession more among the latter than the former.

Because very little serious violent crime is committed by persons without previous records of serious violence, there are at best only modest direct crime control benefits to be gained by reductions in gun possession among noncriminals, although even marginal reductions in gun possession among criminals might have crime-inhibiting effects. Consequently, one has to take seriously the possibility that "across-the-board" gun control measures could decrease the crime-control effects of noncriminal gun ownership more than they would decrease the crime-causing effects of criminal gun ownership. For this reason, more narrowly targeted gun control measures like gun owner licensing and permit-to-purchase systems seem preferable.

People skeptical about the value of gun control sometimes argue that while a world in which there were no guns would be desirable, it is also unachievable. The evidence summarized here raises a more radical possibility—that a world in which no one had guns might actually be less safe than one in which nonaggressors had guns and aggressors somehow did not. As a practical matter, the latter world is no more achievable than the former, but the point is worth raising as a way of clarifying what the goals of rational gun control policy should be. If gun possession among prospective victims tends to reduce violence, then reducing such gun possession is not, in and of itself, a social good. Instead, the best policy goal to pursue may be to shift the distribution of gun possession as far as practical in the direction of likely aggressors being disarmed and likely nonaggressors being armed. To disarm noncriminals in the hope this might indirectly help reduce access to guns among criminals is not a cost-free policy . . .

Guns in the hands of prospective victims of violence can deter criminal attempts or disrupt crimes once they are attempted, thereby exerting a violence-reducing effect. Oddly enough, guns in the hands of aggressors also have certain violence-reducing effects, along with the more obvious violence-increasing effects.

The power which weaponry confers has conventionally been treated as exclusively violence-enhancing—it has commonly been assumed that weapon possession and use serves only to increase the likelihood of the victim's injury and death (e.g., Newton and Zimring 1969). This is an unduly restrictive conceptualization of the significance of weaponry. A broader perspective starts with a recognition of weaponry as a source of power, frequently used instrumentally to achieve goals by inducing compliance with the user's demands. The ultimate goal behind an act of violence is not necessarily the victim's death or injury, but rather may be money, sexual gratification, respect, attention, or the terrorizing, humiliation, or domination of the victim. Power can be, and usually is, wielded so as to obtain these things without inflicting physical injury.

Threats, implied or overt, usually suffice and are often preferred to physical attack.

The effects of guns in the hands of aggressors can be better understood if we view violent events as being composed of an ordered series of stages, with the occurrence and outcome of each stage being contingent on previous stages.

(1) Confrontation. First, the prospective aggressor and victim coincide in time and space, entering into a potentially conflictual encounter with each other. Possession of a gun can embolden both victims and aggressors to go where they like, including dangerous places where they might adventitiously encounter a stranger who, in the course of the interaction, becomes an adversary, or it may even encourage them to stop avoiding, or even deliberately seek out, contact with persons with whom they already had a hostile relationship. Thus, gun ownership could increase the rate of assaultive violence by giving people freedom of movement without regard to the risks of entering into dangerous circumstances, thereby increasing the rate of hostile encounters. There is, however, no systematic evidence on these possible effects.

(2) Threat. Once aggressor and victim find themselves confronting one another in a hostile encounter, a gun in the possession of the aggressor could encourage him to threaten the victim, with words or a gesture, possibly alluding to the gun. On the other hand, the prospective victim's possession of a gun could, if it was known to the wouldbe aggressor, discourage the aggressor from expressing a threat. Again, there is no systematic evidence bearing directly on this effect.

(3) Attack. Some hostile encounters go beyond verbal or gestural threats, escalating to an attempt to physically injure the victim, i.e., pro-

ceeding to an attack. An aggressor's possession of a gun can either increase or decrease the probability that he will attack his victim. At least four categories of effects on attack can be conceptualized, and they can be labelled facilitation, triggering, inhibition and redundancy.

Facilitation. A gun could make possible or easier an attack which would otherwise be physically or emotionally impossible, dangerous, or difficult to carry out. It has often been remarked that a gun serves as an "equalizer," that it is a way of making power relations more equal than they otherwise would be. Just as a prospective victim's possession of a gun can give him power greater than or equal to his adversary and discourage an attack, the aggressor's possession of a gun could encourage it. The gun might assure the aggressor that his attack will so effectively hurt his victim that counterattack will be impossible, or at least that his victim will be afraid to strike back, even if physically capable of doing so. Guns can thereby encourage weaker adversaries to attack stronger ones. Thus guns are more commonly used when women attack men than when women attack other women, are more common when an individual attacks a group than when the situation is reversed, and so forth. Guns also facilitate attack from a distance. As someone once observed . . . , "a gun may not be absolutely necessary to kill, but at fifty yards it's certainly a help." Further, a gun may facilitate an attack by a person who is unwilling to attack in a way which involves physical contact with his victim, or by a person too squeamish to use a messier weapon like a knife or club.

Triggering. This is the effect which experimental psychologists label the "weapons effect." Since it is but one of many effects of weaponry, this term is unsuitable, so I have relabelled it the triggering effect. Psychologists have argued that a person who is already angered may attack when they see a weapon, due to the learned association between weapons and aggressive behavior. The experimental research literature on this hypothesis is almost exactly divided between studies supporting it and studies failing to support it. Generally, the more realistic the study's conditions and the more relevant to real-world aggression, the less supportive the results were. There may be triggering effects, but they appear to be very contingent effects, which depend on settings and conditions not yet very well-specified.

Inhibition. Some of the "weapons effect" studies found evidence that weapons could inhibit aggression as well as trigger it. While the reasons for these experimental findings are not clear, in real world violence, one reason for such an effect might be that a gun provides an aggressor with a more lethal weapon than he wants. Most aggressors do not want to kill, but this could easily happen if they attacked with a gun. Therefore, an aggressor may refrain from attacking altogether, for fear that he might . . . end up inflicting more harm than he wanted to.

Redundancy. This inelegant term alludes to the possibility that possession of a gun could make a physical attack unnecessary, by making it possible for an aggressor to get what he wants without attacking.

Weapons are an important source of power frequently wielded to achieve some emotional or material goal—to obtain sexual gratification in a rape or money in a robbery, or, more frequently, to frighten and dominate victims in some other assault. All of these things can be gained without an attack, and indeed the possession of a gun can serve as a substitute for attack, rather than its vehicle. In robberies, offenders without guns often feel they must attack their victim in order to insure that the victim will not resist, while robbers with guns are confident they can gain the victim's compliance merely by pointing their gun at them.

In assaults, a gun can enable an aggressor to terrify his victim or emotionally hurt him, making a physical attack unnecessary. It is not yet possible to separately assess the relative importance of each of these possible causal effects. However, the total effect of all of them considered together is fairly clear. The net effect of aggressor gun possession on whether the aggressor attacks is negative. In at least 17 prior studies, mostly of robbery, but also of assault, aggressors with guns were less likely to attack and/or injure their victim.

(4) Injury. Once an aggressor makes an attack, it may or may not result in injury. That is, only some attempts to injure are successful. The rate at which attacks result in physical injury to the victim is lower when the attacker fires a gun than when he throws a punch, attempts to cut or stab his victim, or tries to strike the victim with a blunt instrument of some kind. This presumably is because it is difficult to shoot a gun (usually a handgun) accurately, especially under the emotionally stressful conditions which prevail in most violent encounters. Only about 19% of incidents where an aggressor shot at a victim result in the victim suffering a gunshot wound, while the comparable attack completion rate is about 55% for knife attacks. Since guns facilitate attacks at a distance and attacks against more difficult targets, they may thereby also reduce the attack completion rate.

(5) Death. Finally, if the aggressor does inflict a physical injury on the victim, it may or may not result in death. Less than 1% of all criminal assaults result in death, and the measured fatality rate is under 15% even if we limit attention just to gunshot woundings. Further, because non-fatal attacks are substantially undercounted, while fatal attacks are fairly completely counted, the true fatality rate in gunshot woundings is actually still lower, probably under 10%.

Nevertheless, the measured wounding fatality rate for guns is about four times higher than that of woundings with knives, the next most lethal weapon, among those which could be used in the same circumstances as guns. This might seem to indicate that if guns became scarce and attackers used knives rather than guns, only one fourth as many victims would die. This reasoning, however, is invalid because it implicitly attributes all of the difference in fatality rates to the weapon itself, and assumes that all else, including the intentions and motives of the aggressors, is equal in gun and knife attacks. This assumption is unrealistic. Evidence indicates that aggressors who use guns choose them over other available weapons—a gun is not used just because "it was there"; weapon choice is not random. Rather, more serious aggressors use more serious weaponry. For example, aggressors with longer records of violence in their past are more likely to use guns. Thus, some of the 4-to-1 difference in fatality rates between guns and knives is due to differences in the people who used the weapons, rather than just the technical differences between the weapons themselves.

Since weapon scarcity would presumably not alter the intentions and aggressive drive of aggressors, this implies that the fatality rate would drop by a factor of less than four if knives were substituted for guns. It is impossible to say how much less, since it is impossible to measure and control for the intentions and intensity of an aggressor's anger and willingness to hurt his victim at the moment of the attack. Nevertheless, studies that have imperfectly controlled for aggressor traits thought to be correlated with these factors indicate that guns still appear to be more lethal than knives.

To summarize, an aggressor's possession and use of a gun apparently reduces the probability that he will attack, reduces the probability that the attack will result in an injury, and increases the probability that the injury will be fatal. Therefore, it is not at all obvious that threatening situations with a gun-armed aggressor are more likely to result in the victim's death, since it is not obvious what the relative balance of these three countervailing effects is. The best empirical evidence on real-life violent incidents indicates that the net effect is essentially zero. That is, the overall probability of a threatening situation ending in the victim's death is about the same when the aggressor is armed with a gun as it is when the aggressor is unarmed. In short, guns have many strong effects on violent encounters, but they work in both violence-increasing and violence-decreasing directions, and these effects apparently more or less cancel each other out.

Note that this conclusion takes no account of gun effects on confrontations and threats. It is still possible that gun availability in a population could affect the rates of assault and murder, despite the foregoing conclusions, if it significantly encouraged people to more frequently enter into dangerous confrontations and to issue threats or otherwise initiate hostile interactions. Also, an analysis focusing solely on individual violent incidents cannot take account of possible deterrent effects of victims having guns, which would tend to discourage aggressors from seeking contact with victims or threatening them.

Consequently, the net impact of widespread gun ownership must be assessed using data on aggregates like cities or states, where the combined impact of all of these separate effects can be estimated.

Source: Paper presented at 1991 Annual Meeting of the American Political Science Association, Washington Hilton, August 29 through September 1, 1991.

Document 151: "10 Myths of Gun Control," National Rifle Association (1994)

MYTH: "Since a gun in a home is many times more likely to kill a family member than to stop a criminal, armed citizens are not a deterrent to crime."

This myth, stemming from a superficial "study" of firearm accidents in the Cleveland, Ohio, area, represents a comparison of 148 accidental deaths (including suicides) to the deaths of 23 intruders killed by home owners over a 16-year period.

Gross errors in this and similar "studies"—with even greater claimed ratios of harm to good—include: the assumption that a gun hasn't been used for protection unless an assailant dies; no distinction is made between handgun and long gun deaths; all accidental firearm fatalities were counted whether the deceased was part of the "family" or not; all accidents were counted whether they occurred in the home or not, while self-defense outside the home was excluded; almost half the self-defense uses of guns in the home were excluded on the grounds that the criminal intruder killed may not have been a total stranger to the home defender; suicides were sometimes counted and some self-defense shootings misclassified . . .

The "guns in the home" myth has been repeated time and again by the media, and anti-gun academics continue to build on it. In 1993, Dr. Arthur Kellermann of Emory University and a number of colleagues presented a study that claimed to show that a home with a gun was much more likely to experience a homicide. However, Dr. Kellermann selected for his study only homes where homicides had taken place—ignoring the millions of homes with firearms where no harm is done—and a control group that was not representative of American households. By only looking at homes where homicides had occurred and failing to control for more pertinent variables, such as prior criminal record or histories of violence, Kellermann et al. skewed the results of this study.

Prof. Kleck wrote that with the methodology used by Kellermann, one could prove that since diabetics are much more likely to possess insulin than non-diabetics, possession of insulin is a risk factor for diabetes. Even Dr. Kellermann admitted this in his study: "It is possible that reverse causation accounted for some of the association we observed between gun ownership and homicide." Law Professor Daniel D. Polsby went further, "Indeed the point is stronger than that: 'reverse causation' may account for most of the association between gun ownership and homicide. Kellermann's data simply do not allow one to draw any conclusion."

Research conducted by Professors James Wright and Peter Rossi for a landmark study funded by the U.S. Department of Justice, points to the armed citizen as possibly the most effective deterrent to crime in the nation. Wright and Rossi questioned over 1,800 felons serving time in prisons across the nation and found:

- 81% agreed the "smart criminal" will try to find out if a potential victim is armed.
- 74% felt that burglars avoided occupied dwellings for fear of being shot.
- 80% of "handgun predators" had encountered armed citizens.
- 40% did not commit a specific crime for fear that the victim was armed.
- 34% of "handgun predators" were scared off or shot at by armed victims.
- 57% felt that the typical criminal feared being shot by citizens more than he feared being shot by police.

Professor Kleck estimates that annually 1,500–2,800 felons are legally killed in "excusable self-defense" or "justifiable" shootings by civilians, and 8,000–16,000 criminals are wounded.

This compares to 300–600 justifiable homicides by police. Yet, in most instances, civilians used a firearm to threaten, apprehend, shoot at a criminal, or to fire a warning shot without injuring anyone.

Based on his extensive independent survey research, Kleck estimates that each year Americans use guns for protection from criminals more than 2.5 million times annually. U.S. Department of Justice victimization surveys show that protective use of a gun lessens the chance that robberies, rapes, and assaults will be successfully completed while also reducing the likelihood of victim injury. Clearly, criminals fear armed citizens.

Source: National Rifle Association, "10 Myths of Gun Control," 1994.

Next, two criminologists explain the survey and methods they used to determine the number of times guns are used defensively.

DOCUMENT 152: "Armed Resistance to Crime: The Prevalence and Nature of Self-Defense with a Gun," Gary Kleck and Marc Gertz (1995)

However consistent the evidence may be concerning the effectiveness of armed victim resistance, there are some who minimize its significance by insisting that it is rare. This assertion is invariably based entirely on a single source of information, the National Crime Victimization Study (NCVS).

Data from the NCVS imply that each year there are only about 68,000 defensive uses of guns in connection with assaults and robberies, or about 80,000 to 82,000 if one adds in uses linked with household burglaries. These figures are less than one ninth of the estimates implied by the results of at least thirteen other surveys . . .

[This] present survey is the first survey ever devoted to the subject of armed self-defense. It was carefully designed to correct all of the known correctable or avoidable flaws of previous surveys which critics have identified . . .

Are [our] estimates plausible? Could it really be true that Americans use guns for self-protection as often as 2.1 to 2.5 million times a year? The estimate may seem remarkable in comparison to expectations based on conventional wisdom, but it is not implausibly large in comparison to various gun-related phenomena. There are probably over 220 million guns in private hands in the U.S., implying that only about 1% of them are used for defensive purposes in any one year—not an impossibly high fraction . . .

Huge numbers of Americans not only have access to guns, but the overwhelming majority of gun owners, if one can believe their statements, are willing to use a gun defensively. In a December 1989 national survey, 78% of American gun owners stated that they would not only be willing to use a gun defensively in some way, but would be willing to shoot a burglar. The percentage willing to use a gun defensively in some way, though not necessarily by shooting someone, would presumably be even higher than this . . .

Guns were most commonly used for defense against burglary, assault, and robbery. Cases of "mutual combat," where it would be hard to tell who is the aggressor or where both parties are aggressors, would be a subset of the 30% of cases where assault was the crime involved. However, only 19% of the defensive gun use (DGU) cases involved *only* assault and no other crime where victim and offender could be more easily distinguished . . .

While victims face multiple offenders in only about 24% of all violent crimes, the victims in our sample who used guns faced multiple offenders in 53% of the incidents. This mirrors the observation that criminals who use guns are also more likely than unarmed criminals to face multiple victims. A gun allows either criminals or victims to handle a larger number of adversaries. Many victims facing multiple offenders probably would not resist at all if they were without a gun or some other weapon. Another possible interpretation is that some victims will resort to a defensive measure as serious as wielding a gun only if they face the most desperate circumstances. Again, this finding contradicts a view that gun defenders face easier circumstances than other crime victims . . .

If one were committed to rejecting the seemingly overwhelming survey evidence on the frequency of DGU, one could speculate, albeit without any empirical foundation whatsoever, that nearly all of the people reporting such experiences are simply making them up. We feel this is implausible. A respondent who had actually experienced a DGU would have no difficulty responding with a "no" answer to our DGU question because a "no" response was not followed up by further questioning. On the other hand, lying with a false "yes" answer required a good deal more imagination and energy. Since we asked as many as nineteen questions on the topic, this would entail spontaneously inventing as many as nineteen plausible and internally consistent bits of false information and doing so in a way that gave no hint to experienced interviewers that they were being deceived . . .

The banal and undramatic nature of the reported incidents also undercuts the dishonest respondent speculation. While all the incidents involved a crime, and usually a fairly serious one, only 8% of the alleged gun defenders claim to have shot their adversaries, and only 24% claim to have fired their gun. If large numbers of respondents were inventing their accounts, one would think they would have created more exciting scenarios . . .

The policy implications of these results are straightforward. These findings do not imply anything about whether moderate regulatory measures such as background checks or purchase permits would be desirable. Regulatory measures which do not disarm large shares of the population would not significantly reduce beneficial defensive uses of firearms by noncriminals. On the other hand, prohibitionist measures, whether aimed at all guns or just at handguns, are aimed at disarming criminals and noncriminals alike. They would therefore discourage and presumably decrease the frequency of DGU among noncriminal crime victims because even minimally effective gun bans would disarm at least some noncriminals. The same would be true of laws which ban gun carrying. In sum, measures that effectively reduce gun availability among the noncriminal majority also would reduce DGUs that otherwise would have saved lives, prevented injuries, thwarted rape attempts, driven off burglars, and helped victims retain their property.

Since as many as 400,000 people a year use guns in situations where the defenders claim that they "almost certainly" saved a life by doing so, this result cannot be dismissed as trivial. If even one-tenth of these people are accurate in their state[d] perceptions, the number of lives saved by victim use of guns would still exceed the total number of lives taken with guns . . .

This is also too serious a matter to base conclusions on silly statistics comparing the number of lives taken with guns with the number of criminals killed by victims. Killing a criminal is not a benefit to the victim, but rather a nightmare to be suffered for years afterward. Saving a life through DGU would be a benefit, but this almost never involves killing the criminal; probably fewer than 3,000 criminals are lawfully killed by gun-wielding victims each year, representing only about 1/1000 of the number of DGUs, and less than 1% of the number of purportedly life-saving DGUs.

Source: The Journal of Criminal Law and Criminology 86 (Fall 1995): 150–87.

In the following entry, researchers tried to determine whether "gun ownership raises or lowers the *perceived* safety of others in the community by looking at subjective beliefs." Researchers asked respondents about crime in the neighborhood and how safe they feel. They also asked if respondents would feel more or less safe or the same if more people in the area were to get guns.

DOCUMENT 153: "Firearms and Community Feelings of Safety," David Hemenway, Ph.D., Sara J. Solnick, and Deborah R. Azrael (1995)

Eighty-five percent of non-gun owners report they would feel less safe if more people in their community acquired guns; only 8% would feel more safe. By a ten-to-one margin, they prefer others not to acquire firearms. Over 80% of non-gun owners would feel less safe if others acquire guns whether respondents are male or female, white or non-white, live in urban or suburban/rural areas, have high or low income, are young or old, have children living at home or not, and had a gun in the house when growing up or not.

For gun owners, the acquisition of firearms by others in the community would leave about equal numbers feeling less safe as feeling more safe. Among gun owners, those likely to feel less safe are females, non-whites, urban dwellers, those who did not have a gun in the home when growing up, and those who own a gun for reasons other than protection.

[Because gun owners were oversampled, extrapolating data to the United States as a whole shows that of] gun owners and non-gun owners together—71% feel less safe and 19% feel more safe when others in the community acquire firearms . . .

Most people feel the external effects of gun ownership. Our study demonstrates that the vast majority of Americans believe they will either be more or less safe when others in the community acquire guns. Most people probably do not know much about or may not care enough about the preferences of others when making the decision to obtain a firearm. If the externalities are primarily negative, then individual decision-making may lead to too many people obtaining firearms. The result could be an equilibrium in which, compared to the optimum, too many households contain guns . . .

While the decision to acquire a firearm is personal, it has public ramifications . . .

Source: The Journal of Criminal Law and Criminology 86 (1995): 121–32.

In discussions of safety, it follows that those who feel most vulnerable stand to gain a greater sense of security. After all, that is why a gun is sometimes called "the great equalizer." And as several earlier entries have noted, women are often viewed, and view themselves, as vulnerable. Sociologist James D. Wright said, "Firearms equalize the means of physical terror between men and women. In denying the wife of an abusive man the right to have a firearm, we may only be guaranteeing her husband the right to beat her at his pleasure."

Much has been written on women and guns, but in general, the arguments for and against women owning guns for self-defense are no different than the arguments for and against anyone owning guns for self-defense. There have been reports in the media and by those involved in the gun control debate that an increasing number of women own and carry guns—for good or bad. Indeed, the gun industry has contributed to the perception—or reality—by promoting "women's" guns, magazines, and accessories such as purses with compartments for carrying concealed weapons. But is that really true? One report says those numbers might be exaggerated.

DOCUMENT 154: "Changes in Firearms Ownership among Women, 1980–1994," Tom W. Smith, Ph.D., and Robert J. Smith, J.D. (1995)

Since the mid-1980s, pro-gun groups . . . have promoted gun owner-ship among women. They claim that the purchase and ownership of firearms by women has greatly increased. This claim has been accepted by most journalists and repeated in dozens of stories about the femini-zation of gunnery. . . . The typical news story describes women who buy handguns and take firearms training courses because they have been the victims of crime or are afraid of becoming victims. Most of these women are unmarried and live in large cities. The typical article asserts that the level of ownership among women is already high, that their ownership is rapidly increasing, and that women account for a large number of trainees, gun sales, and new permit holders . . .

In support of media claims that the number of women owning guns is increasing is a frequently cited Smith & Wesson survey which found that gun ownership among women increased by 53% from 1983 to 1986. . . . In particular, the Smith & Wesson/Gallup surveys found that there were 15.6 million potential female gun purchasers in 1989 and that this figure was 100% higher than in 1983 . . .

Pro-gun groups are, as expected, doing all that they can to further this supposed development. . . . The NRA targeted women in their member-ship drives in the 1980s, set up an Office on Women's Issues and Infor-mation in 1990, and launched a massive public relations and recruitment campaign in October 1993 called "Refuse to Be a Victim." It urged women to take self-protection and anti-crime measures and equated owning a gun to female empowerment. Female gun ownership has been characterized as the "last frontier of feminism." . . .

First, on what does the NRA base its estimates? Elizabeth Swasey, director of the Office on Women's Issues and Information at the NRA and main NRA spokesperson on this issue, cites (1) the Smith & Wesson Gallup polls, (2) industry sources, (3) information from the NRA's 33,000 certified instructors, and (4) magazine surveys such as a 1992 readership survey by Self magazine which indicated that 16% of gun owners pur-chased a gun to protect themselves.

How these various bits of information are put together to yield esti-mates on how many women own guns is not explained. Of the sources cited, only the Gallup polls are possibl[y] a credible and scientifically reliable source; yet Smith & Wesson has never presented any detailed analysis of their Gallup polls, has refused to allow scholars to examine the data, and has been corrected by Gallup for misusing data on potential gun purchases from these same surveys . . .

The best available data on the ownership of firearms by gender are the General Social Surveys (GSS) conducted by the National Opinion Research Center, University of Chicago [with which author Tom Smith is affiliated]. [From 1980 to 1994] for both men and women and for both handguns and all guns, there has been no statistically significant trend in the ownership of firearms. Neither women nor men are more likely to own either a gun or handgun now than they were in 1980. The notion that women are rapidly purchasing guns and increasing their ownership of firearms receives no support from these data. And the gender gap in weapons has not changed. From 1980 to 1994 male ownership of firearms exceed[ed] female ownership by a constant 31.1 percentage points, better than four-to-one, and male ownership of handguns surpassed ownership by women by 19.7 percentage points, or almost four-to-one.

Second, the level of gun ownership is substantially below that cited by the NRA and the mass media. As detailed above, the typical claims are that 17 to 20% of women own guns, and these soar to as high as 43.5%. However, the GSS indicates that from 1980 to 1994 about 11.6% of women owned a gun and 7.4% of women had a handgun.

Third, contrary to the heavy media emphasis on handguns, many of the weapons owned by women are long guns. From 1988 to 1993, 88.7% of women did not personally own a gun and only 11.3% had a weapon in their households (32.% owned only handguns, 3.1% owned only long guns, 4.7% owned both types, and 0.3% some other or unknown type). This means that from 3.2% to 7.9% of women personally owned a handgun. If we assume that women living without another adult personally owned the handgun(s) reported, then the female ownership range would be from 4.5% to 7.9% . . .

Nor is the typical female gun owner an unmarried women living in a large city or a past or fearful victim of violent crime. Gun ownership is higher among married women living outside large cities, and it is associated more with hunting than with either fear of crime or past victimization.

Source: The Journal of Criminal Law and Criminology 86, no. 1 (Fall 1995): 133–49.

Much has been written on women and guns on both sides of the issue. The National Rifle Association offers a different perspective, which can be viewed on its World Wide Web page or requested from the organization. (See Resources, Appendix IV.)

Another researcher and physician wrote recently on the relationship between gun design and violence, noting the trend toward smaller, concealable handguns.

DOCUMENT 155: "The Relationship between Firearm Design and Firearm Violence, Handguns in the 1990s," Garen J. Wintemute, M.D., M.P.H. (June 12, 1996)

In 1994, an estimated 39,720 persons died from firearm-related injuries. Firearms now rank a close second to motor vehicles as a cause of traumatic death nationwide. This convergence results not so much from an increase in the firearm-related death rate, which has remained relatively stable for the past 15 years, as from a steady decrease in the death rate from motor vehicle injuries. That decrease stems in large part from an explicit focus on the contribution to motor vehicle death rates made by the design and marketing of motor vehicles themselves.

The Changing Nature of Handgun Design and Marketing

Not surprisingly, trends in the nature of crime- and violence-involved handguns reflect general trends in the design and marketing of these consumer products. The most important of these trends is the emergence, for the first time, of the semiautomatic pistol as the dominant handgun design. In the early 1980s, US firearm manufacturers produced more than twice as many revolvers as pistols; by 1994, pistols outnumbered revolvers by more than 3:1. The substantial growth in pistol production since the mid 1980s has been limited almost entirely to medium- and large-caliber guns. The disparate findings of the medical and criminal justice statistics result from the development of two largely distinct classes of pistols. The first is made up of relatively expensive, large-capacity guns of a caliber of 9 mm or greater; their prominence in most studies of fatalities results in part from the higher wounding potential of their more powerful ammunition. The second class is made up of small, inexpensive, small- and medium-caliber guns that are replacing earlier Saturday night special revolvers. The low price and easy availability of these guns have been implicated in their frequent criminal use. A third group is now emerging that combines the characteristics of the other two and takes advantage of recent technical innovations. These guns are designed specifically for the concealed-carry market. Many of them are simpler to operate than conventional pistols. . . .

In the third development, pistols are becoming simpler to operate. The original Colt pistol and many of those manufactured today are of what is called single-action design: For the gun to fire, its hammer must be cocked before the trigger is pulled. This is done manually before the first round is fired; the hammer is recocked automatically, and another round is brought into firing position, by the explosive forces of each discharge. For a single-action pistol to be ready for immediate use, it must be carried cocked and with a round of ammunition in the firing position; the safety is engaged to prevent unintentional firing.

Two relatively recent modifications of the operating mechanism, or action, of pistols have made them easier to use and therefore potentially accessible to a larger market. These operating mechanisms are referred to as double-action and double-action-only. Both mechanisms eliminate the need for the gun to be cocked manually; the first pull of the trigger cocks and then drops the hammer, firing the first round.

In conventional double-action pistols, the explosive forces of the first firing recock the hammer and bring a new round into firing position; the gun operates in single-action mode thereafter. The first (double-action) trigger pull is heavier than the single-action pulls that follow, which can be confusing to untrained users. After the user has finished firing, the gun remains cocked with ammunition in firing position unless it is empty. Such guns are equipped with a manually operated decocking device, which allows the cocked hammer to be lowered without firing the gun. Many have other user-operated safety devices as well.

By contrast, in double-action-only pistols the explosive forces of each firing bring the next round into firing position, but do not cock the hammer. Many such guns carry no external, user operated safety devices; these "slick-slide" guns are promoted as "more snag-resistant" for concealed-carry use.

Their simplicity is seen by some as a strong advantage: "Just draw and shoot." Their relatively long and difficult trigger pull has made them hard to control in some cases, and some early models have been unreliable. The absence of any user-operated safety devices in many of these guns has also caused concern. With the exception of companies producing only the most inexpensive guns, every large manufacturer of medium- or large-caliber pistols now produces double-action and double-action-only models. Some industry analysts expect them eventually to dominate the handgun market; they approximate the ease of operation of revolvers but have a substantially larger ammunition capacity.

Finally, the past decade has seen a rapid increase in the use of polymer and other lightweight materials in this group of pistols. Polymer technology was popularized in the mid 1980s by Glock, a US-Austrian importer. Many manufacturers make extensive use of polymers in guns designed for concealed carrying, in which weight reduction is seen as an important advantage. Such guns can also be made less expensively, as machining costs are reduced. . . .

Technology and opportunity are now coming together. A rapidly growing number of manufacturers have introduced lightweight, easily concealable, double-action or double-action-only, medium- or large-caliber pistols; some smaller companies produce nothing else. The trend has given rise to a resurgence in what might be called "palmshot" advertising in gun consumer magazines, in which manufacturers emphasize photographically that their pistols can be hidden entirely behind the hand. Advertisements and promotional articles refer to these guns as "pocket rocket[s]" and "pocket battleship[s]."

These new pistols retain substantial ammunition capacity: 7 to 9 rounds for medium-caliber guns (.380, 9 mm) and 5 to 7 rounds at larger calibers (.40 S&W, .45 ACP).

In 1995, major producers S&W and Glock introduced guns targeting this market. Smith & Wesson's gun, the double-action-only Sigma .380, is of particular significance. Made in part of the zinc alloy used by the Southern California manufacturers, it represents the first contemporary instance of a large, arguably high-end firearm manufacturer entering the low end of the market. The gun is targeted at "the utilitarian, even the reluctant, gun buyer who . . . keeps a pistol for peace of mind." As the first "expensive-name, low-price pistol," it is predicted to be "one of the hottest selling handguns of the decade."

In addition to marketing entirely new guns, many pistol manufacturers have redesigned existing larger pistols to produce "compact" and "subcompact" models in which the barrel is shortened by an inch or more for concealed-carry use. And to facilitate concealed carrying of revolvers, manufacturers are reviving the "hammerless" or bobbed hammer design, in which the hammer is recessed entirely within the frame of the gun or rounded off to a lower profile so that it "can be drawn from purse or fanny pack without snagging." Every major manufacturer of revolvers has added such guns to its product line in the past 3 years. The most recent introductions have been 5-shot .357-caliber guns.

As with the latter-day Saturday night specials, many of these new and redesigned handguns are legally sold in the United States only because they are made here. The pistols frequently fail the minimum size criterion applied to imports. Some pistols, particularly the "slick-slide" double-action-only models, are not equipped with a user-operated safety as imported pistols must be. The new concealed-carry revolvers often have 2-in barrels, below the 3-in minimum for imports. As with any other consumer product, the design of handguns is evolving in response to changing consumer demand and the opportunities and limitations created by statute. This evolution will affect rates of firearm violence. The small-caliber Saturday night special is being replaced by inexpensive me-

dium-caliber guns. The general trend toward higher caliber among handguns may well lead to an increase in the case-fatality rate for all types
of shootings. The increased availability of handguns designed to be carried concealed in public may increase the number of shootings. Frequent
depictions of laser-equipped and very high-caliber handguns in broad-
cast entertainment may lead to selective increases in their involvement
in violence, as is believed to have occurred with both conventional pistols and assault weapons in the 1980s.

Current health and criminal justice surveillance systems are not capable of detecting these changes except where special efforts are being
made. The case for establishing a comprehensive firearm fatality reporting system has been made previously. If we are to understand the relationship between firearms as products and firearm violence, such a
system remains urgently needed.

If formulated without adequate data, future policies to control firearm
violence can be expected to have both intended and unintended effects
on the design and marketing of firearms; some of the latter may be coun-
terproductive. Policymakers should consider adopting a comprehensive,
rational, and continuing focus on product-based approaches to the prevention of firearm violence.

Source: Journal of the American Medical Association 275, 12 June 1996.

In the following public health study, researchers tried to determine
the frequency with which firearms are used to resist home invasion
crimes. Researchers screened Atlanta, Georgia, police department reports for every unwanted entry into occupied homes between June 1
and August 31, 1994.

DOCUMENT 156: "Weapon Involvement in Home Invasion Crimes," Arthur L. Kellermann et al. (1995)

A total of 198 cases were identified during the study interval. Half (99
cases) involved forced entry into the home. The victim and offender were
acquainted in one third of cases. A firearm was carried by one or more
offenders in 32 cases (17%). Seven offenders (3.5%) carried knives. In
42% of cases, the offender fled without confronting the victim. Victims
who avoided confrontation were more likely to lose property but much
less likely to be injured than those who were confronted by the offender.
Resistance was attempted in 62 cases (31%), but the odds of injury were

not significantly affected by the method of resistance. Forty cases (20%) resulted in one or more victims' being injured, including six (3%) who were shot. No one died. Three victims (1.5%) employed a firearm in self-protection. All three escaped injury, but one lost property.

A minority of home invasion crimes result in injury. Measures that increase the difficulty of forced entry or enhance the likelihood of detection could be useful to prevent these crimes. Although firearms are often kept in the home for protection, they are rarely used for this purpose.

Almost half of all homes in the United States contain one or more firearms.

Source: Journal of the American Medical Association 273, no. 22 (June 14, 1995): 1759–762.

ADDITIONAL READING

Bordua, David J. "Firearms Ownership and Violent Crime: A Comparison of Illinois Counties." In *The Social Ecology of Crime*, edited by James M. Byrne and Robert J. Sampson, 156–88. New York: Springer-Verlag, 1986.

Brill, Steven. *Firearm Abuse: A Research and Policy Report*. Washington, D.C.: Police Foundation, 1977.

Cook, Philip J. "The Role of Firearms in Violent Crimes: An Interpretive Review of the Literature with Some New Findings and Suggestions for Further Research." In *Criminal Violence* 236 (1982).

Crocker, Royce. "Attitudes toward Gun Control: A Survey." In *Federal Regulation of Firearms*, edited by Harry L. Hogan. Washington, D.C.: U.S. Government Printing Office, 1982.

Deutsch, Stephen Jay, and Francis B. Alt. "The Effect of Massachusetts' Gun Control Law on Gun-Related Crimes in the City of Boston." *Evaluation Quarterly* 1 (1977): 543–68.

DeZee, Matthew R. "Gun Control Legislation: Impact and Ideology." *Law and Policy Quarterly* 5 (1983): 367–79.

Geisel, Martin S., Richard Roll, and R. Stanton Wettick. "The Effectiveness of State and Local Regulations of Handguns." *Duke University Law Journal* 4 (1969): 647–76.

Hay, Richard, and Richard McCleary. "Box-Tiao Times Series Models for Impact Assessment." *Evaluation Quarterly* 3 (1979): 277–314.

Jones, Edward D., III. "The District of Columbia's 'Firearms Control Regulations Act of 1975': The Toughest Handgun Control Law in the United States— Or Is It?" *The Annals* 455 (1981): 138–49.

Jung, Roy S., and Leonard A. Jason. "Firearm Violence and the Effects of Gun Control Legislation." *American Journal of Community Psychology* 16 (1988): 515–24.

Kleck, Gary. "Capital Punishment, Gun Ownership, and Homicide." *American Journal of Sociology* 84 (1979): 882–910.

————. "The Relationship between Gun Ownership Levels and Rates of Violence in the United States." In *Firearms and Violence: Issues of Public Policy*, edited by Don B. Kates, Jr., 99–135. Cambridge, Mass.: Ballinger, 1984.

————. *Point Blank: Guns and Violence in America*. Hawthorne, N.Y.: Aldine de Gruyter, 1991.

Krug, Alan S. "A Statistical Study of the Relationship between Firearms Licensing Laws and Crime Rates." *Congressional Record*, 25 July 1967, pp. H9366–H9370.

Lester, David. "The Use of Firearms in Violent Crime." *Crime & Justice* 8 (1985): 115–20.

Loftin, Colin, Milton Heumann, and David McDowall. "Mandatory Sentencing and Firearms Violence: Evaluating an Alternative to Gun Control." *Law & Society Review* 17 (1983): 287–318.

Loftin, Colin, and David McDowall. "The Deterrent Effects of the Florida Felony Firearm Law." *Journal of Criminal Law & Criminology* 75 (1984): 250–59.

Magaddino, Joseph P. "An Empirical Analysis of Federal and State Firearm Control Laws." In *Firearms and Violence: Issues of Public Policy*, edited by Don B. Kates, Jr., 225–58. Cambridge, Mass.: Ballinger, 1984.

Magaddino, Joseph P., and Marshall H. Medoff. "Homicides, Robberies and State 'Cooling-off' Schemes." In *Why Handgun Bans Can't Work*, edited by Don B. Kates, Jr., 101–12. Bellevue, Wash.: Second Amendment Foundation, 1982.

Markush, Robert E., and Alfred A. Bartolucci. "Firearms and Suicide in the United States." *American Journal of Public Health* 74 (1984): 123–27.

McDowall, David. "Gun Availability and Robbery Rates: A Panel Study of Large U.S. Cities, 1974–1978." *Law & Policy* 8 (1986): 135–48.

McPheters, Lee R., Robert Mann, and Don Schlagenhauf. "Economic Response to a Crime Deterrence Program." *Economic Inquiry* 22 (1984): 550–70.

Medoff, Marshall H., and Joseph P. Magaddino. "Suicides and Firearm Control Laws." *Evaluation Review* 7 (1983): 357–72.

Murray, Douglas R. "Handguns, Gun Control Laws and Firearm Violence." *Social Problems* 23 (1975): 81–92.

Newton, George D., and Franklin Zimring. *Firearms and Violence in American Life*. A staff report to the National Commission on the Causes and Prevention of Violence. Washington, D.C.: U.S. Government Printing Office, 1969.

Nicholson, Robert, and Anne Garner. *The Analysis of the Firearms Control Act of 1975*. Washington, D.C.: U.S. Conference of Mayors, 1980.

Seitz, Stephen T. "Firearms, Homicides, and Gun Control Effectiveness." *Law and Society Review* 6 (1972): 595–614.

Smith, Tom W. "The 75% Solution: An Analysis of the Structure of Attitudes on Gun Control, 1959–1977." *Journal of Criminal Law & Criminology* 71 (1980): 300–316.

Snyder, Jeffrey R. "A Nation of Cowards." *The Public Interest* 113 (1993): 40–55.

Sommers, Paul M. "Deterrence and Gun Control: An Empirical Analysis." *Atlantic Economic Journal* 8 (1980): 89–94.

Wright, James D., and Linda Marston. "The Ownership of the Means of Destruction: Weapons in the United States." *Social Problems* 23 (October 1975): 93–107.

Wright, James, and Peter Rossi. *Armed and Considered Dangerous: A Survey of Felons and Their Firearms*. Hawthorne, N.Y.: Aldine de Gruyter, 1986.

Zimring, Franklin E. "Is Gun Control Likely to Reduce Violent Killings?" *The University of Chicago Law Review* 35 (1968): 721–37.

———. "Firearms and Federal Law: The Gun Control Act of 1968." *Journal of Legal Studies* 4 (1975): 133–98.

———. "Street Crime and New Guns: Some Implications for Firearms Control." *Journal of Criminal Justice* 4 (1976): 95–107.

Part X

The 1990s— The Debate Takes Center Stage

There has been significant gun control activity in the past decade. Several states have enacted right-to-carry laws; other states have limited the number of guns available at each purchase. On the federal level, the Brady Bill (see Document 92) waiting period was passed after several years of trying.

Just as gun control can generally be viewed as an urban versus a rural issue, it can also be viewed as a Democrat versus a Republican issue. As with any generalization, there are exceptions to the rule. Presidential election year party platforms reflect the philosophies of the two parties.

DOCUMENT 157: "Uniting the Family," The Republican Party Platform (1992)

Republicans defend the constitutional right to keep and bear arms. We call for stiff mandatory sentences for those who use firearms in a crime. We note that those who seek to disarm citizens in their homes are the same liberals who tried to disarm our Nation during the Cold War and are today seeking to cut our national defense below safe levels. We applaud congressional Republicans for overturning the District of Columbia's law blaming firearms manufacturers for street crime.

Source: The Republican Party Platform, adopted 17 August 1992.

DOCUMENT 158: "A New Covenant with the American People," The Democratic Party Platform (1992)

It is time to shut down the weapons bazaars. We support a reasonable waiting period to permit background checks for purchases of handguns, as well as assault weapons controls to ban the possession, sale, importation and manufacture of the most deadly assault weapons. We do not support efforts to restrict weapons used for legitimate hunting and sporting purposes. We will work for swift and certain punishment of all people who violate the country's gun laws and for stronger sentences for criminals who use guns. We will also seek to shut down the black market for guns and impose severe penalties on people who sell guns to children.

Source: The Democratic Party Platform, 1992.

Not surprisingly, a policy on gun control made it into the platforms of the Republicans and Democrats again in 1996. It is important to note that the Republican and Democratic crime and violence initiatives go beyond "gun control," but for purposes of this text, only those sections of the platforms dealing with firearms have been excerpted.

DOCUMENT 159: "Individual Rights and Personal Safety," The Republican Party Platform (1996)

We defend the constitutional right to keep and bear arms. We will promote training in the safe usage of firearms, especially in programs for women and the elderly. We strongly support Bob Dole's National Instant Check Initiative, which will help keep all guns out of the hands of convicted felons. The point-of-purchase instant check has worked well in many states, and now it is time to extend this system all across America. We applaud Bob Dole's commitment to have the national instant check system operational by the end of 1997. In one of the strangest actions of his tenure, Bill Clinton abolished Operation Triggerlock, the Republican initiative to jail any felon caught with a gun. We will restore that effort and will set by law minimum mandatory penalties for the use of guns in committing a crime: 5 years for possession, 10 years for brandishing, and 20 for discharge.

Source: The Republican Party Platform, adopted 12 August 1996.

DOCUMENT 160: "Protecting Our Children, Our Neighborhoods, and Our Police from Criminals with Guns," The Democratic Party Platform (1996)

Bob Dole, Newt Gingrich, and George Bush were able to hold the Brady Bill hostage for the gun lobby until Bill Clinton became President. With his leadership, we made the Brady Bill the law of the land. And because we did, more than 60,000 felons, fugitives, and stalkers have been stopped from buying guns. President Clinton led the fight to ban 19 deadly assault weapons, designed for one purpose only—to kill human beings.

We oppose efforts to restrict weapons used for legitimate sporting purposes, and we are proud that not one hunter or sportsman was forced to change guns because of the assault weapons ban. But we know that the military-style guns we banned have no place on America's streets, and we are proud of the courageous Democrats who defied the gun lobby and sacrificed their seats in Congress to make America safer.

Today's Democratic Party stands with America's police officers. We are proud to tell them that as long as Bill Clinton and Al Gore are in the White House, any attempt to repeal the Brady Bill or assault weapons ban will be met with a veto. We must do everything we can to stand behind our police officers, and the first thing we should do is pass a ban on cop-killer bullets. Any bullet that can rip through a bulletproof vest should be against the law; that is the least we can do to protect the brave police officers who risk their lives to protect us.

Source: Democratic Party Platform, section on Responsibility, adopted August 1996.

When a gun control proposal reaches the federal level, the lobbying rises to a fevered pitch. As with every other greatly polarized issue, each side accuses the other of sneaky politics, obstructionism, playing to emotions, or outright vote buying. Emotions run high, but that is to be expected when each side believes so fervently in its position.

One example of that is what has happened with the "assault weapons" ban. This law has fierce supporters and opponents. In early 1996, the U.S. House of Representatives voted to repeal the law. President Clinton vowed to keep it in place. (As of this edition, the Senate had not taken action on its repeal.) There are relatively few assault weapon fatalities—but those that occur are always big news. For example, on January 17, 1989, Patrick Purdy, a 24-year-old drifter walked into the playground of an elementary school in Stockton, California, with a semiautomatic assault rifle and killed 5 students and injured 30 others, before turning a handgun on himself. Such shootings draw immediate media attention, another point of contention in the gun control debate. The following entry describes an analysis done by the Media Research Center (MRC) that shows how television networks covered firearms issues (with the exception of assault weapon stories) from December 1, 1991, to November 30, 1993.

DOCUMENT 161: "Guns, Bias, and the Evening News," National Rifle Association Institute for Legislative Action (1994)

In all, 107 stories were examined, and MRC reports that "a clear pattern emerged, emphasizing the agendas, spokesmen, labels, and academic research of gun control supporters. Overall, 62 percent of the stories devoted substantially more time to pro- than anti-gun control arguments; talking heads who endorsed gun control outnumbered opponents by nearly 2-to-1; in stories concerning the Brady bill, the bias against gun control opponents was even greater, a ratio of 3 to 1.... Brady bill supporters amounted to 69% of all the sources quoted, compared to 22% opposed and 8% who were neutral." ...

In these 78 stories [not relating to the Brady bill], the networks clearly gave anti-gun spokesmen greater access to the airwaves. Of the 272 "talking heads" shown, 146 advocated gun control, 26 were neutral, and 100 presented pro-gun points of view ...

The research done by the staff at the Media Research Center confirms what most gun owners already knew all too well—when it comes to the national media reporting the gun issue, objectivity is lost as emotion replaces fact.

Source: National Rifle Association Institute for Legislative Action, 1994.

In his book, Osha Gray Davidson explained how differently the two sides on this issue interpret spectacular news events like the above mentioned massacre of school children in Stockton, California. Davidson described the reactions of two representatives, in the days following the shooting—NRA lobbyist James Jay Baker and gun control proponent U.S. Sen. Howard Metzenbaum.

DOCUMENT 162: *Under Fire: The NRA and the Battle for Gun Control*, Osha Gray Davidson (1993)

It was battle, and not hearing, that was on James Jay Baker's mind as the thirty-five-year-old lobbyist sat in his office in a posh section of Washington, D.C. Just days after the Stockton massacre, Baker was preparing for his upcoming appearance before a congressional subcommittee hearing on a bill to virtually ban the type of rifle used by Eddie Purdy.

The Stockton incident was anything but inexplicable to him. He took a long drag on his Vantage filter cigarette, set it on his desk ashtray, and wrote: "The real lesson to be drawn from the Purdy crime is that Patrick Edward Purdy was a criminal who ought to have been in jail rather than left free to roam the streets. . . . It was the criminal justice system that failed those five schoolchildren."

According to Baker, this was the Stockton lesson: Our society is too soft on criminals.

At the opposite end of the Washington Mall, the long grassy strip that stretches from the Lincoln Memorial to the Capitol Building, in his spacious office in the Russell Senate Office Building, Senator Howard M. Metzenbaum also prepared for battle. Like Baker, the white-haired, three-term senator from Ohio was clear about the "real lesson" of the Stockton killings. His conclusions, however, were 180 degrees from Baker's.

"Assault weapons are designed for one purpose, and one purpose alone, for killing human beings," he read aloud, practicing his opening statement before the subcommittee he chaired. To attack the problem as he saw it—easy access to these guns of war—Metzenbaum was championing a bill that would make it difficult to buy these weapons.

"If such a procedure had been in effect last August," he continued, "the local police would not have allowed Patrick Edward Purdy to buy the AK-47 he used to massacre five children in a California schoolyard."

According to Metzenbaum, *this* was the Stockton lesson: Our society has too many guns that are too powerful and are too readily available.

What was taking place on either end of the Mall was a time-honored ritual of transformation. An act of appalling violence—in this case, the massacre of five schoolchildren by a berserk loner—was being converted into ammunition for one of this country's most bitter and intractable political debates: the fight for and against gun control. There was nothing new about either the situation or the major players, or even about the debate itself. What *was* new was that the organization James Baker represented was on the defensive.

Source: Osha Gray Davidson, *Under Fire: The NRA and the Battle for Gun Control* (New York: Henry Holt, 1993), 18–19.

The assault weapons debate raged for years, with politicians, law enforcement officials, medical researchers, and opinion pollers getting in on the act.

DOCUMENT 163: "Assault Weapons as a Public Health Hazard in the United States," Sona Kalousdian, M.D., M.P.H., and Sharon B. Buchbinder, R.N., M.A. (1992)

The Bureau of Alcohol, Tobacco, and Firearms (BATF) estimates that there are 1 million assault weapons in private hands in the United States. Another BATF estimate is much higher—2 to 3 million—when 1.5 million M-1 semiautomatic Garands are included . . .

In 1989, Stewart and Alexander of the Cox Newspaper Bureau analyzed gun trace requests to estimate the approximate prevalence of assault weapon use by criminals. They examined 42,758 requests submitted to the BATF during the period January 1, 1988, through March 27, 1989. . . . Stewart and Alexander concluded that one of every 10 firearms traces involves an assault weapon. . . . Los Angeles, and Miami had the highest percentages of assault weapons traces (19% and 18%, respectively); Washington, DC, had 13% and Detroit and New York City both had 11%. Two thirds of traced assault weapons were domestically manufactured. . . .

The actual numbers of deaths and injuries caused by assault weapons are not known. . . . The reported number of firearm homicides was 11,084 in 1988, and 8.1% of the gun traces for homicides during the same period were assault weapons. Even given the limitations of these data, these figures may still be used to give a crude approximation of the number of reported homicides due to assault weapons: 898. This figure is similar to the number of homicides in which rifles (764) or shotguns (1117) were used and is considerably lower than the number of homicides due to handguns (8278) in the same year. . . .

Semiautomatic weapons have been described as the weapon of choice for drug gangs, and officials have noticed their use had increased in areas where crack cocaine is endemic. In Los Angeles, at least 20 percent of those seen in emergency departments for injuries from assault weapons were innocent bystanders who became victims of drive-by shootings. . . . Clearly, the injuries from assault weapons are taxing hospital emergency departments in large urban areas. For this reason, military trauma physicians are being recruited to relieve the work load at the Washington (DC) Hospital Center and at Martin Luther King Hospital in Los Angeles. . . . Wounds from high-velocity assault weapons resemble the wounds inflicted in the Vietnam War: they are often multiple and massive, and immediate treatment is critical to survival. . . . A spokesman for the Hospital Council of Southern California has stated that mortality rates from high-velocity bullet wounds are four to five times higher than those from low-velocity bullet wounds and stab wounds.

The estimated cost of treating a case penetrating trauma (like that from an assault weapon) varies from $1500 to $20,000. A stay in intensive care is not unusual and may cost as much as $150,000, and patients may require long rehabilitation. . . .

Baker et al. have identified four times a "gun's life span" when legal regulations can occur: (1) the time of manufacture or importation, (2) the time of sale or transfer, (3) the period of possession, and (4) the period of use. . . .

The single greatest barrier to the enactment of federal legislation restricting or banning access to semiautomatic assault weapons is a precise definition of the weapons. . . .

Source: Sona Kalousdian, M.D., M.P.H., and Sharon B. Buchbinder, R.N., M.A., *Journal of the American Medical Association* 267, no. 22 (June 10, 1992): 3067–3070.

That report had its share of detractors, as represented by the following entry. Dr. Suter took issue with some key data in the report, noting that gun trace requests do not provide a reliable statistic on the criminal misuse of a type of gun. He also argued that the term "assault weapons" is a difficult one to identify and of little relevance.

DOCUMENT 164: " 'Assault Weapons' Revisited—An Analysis of the AMA Report," Edgar A. Suter, M.D. (May 1994)

Whether or not a gun has a large ammunition capacity is generally irrelevant because few criminals or police officers even use the capacity of an old-fashioned "six-shooter." Of course, the rare exceptions, such as the 1989 Stockton incident . . . are, because of their rarity, "newswor-thy" and highly sensationalized. For example, in the average 1989 New York City shooting incident, the perpetrator fired 2.55 shots, of which 11.8% hit someone. The situation was relatively unchanged in 1992, and contrary to frequent, but vague and unsubstantiated, assertions about the police being "outgunned," the New York City Police fire 40% more rounds per incident than criminals. . . .

These figures undercut the Council's assertion of increased criminal firepower from assault weapons. The Council cited only anecdotal and unsubstantiated sources to conclude: "Clearly the injuries from assault weapons are taxing hospital emergency departments in large urban ar-eas." . . .

The public policy debate should focus upon effectual and constitu-tional measures that are supported by sound data. An unbiased analysis of the council's report must conclude that they have made neither a careful, a complete, nor a convincing case for an assault weapon ban. Instead of attacking the actual roots of violence, the Council's effort was misdirected against certain guns that, without good reason, are symbols of violence . . .

Responsible ownership of any kind of firearm by mentally competent and lawabiding adults causes no social ill and leaves no victims. For predatory criminals, however, there should be inescapable punishment for violent crime regardless of instrumentality. The demonstrated effect-iveness of mandatory prison sentencing for gun crimes evaporates when bartered away in plea bargains . . .

Source: Edgar A. Suter, M.D., " 'Assault Weapons' Revisited—An Analysis of the AMA Report," *Journal of the Medical Association of Georgia* 85, May 1994.

DOCUMENT 165: *Guns, Crime and Freedom*, Wayne LaPierre (1994)

What the public doesn't know is that fully automatic "assault rifles" have been virtually banned for over fifty years under the National Fire-arms Act of 1934. They don't know that semi-automatic firearms have been around for over a hundred years and are owned and lawfully used by millions of law-abiding people. They don't know that some semi-automatic firearms only look different from other semi-automatic fire-arms. And the media certainly aren't going to tell them.

During the late 1960s, the cosmetics of firearms began to change. Man-ufacturers of firearms, looking for new ways to keep costs down, turned to modern technology. As traditional woods suitable for gun stocks became expensive, the miracle of plastics made it possible to produce replicas of wood stocks economically. Plastic stocks first appeared on popular, less expensive models of firearms. At a distance, they looked like very expensive fine quality wood.

Some firearms owners rejected the cosmetic changes; others welcomed them. For utility in hunting and for recreational shooting, plastic stocks have benefits. They don't warp and crack from moisture. Scratches and dents on plastic don't matter as they do on expensive wood stocks. With acceptance of plastic and the evolution of better grades of plastic, less traditional stocks—more convenient and easier to carry and handle than conventional stocks—emerged. The look of fake wood on some stocks was replaced with color—black or green or even camouflage.

This cosmetic transformation in appearance gave birth in the 1980s to a deception concerning semi-automatic guns and their owners. The black color, utilitarian shape, convenient pistol grip, and barrel shroud gave rise to the "assault weapons" description of the gun control crowd. No one could have predicted that innocent cosmetics would be used to symbolize criminal intent and tragedy, or to evoke fear and disgust in the uninformed.

Source: Wayne LaPierre, *Guns, Crime and Freedom* (Washington, D.C.: Regnery, 1994), 53–54.

The debate on assault weapons raged for years. The following is a sampling of testimony presented before the U.S. Senate Committee on the Judiciary on August 3, 1993.

DOCUMENT 166: Testimony Presented by Sarah Brady, Chair of Handgun Control, Inc. (August 3, 1993)

From 1986 to 1991, 20,526 assault weapons were traced to crimes by the Bureau of Alcohol, Tobacco and Firearms. More than 1,300 of these were specifically traced to murders in the United States, but nothing has happened. A survey of State prison inmates was recently released by the Department of Justice. It found that of all inmates who admitted to owning or possessing a gun, more than 21 percent said they had owned or possessed either a military type or fully automatic weapon. By comparison, less than 1 percent of law abiding gun owners have these types of guns, but nothing has happened. . . .

We also need to fashion a definition of assault weapons that will prevent gun makers from continually designing new assault weapons or redesigning old ones. Without such a definition, the law will always lag behind the latest in assault weapon manufacture.

Finally, we must also ban large-capacity ammunition magazines. These are an integral part of combat hardware for assault weapons and were used in the Nation's worst mass slaying in Kileen, Tx. Many states limit the magazine capacity . . . for hunters usually to between three and seven rounds. It is unconscionable that we protect our game better than we protect our fellow human beings. . . .

Source: Testimony before U.S. Senate Committee on the Judiciary, 3 August 1993.

DOCUMENT 167: Statement of Johnny Mack Brown, President of the National Sheriffs Association (August 3, 1993)

In 1989, the National Sheriffs Association passed a resolution in support of a federal ban on assault weapons. We all know that crime in the nation is increasing in enormous strides. The United States is statistically one of the most violent nations in the world.

According to the Bureau of ATF, there are more than 1 million semi-automatic weapons currently in circulation. While there is no reporting requirement on assault weapons, law enforcement across America reports that semi-automatic weapons have become quickly the weapons of choice among drug traffickers and gangs.

From 1986 to 1990, 1,088 assault weapons were traced to murders in the United States, and 3,404 were linked to drug traffickers. Since only about 10 percent of all gun crimes actually result in firearm traces, it is estimated that assault weapons have been used in 10 times more crimes . . .

When considering the problems of crime in America, there exists a universal feeling that something must be done. Poll after poll shows that Americans favor a ban on assault weapons. Law enforcement officials from around the country agree that the increasing presence of assault type weapons in the drug trade and other types of crime constantly jeopardizes the safety and the lives of the American public and also poses an enormous threat to the lives of the Federal, State, and local law enforcement officers who are outgunned by the criminals that they face on the street.

Source: Testimony before U.S. Senate Committee on the Judiciary, 3 August 1993.

DOCUMENT 168: Statement of Kenneth T. Lyons, International Brotherhood of Police Officers (August 3, 1993)

[I]n the 1930s, our country saw a dramatic increase in gangster activity, violence, and general lawlessness. It was a time when the Mafia held all of the cards and the police were increasingly powerless to protect the innocents. One of the actions then taken by Congress was to severely restrict the purchase and transfer of machine guns, or fully automatic assault weapons. The result was a virtual elimination of machine guns within a few years. In the 1990s, our country is once again seeing a dramatic increase in gangster activity, violence, and general lawlessness. Times, of course, have changed. Today's gangsters often wear sneakers rather than wing-tips, bandannas rather than pin-stripes, and deal drugs rather than alcohol. There is one thing, however, that the two brands of criminals have in common: their choice of high powered weapons of destruction.

Don't be misled by the seemingly low number of assault weapons found in various surveys. The cop on the street is being outgunned . . . assault weapons make up about 1.5 to 3% of the guns in the country, but make up 7% of the guns which law enforcement asks ATF to trace.

Source: Testimony before U.S. Senate Committee on the Judiciary, 3 August 1993.

Although many police agencies did line up to support the assault weapons ban, as is true of all aspects of the debate, this opinion is not universally held. For example, a New Jersey police officer testified that the assault weapons ban in his state has created more problems than it has solved.

DOCUMENT 169: Statement of Joseph Constrance, Trenton, New Jersey, Police Department (August 3, 1993)

At best, the state's assault weapons ban is a fig leaf behind which frightened politicians hide their impotence in the face of rising crime.

Rest assured that rank-and-file officers in New Jersey knew to a certainty that criminals would continue to obtain guns illegally, no matter how strict we made our gun laws. Our prediction of failure has been borne out.

You should not think, however, that the law has had no effect. It has driven a wedge between the honest gun-owning citizens and those sworn to protect them. Many of the guns outlawed are used by the police, as well as citizens, for protection and recreation.

Source: Testimony before U.S. Senate Committee on the Judiciary, 3 August 1993.

An NRA representative testified before the committee that the organization finds some irony in the current debate. She said it also serves to flush out the true goals of gun control advocates.

DOCUMENT 170: Testimony of Susan R. Lamson, Director, Federal Affairs, National Rifle Association (August 3, 1993)

Advocates of gun control have finally admitted that they are not interested in protecting the rights of law-abiding gun owners—they are merely interested in eliminating any type of firearm whenever presented with an emotionally charged opportunity to do so . . .

Sportsmen have been told for years that the reason gun control advocates targeted handguns was because they were not suitable for militia use, hunting or self protection and were therefore not included under the constitutional safeguard of the Second Amendment. We are now being told by antigun advocates and certain politicians that precisely because many semi-automatic firearms useful for hunting and target shooting are patterned after their military counterparts, they should be banned or heavily restricted in the interest of public safety. . . .

Equally common to these bills is that they provide no meaningful definition of an "assault weapon" but instead rely on the existence of cosmetic accoutrements as the means of determining the firearms to be banned. . . .

There can be no legitimate public policy goal served which bans firearms based on appearance. Additionally, attempts to control high capacity magazines and the parts from which such magazines may be assembled, . . . has no legitimate criminal justice purpose. Advocates of such proposals are unaware of the relative ease with which a magazine may be manufactured.

Any firearm, semiautomatic or otherwise, capable of accepting a detachable magazine can accept a magazine of any capacity . . .

. . . The designation of "assault weapon" for certain semi-automatic firearms with military styling is part of an ongoing effort to capitalize on the confusion over the difference between semi-automatic firearms and those capable of a fully automatic rate of fire. Because proponents of a semi-automatic ban cannot provide any compelling legitimate justification, they resort to terminology that is without specific definition.

"Assault rifle" is a military term originated during World War II to describe selective fire military rifles of intermediate power cartridge and capable of fully automatic fire. Selective fire firearms mean those firearms capable of producing variable firing patterns including the discharge of a single shot, a burst of shots, or the continuous discharge of ammunition with a single depression of the trigger.

Semi-automatic firearms do not meet these criteria, since they discharge one round of ammunition with each depression of the trigger, rather than multiple rounds. Fully automatic firearms, which fire multiple rounds with a single depression of the trigger, have been stringently controlled since 1934.

Source: Testimony before U.S. Senate Committee on the Judiciary, 3 August 1993.

But one gun control supporter had testified earlier before the U.S. House Subcommittee on Crime and Criminal Justice that classifying certain guns as "assault weapons" came about because of actions of gun manufacturers and dealers, not gun control activists.

DOCUMENT 171: Testimony of Michael K. Beard, President, Coalition to Stop Gun Violence (July 25, 1991)

The arguments against assault weapons law center on the belief that assault weapons are not definable, and in fact, the term was made up by gun control advocates. Neither of the assertions is true.

Gun manufacturers and dealers were using the term assault weapons to describe paramilitary style semiautomatic firearms long before we were. Although, today, the gun lobby will tell you that the term assault weapon only refers to select fire weapons capable of being fired either automatically or semi-automatically, a few years ago the gun industry was singing a different tune. . . . Just three years ago, the "Shooters Bible" listed a separate section for paramilitary style weapons. Today, "Shooters Bible" blends those guns in with other shotguns, rifles, and handguns. . . .

Source: Hearings before the U.S. House Subcommittee on Crime and Criminal Justice, 25 July 1991.

Indeed, the table of contents in a 1986 book, *Gun Digest Book of Assault Weapons*, edited by Jack Lewis, has sections on 28 guns and manufacturers. The book starts with "A Matter of Mystique," which notes, "There are varying views regarding the increasing interest in today's assault-type armament."

Despite heavy lobbying from gun control opponents, the Violent Crime and Law Enforcement Protection Act was passed in 1994. It banned assault weapons by make, manufacturer, and certain characteristics.

DOCUMENT 172: Violent Crime Control and Law Enforcement Act, PL-103–322 (1994)

DEFINITION OF SEMIAUTOMATIC ASSAULT WEAPON

Section 921(a) of title 18, United States Code, is amended by adding at the end the following new paragraph:

(30) The term "semiautomatic assault weapon" means—

(A) any of the firearms, or copies or duplicates of the firearms in any caliber, known as—

(i) Norinco, Mitchell, and Poly Technologies Avtomat Kaiashnikovs (all models);

(ii) Action Arms Israeli Military Industries UZI and Galil;

(iii) Beretta Ar70 (SC-70);

(iv) Colt AR-15;

(v) Fabrique National FN/FAL, FN/LAR, and FNC;

(vi) SWD M-10, M-11, M-11/9, and M-12;

(vii) Steyr AUG;

(viii) INTRATEC TEC-9, TEC-DC9 and TEC-22; and

(ix) revolving cylinder shotguns, such as (or similar to) the Street Sweeper and Striker 12;

(B) a semiautomatic rifle that has an ability to accept a detachable magazine and has at least 2 of—

(i) a folding or telescoping stock;

(ii) a pistol grip that protrudes conspicuously beneath the action of the weapon,

(iii) a bayonet mount;

(iv) a flash suppressor or threaded barrel designed to accommodate a flash suppressor; and

(v) a grenade launcher;

(C) a semiautomatic pistol that has an ability to accept a detachable magazine and has at least 2 of—

(i) an ammunition magazine that attaches to the pistol outside of the pistol grip;

(ii) a threaded barrel capable of accepting a barrel extender, flash suppressor, forward handgrip, or silencer;

(iii) a shroud that is attached to, or partially or completely encircles, the barrel and that permits the shooter to hold the firearm with the nontrigger hand without being burned;

(iv) a manufactured weight of 50 ounces or more when the pistol is unloaded; and

(v) a semiautomatic version of an automatic firearm; and

(D) a semiautomatic shotgun that has at least 2 of—

(i) a folding or telescoping stock;

(ii) a pistol grip that protrudes conspicuously beneath the action of the weapon;

(iii) a fixed magazine capacity in excess of 5 rounds; and

(iv) an ability to accept a detachable magazine. . . .

The term "large capacity ammunition feeding device"—

(A) means a magazine, belt, drum, feed strip, or similar device manufactured after the date of enactment of the Violent Crime Control and Law Enforcement Act of 1994 that has a capacity of, or that can be readily restored or converted to accept, more than 10 rounds of ammunition; but

(B) does not include an attached tubular device designed to accept, and capable of operating only with, .22 caliber rimfire ammunition.

Source: PL-103–322, the Violent Crime Control and Law Enforcement Act, Section 921, amending Section 921(a) of title 18 of the U.S. Code, 1994.

The passage of the law, however, did not end the debate. On March 22, 1996, the U.S. House of Representatives voted 239 to 173 to repeal the assault weapons ban. (Nineteen representatives did not vote.)

The following two entries show some of the passion in the heated debate that led to the repeal vote in the House.

DOCUMENT 173: Speech of Rep. Charlie Norwood of Georgia (March 22, 1996)

In spite of what the liberal media would have us believe, the semiautomatic weapons outlawed by the 1994 assault weapons ban are seldom used in crimes. According to the Bureau of Alcohol, Tobacco and Firearms, for every 4000 violent crimes reported in this country, there was only one of these weapons involved. In fact, we would accomplish more by banning kitchen knives . . .

The sheriffs and district attorneys in my district tell me they don't need more gun control, they need the ability to take gun-carrying criminals off the street, and that's what H.R. 125 does.

For any criminal in possession of a gun while committing a crime, this bill provides for a mandatory minimum sentence of 5 years in prison. For pulling that gun during a crime, 10 years. For firing it, 20 years. And if the weapon used is a sawed-off rifle or shotgun, they automatically get an extra 10 years in prison added to these sentences.

Furthermore, subsequent violent or drug-related crimes are punished by 20 years for having a gun, 25 years for pulling it, and 30 years for firing it. And if that gun is a machine gun, or has a silencer or flash suppressor, the sentence is life in prison.

Compare this to the 1994 crime bill's 10-year sentence for crimes involving semiautomatic assault weapons, and it's easy for both sides of the aisle to determine that this bill does for gun-crime prevention what the assault-weapons ban will never do.

Source: Congressional Record, 22 March 1996.

The next exchange took place between Rep. Patrick Kennedy, the son of Sen. Edward Kennedy and nephew of President John F. Kennedy and Sen. Robert Kennedy, both assassinated, and Rep. Gerry Solomon, who advocated the repeal of the assault weapons ban. It shows that emotionalism ran high during the debate.

DOCUMENT 174: Remarks of Rep. Patrick Kennedy of Rhode Island and Comments by Rep. Gerry B. H. Solomon of New York (March 22, 1996)

Rep. Kennedy. This notion that we cannot make a difference because if we ban so many, we are not banning all of them, or if you cannot save all crime, you are not going to try to save any at all, is just bogus.

Our responsibility in this House is to do what we are able to do. That is our responsibility. If we are able to save anyone's life because we ban these weapons of war that spray bullets and kill people indiscriminately, then we should do so. I cannot believe in this House, a week after the kids were mowed down in Scotland, that you have the nerve to bring this bill up.

In the opening of this debate, you said we should have known about this bill before we were elected to the 104th Congress. I will tell you, we knew about this bill. Americans knew about this bill, my family knew about this bill. We did not have to read the NRA questionnaire to know about this bill. Families like mine all across this country know all too well what damage weapons can do, and you want to arm our people even more. You want to add more magazines to the assault weapons so they can spray and kill even more people.

Shame on you. What in the world are you thinking when you are opening up the debate on this issue? Mr. Speaker, this is nothing but a sham, to come on this floor and say you are going to have an open and fair debate about assault weapons. My God, all I have to say to you is, play with the devil, die with the devil.

There are families out there, Mr. Speaker, and the gentleman will never know what it is like, because they do not have someone in their family killed. It is not the person who is killed, it is the whole family that is affected.

Furthermore, people will say, and I have heard this argument already, this is not effective because it is not cutting crime, you are not cutting crime. That is the wrong question. It is not about cutting crime, it is about cutting the number of people who get killed by these assault weapons. You are asking the wrong question. It is not about crime, it is about the families and victims of crime. That is what we are advocating, in proposing this ban. That is why we should keep this ban in place.

Rep. Solomon. . . . Before the gentleman leaves the floor, and I have a great respect for him and his family, but I am going to tell him something, when he stands up and questions the integrity of those of us that have this bill on the floor, the gentleman ought to be a little more careful. Let me tell you why.

Rep. Kennedy. Tell me why.

Rep. Solomon. My wife lives alone 5 days a week in a rural area in upstate New York. She has a right to defend herself when I am not there, and don't you ever forget it.

Rep. Kennedy. You know the facts about this. You have guns in the home that are going to be used against your own family members. You know what the evidence is.

Source: Congressional Record, 22 March 1996, p. H2675.

Following the March 22, 1996, vote, the NRA and other gun rights advocates rejoiced. The NRA issued a press release, commending those legislators who voted to repeal the ban and commenting on several other reactions to existing gun restrictions. It said that the Congress "reaffirmed the value of the Second Amendment and the civil right of self-defense this amendment guarantees."

Just before the vote, then-Senate Majority Leader Robert Dole wrote a letter to the NRA's executive director, Tanya Metaksa, affirming his alignment with the group on gun control issues.

DOCUMENT 175: Letter from Senator Bob Dole to NRA Executive Director (March 10, 1996)

In my view, vigorous protection of the individual freedoms secured by the Bill of Rights—including the Second Amendment—is crucial to our nation's future. It should go without saying that as long as I am Senate Majority Leader, I will continue to do everything within my power to prevent passage of anti-Second Amendment legislation in the Senate.

Repealing the ill-conceived gun ban passed as part of President Clinton's crime bill last year is one of my legislative priorities. The Senate will debate this issue in the near future, and I hope to have a bill on President Clinton's desk by this summer. President Clinton has said he will oppose repealing this measure, an indication of one of our many differences. I voted against the gun ban in 1994, and I will vote to repeal it in 1996.

Experience, and I might add common sense, has taught me that because criminals don't obey the law, gun control will only limit those who do. It may be old fashioned, but keeping criminals behind bars still seems [to] be the most effective approach in fighting crime. Gun control is a completely ineffective approach to the lack of safety and security in our communities. Disarming law-abiding citizens only places them at the mercy of those who break the law.

Source: Letter from U.S. Sen. Bob Dole to Tanya Metaksa, Executive Director, National Rifle Association, March 10, 1996.

A few months later, however, after Senator Dole resigned his Senate position to run for president, he seemed to move away from his call for a repeal on the assault weapons ban. In a speech before Virginia state and county troopers, he emphasized that he would implement an instant background check like Virginia's in all 50 states by the end of 1997, a year before such a nationwide system is required by the Brady law.

DOCUMENT 176: Remarks by Republican Nominee for President Bob Dole (July 9, 1996)

We have a ban on so-called assault weapons. But let's be realistic: of the 17 weapons that were specifically outlawed, 11 are already back on the market in some other form. So what I say, let's move beyond the debate. . . . We've got to move beyond banning assault weapons. And instead of endlessly debating which guns to ban, we ought to be emphasizing what works, what's been tried, in the great Commonwealth of Virginia and other states. And we've seen here what works, we've seen it's an instant check on handguns, shotguns, rifles, all guns period. All guns. Period. And that's the system we should have. And we're not talking about a waiting period of five days or even five hours. We're talking two or three minutes. That should be our goal. You're doing it here, no doubt about it, the people of Virginia are safer because of it. It just seems to me that we ought to do it for all Americans. And plus, you would be even more safe in Virginia because they wouldn't be able to bring guns they could buy from somewhere else.

Source: Remarks by Sen. Bob Dole made at the Virginia State Police Academy, Richmond, Virginia, 9 July 1996. Text found on Bob Dole's Internet home page.

Some public opinion polls show that about 70 percent of the public consistently support the assault weapons ban. That could be one reason this issue is such a political hot potato. The day after Senator Dole made his remarks, President Clinton retorted.

DOCUMENT 177: "Clinton Draws Bead on Dole's Assault Weapons Retreat," *Washington Post* (July 11, 1996)

[President] Clinton and his aides ridiculed their GOP rival for leaving his position unclear, and implied that Dole's vagueness sprang from a desire to not offend the gun lobby.

"I will say one thing that the Republican candidate for president has not said, and probably will not and cannot say . . . I will veto any attempt to repeal the assault weapons ban or the Brady bill."

Dole last year told the National Rifle Association that he would work to overturn the ban on assault weapons . . .

Referring to a recent House vote to overturn the weapons ban, Clinton's tone turned to mockery. "They want to take Uzis out there and shoot deer," he said to a chorus of cheers and chortles from the overwhelmingly Democratic audience. "Wild turkeys fly fast—you need lots of bullets. I'm kind of laughing to keep from crying about this."

Source: Washington Post, 11 July 1996.

The assault weapons debate is just one of the areas where the arguments focus on gun control versus crime control. Opponents of gun control, such as the NRA, say only tough sanctions against criminals will reduce violent crime; further gun restrictions will only hamper individuals who want to choose their own means of self-protection. To this end, Wayne LaPierre (NRA executive vice president) outlines his views.

DOCUMENT 178: "Twenty Elements for an Effective Criminal Justice System," *Guns, Crime and Freedom*, Wayne LaPierre (1994)

1: Legal authority for the pretrial detention of dangerous defendants.

2: Mandatory prison sentences for the most serious offenders.

3: Sentencing laws that require the court to sentence for actual conduct, where it is shown at the time of sentencing by a preponderance of the evidence that the crime involved the use of a deadly weapon or dangerous instrument, or the intentional or knowing infliction of serious physical injury.

4: Mandatory life prison sentence without release, except for executive clemency, for the third conviction for a violent or serious felony including murder, manslaughter, sexual assault, armed robbery, aggravated assault, arson, child abuse or molestation, and kidnapping.

5: The death penalty for the first degree murder with aggravating circumstances.

6: Determinate sentences with "truth-in-sentencing" laws and prison release policies that require every inmate to serve no less than 85 percent of the prison sentence imposed by the court.

7: Prisons and jails that are safe and habitable but which do not allow their inmates to live better than law-abiding person[s] living at the poverty level and that require all able-bodied prisoners to work.

8: Mandatory drug testing for every person convicted of a felony offense and mandatory discipline for continued drug use by a person on any form of conditional release from prison or on probation.

9: Computerized records containing data on crime and punishment for both adult and juvenile criminal justice systems that are reliable, accurate, and timely, and that publicly disclose how cases are handled from arrest to conviction.

10: Effective victim and witness protection programs.

11: A comprehensive and effective juvenile justice system that

(A) provides early intervention strategies for "at risk" youth....

(B) emphasizes discipline and responsibility for nonviolent first time offenders ...

(C) allows juvenile offenders to be treated as adults for committing serious offenses ...

(D) provides for the admissibility and consideration of juvenile criminal history in adult court proceedings.

12: Comprehensive and enforceable rights for victims which must include:

(A) The right to justice and due process.

(B) The right to be treated with fairness, respect, privacy and dignity, and to be free from intimidation, harassment, and abuse throughout the criminal justice process.

(C) The right to be present at all proceedings where the defendant has the right to be present.

(D) The right to be heard at any proceeding involving a post arrest release decision, a negotiated plea, sentencing, or a post conviction release from confinement.

(E) The right to be informed of all proceedings, and to be informed of the release, transfer, or escape of the accused or convicted person.

(F) The right to a speedy trial or disposition and a prompt and final conclusion of the case after the conviction and sentence.

(G) The right to receive full restitution.

(H) The right to confer with the prosecution.

(I) The right to be informed of each of the rights established for victims.

13: Upon the victim's request, HIV testing for those arrested for sexual offenses or any other offense where there is a reasonable likelihood of transmission of the disease.

14: Adequate prison capacity including the legal authority for the states and localities to privatize prisons, jails, and other detention facilities.

15: No release pending appeal for high risk offenders and waiver of appeal as part of a guilty plea.

16: No unsupervised furlough or other temporary or conditional release for violent or repeat offenders.

17: Progressive community punishment programs for non-violent first-time offenders.

18: Protection against civil and criminal liability for a person's exercise of the right to use reasonable force, including deadly force where warranted, in self-defense, in defense of a third person, or to prevent a serious felony, where the use of force is legally justified.

19: Laws to prevent criminals from collecting damages from a private citizen for injuries sustained while committing, attempting to commit, or fleeing from the commission of a felony criminal offense.

20: Effective laws to deter and punish stalking.

Source: Wayne LaPierre, *Guns, Crime and Freedom* (Washington, D.C.: Regnery, 1994), 221–35.

DECLINING DEALERS

Others are taking different measures. For example, as a result of stricter enforcement of existing regulations and new regulations increasing licensing requirements and fees for federally licensed firearm dealers, the number of licensed gun dealers is declining.

According to a General Accounting Office report there has been a steady two-year decline after some of these measures took effect and after President Clinton called for tougher enforcement.

DOCUMENT 179: *Federal Firearms Licenses: Various Factors Have Contributed to the Decline in the Number of Dealers,* **General Accounting Office (1996)**

Since reaching a high point in April 1993, the number of licensed firearms dealers declined steadily and sharply by approximately 35 percent as of September 30, 1995. The decline occurred in every state. ATF received substantially fewer applications for licenses; in particular, applications for new licenses dropped very sharply from April 1993 to April 1994, during the first year of declines. Also, in fiscal years 1993 and 1994, the number of ATF denials of both new and renewal applications remained relatively small, but there was a substantial increase in the number of new applications abandoned and withdrawn. Similarly, during the same years, as a result of ATF inspections, the number of licenses revoked remained small, but the number of licenses voluntarily surrendered was high.

Source: Government Accounting Office, *Federal Firearms Licenses: Various Factors Have Contributed to the Decline in the Number of Dealers* (Washington, D.C.: Government Printing Office, March 1996).

The report states that dealer licenses peaked in April 1993 at 260,703, but by the end of September 1995, there were only 168,395 dealer licensees, the lowest number in more than a decade. The report attributes this decline to a number of factors, including the Federal Firearms License Reform Act of 1993, which raises the cost of a federal firearms license from $10 per year to $200 for three years.

Another factor is that President Clinton urged the ATF to begin enforcing provisions of the 1968 Gun Control Act, such as using the relatively limited definition of "engaged in business."

DOCUMENT 180: Gun Control Act of 1968, Explanation of Terminology "Engaged in Business"

The term "engaged in the business" means—
(C) as applied to a dealer in firearms, as defined in section 921(a)(11)(A), a person who devotes time, attention, and labor to dealing in firearms as a regular course of trade or business with the principal objective of livelihood and profit through the repetitive purchase and resale of firearms, but such term shall not include a person who makes occasional sales, exchanges, or purchases of firearms for the enhancement of a personal collection or for a hobby, or who sells all or part of his personal collection of firearms.

Source: U.S. Code Title 18, Section 921(a)(21)(c).

Since a significant number of gun dealers do not actually do any selling, this enforcement, coupled with the higher licensing fees, could cause many not to renew their licenses.

DOCUMENT 181: *Federal Firearms Licenses: Various Factors Have Contributed to the Decline in the Number of Dealers,* **Government Accounting Office (1996)**

ATF . . . reported that as many as 46 percent of dealer licensees were not selling firearms. Our survey results indicated that similar proportions of the former licensees in our sample period were probably not selling firearms. We asked our respondents how many firearms they sold in an average year when they had a license. On the basis of their responses, we estimated that between 27 percent and 55 percent of licensees had not sold any firearms in an average year. In addition, we estimated that at least 50 percent, and as many as 78 percent, of former licensees had sold fewer than six firearms in an average year. We also found that only 2 of the 56 former licensees had sold 100 firearms or more per year. These results help support ATF's conclusions that part of the decline in the number of licensees involves those not actually selling firearms dropping out of the population of licensees.

Source: Government Accounting Office, *Federal Firearms Licenses: Various Factors Have Contributed to the Decline in the Number of Dealers* (Washington, D.C.: Government Printing Office, March 1996), 27.

How did stricter enforcement come about? In August 1993, President Clinton sent a memo to the Secretary of Treasury—whose department oversees the ATF.

DOCUMENT 182: White House Memo from President Bill Clinton to the Secretary of the Treasury (August 11, 1993)

A major problem facing the Nation today is the ease with which criminals, the mentally deranged, and even children can acquire firearms. The gruesome consequences of this ready availability of guns is found in the senseless violence occurring throughout the country with numbing regularity. While there is not one solution to the plague of gun-related violence, there is more than sufficient evidence indicating that a major part of the problem involves the present system of gun dealer licensing, which encourages a flourishing criminal market in guns.

The Gun Control Act of 1968 established a licensing system for persons engaged in businesses of manufacturing, importing, and dealing in firearms. These licensees are allowed to ship firearms in interstate commerce among themselves, and are required to abide by State laws and local ordinances in their sale of firearms to non-licensees. They are also prohibited from selling firearms to felons, certain other classes of persons, and generally to out of state persons. This Act also established a comprehensive record-keeping system and authorized the Secretary to conduct inspections to ensure compliance with the Act. The statutory qualifications for a licensee are that the applicant is at least 21 years of age, is not a felon or other person prohibited from possessing firearms, has not willfully violated the Gun Control Act, and has premises from which he intends to conduct business. The license fee for a basic dealer's license is only $10 a year.

The minimal qualification standards of the statute, coupled with policies of neglect and opposition to legitimate regulatory efforts by past Administrations, leave us with a situation where in some ways we have made it easier to get a license to sell guns than it is to get and keep a driver's license. Today, there are in excess of 287,000 Federal firearms licensees, and a great number of these persons probably should not be licensed. The Bureau of Alcohol, Tobacco and Firearms (ATF) estimates that only about 30 percent of these are bona fide storefront gun dealers. ATF estimates that probably 40 percent of the licensees conduct no business at all, and are simply persons who use the license to obtain the benefits of trading interstate and buying guns at wholesale. The remaining 30 percent of licensees engage in a limited level of business, typically out of private residences. While the Federal statute creates no minimum level of business activity to qualify for a license, many of the licensees in this category operate in violation of State and local licensing, taxing, and other business-related laws. Since the overall purpose of the Gun Control Act was to assist State and local gun control efforts, at the very least we need to coordinate the Federal licensing process with the appropriate State and local agencies.

This administration is committed to doing more to prevent this criminal market in illegal guns from continuing to flourish. Since all new firearms used in crime have at some point passed through the legitimate distribution system, Federal firearms licenses represent the first line of defense in our efforts to keep guns out of the hands of criminals.

Accordingly, you have informed me that you will direct the Department of the Treasury and ATF to take whatever steps are necessary, to the extent permitted by law, to ensure compliance with present licensing requirements, such as:

(a) improving the thoroughness and effectiveness of background checks in screening dealer license applicants;

(b) revising the application process to require the applicant to supply all information relevant to establishing qualification for a license, and to require more reliable forms of identification of the applicant, such as fingerprinting, to assist in identifying an applicant's criminal or other disqualifying history;

(c) making the "premises" requirement of the statute more meaningful by increasing field checks and the use of other procedures to verify compliance;

(d) increasing the scrutiny of licensees' multiple handgun sales reports and providing automated access to multiple sales report information by serial number for firearms trace purposes;

(e) requiring dealers to obtain more reliable identification from purchasers;

(f) reviewing sanctioning policies to determine the feasibility and desirability of adding the option of license suspension for certain violations;

(g) expanding the use of cooperative agreement with State and local law enforcement agencies to address licensing and trafficking problems;

(h) expanding ATF's capabilities to utilize effectively the firearms transaction records of out-of-business licensees for tracing purposes through the use of automation and other technology.

Source: White House Memorandum from President Bill Clinton to the Secretary of the Treasury, 11 August 1993, as cited in Government Accounting Office, *Federal Firearms Licenses: Various Factors Have Contributed to the Decline in the Number of Dealers* (Washington, D.C.: Government Printing Office, March 1996), 41–43.

In December 1993, the ATF revised its licensing requirements and application forms, requesting greater and more detailed information from applicants. The GAO report said that the NRA and the firearms industry organizations thought that move might be a major factor in the decline of licensees.

As part of the Brady law, the licensing fee rose to $200 for a three-year license. Secretary of the Treasury Lloyd Bentsen made the following remarks shortly after the change.

DOCUMENT 183: Remarks of Treasury Secretary Lloyd Bentsen (January 1994)

One of our responsibilities at ATF is to license firearms dealers. Let me explain our problem. There are 284,000 gun dealers—31 times more gun dealers than there are McDonald's restaurants.

Why so many? It's cheap. Best bargain in town.

A new license costs $66 a year, even though it costs the taxpayer about $600 a year per license. And up until the President signed the Brady Bill, it was only $10 a year for a license.

To sell liquor in the five boroughs of New York, it costs $5,200 for a three-year license. To teach Spanish and history in New York, it costs $200 for a teacher's certificate. But to sell guns in New York, it's only $66 . . .

That isn't ridiculous. That goes all the way to reckless.

The fee under the Brady Bill has gone up—but my friends, it's not enough.

It may stop some people from getting a firearms license. Many people get licenses—not to sell firearms—but to buy them cheap, for themselves. They can plop down $66, call themselves a wholesaler, and buy direct from the manufacturer—so instead of having to pay, say $400, they pay $250 . . .

We've done studies at ATF, and found 45 percent of licensed dealers don't acquire any firearms. Another 36 percent acquire less than 10 a year. I can tell you that you don't rent retail space to sell 10 guns. You do that out of your kitchen or your car trunk . . .

One other thing—I'm not up here pretending these initiatives will solve all our violence. Back in 1968, Congress passed a gun bill that set forth the licensing system, right after Martin Luther King and Robert Kennedy were killed. It hasn't stopped the violence, because there's an awful lot we don't know.

Some things we don't know because ATF is prohibited from collecting information.

And we don't know where these guns are all coming from. . . . Maybe one third of the guns criminals get are from licensed dealers. Then there's the other two-thirds. The off-the-street-sales; the criminals who trade drugs for guns, or who pick them up during burglaries; the black market; the flea markets; or the kids who get them from their parents. No law enforcers—not 400, not 4,000, not 400,000—can stop that. . . .

We don't want to get rid of the actual dealers—just everybody else. It's time to change.

We'll ask that the licensing fee be raised to $600 annually. This should eliminate 200,000 dealers, leaving only the actual ones in place. And it will end the defacto taxpayer subsidizing of the gun business.

Source: Remarks of Treasury Secretary Lloyd Bentsen, Federal Law Enforcement Training Center Awards Ceremony, Washington, D.C., Treasury Department Press Release, 4 January 1994.

Gun control supporters generally see the decline in the number of dealer licenses as a positive move. The GAO interviewed seven organizations on their views of the decline. They saw both positive and negative aspects of this trend.

DOCUMENT 184: *Federal Firearms Licenses: Various Factors Have Contributed to the Decline in the Number of Dealers,* General Accounting Office (1996)

Several organizations saw declines as advantageous to regulatory enforcement efforts. The Executive Director of American Shooting Sports Council, Inc. (ASSC) indicated that reducing the number of licensed dealers would allow better use of regulatory resources. The President of National Association of Federally Licensed Firearm Dealers (NAFLFD) stated that with fewer licensed firearms dealers, ATF's firearms tracing operations should become more efficient and effective. International Association of Chiefs of Police (IACP) indicated that reducing the number of federally licensed firearms dealers would enable the limited number of [ATF] inspectors to do their jobs. Similarly, Handgun Control and Violence Policy Project (VPC) stated that when the number of licensed dealers was about 244,000, ATF could not effectively monitor them. They stated that with fewer licensed dealers, ATF would be able to more efficiently and effectively monitor dealer compliance with federal law. As a disadvantage, the President of NAFLFD raised a concern that reducing the number of licensed dealers too much could lead to an "underground economy," an environment where firearms transactions would go unregulated and firearms tracing would be difficult.

Two firearms industry organizations—NAFLFD and ASSC—expressed concerns that a reduction in the number of retail dealers could negatively affect competition. NRA representatives said they were less concerned with the number of dealers than with ATF artificially reducing the number of dealers due to its policies and enforcement efforts. NRA indicated that as a representative of firearm consumers, it is vitally interested in ensuring that government policies do not have a detrimental effect on the legal supply and availability of firearms. The President of NAFLFD indicated that the smaller firearms dealers did not represent competition for successful storefront dealers; therefore, the elimination of smaller dealers would not affect the availability or prices of legally traded firearms. IACP indicated that the reduction in the number of dealers had not made it any more difficult for law-abiding citizens to purchase firearms.

Source: General Accounting Office, *Federal Firearms Licenses: Various Factors Have Contributed to the Decline in the Number of Dealers* (Washington, D.C.: Government Printing Office, March 1996).

KIDS, GUNS, AND SCHOOLS

One area that many people find alarming is the reported increase in students and other young people bringing guns to or near school grounds. The following entry attempts to document the problem.

DOCUMENT 185: Basic Facts of Guns in Our Schools, Coalition to Stop Gun Violence (1995)

Gun violence in our nation's schools is becoming more prevalent. A 1994 Gallup poll of Americans shows that for the first time, fighting, violence, and gangs moved to the top of the list to tie with lack of discipline as the biggest problem facing schools. No longer a safe haven for learning, schools have come to reflect the violence found on the streets. Many students fear violent attacks traveling to and from school as well as within school itself. This fear leads many young people to conclude mistakenly that a gun is their best means of defense. It is difficult to determine what effect the threat of violence has upon the learning of each student, but clearly education takes a back seat to one's own sense of security and well-being.

How violent have our schools become, and how do today's students cope with this violence? A 1994 poll conducted by Lou Harris found that only 1 in 5 students would tell a teacher if he or she knew of another student carrying weapons to school.

Theories differ about where young people get their guns. School security experts and law enforcement officials estimate that 80% of the firearms students bring to school come from home, while students estimate that 40% of their peers who bring guns to school buy them on the street. The Chicago-based Joyce Foundation conducted a poll which found that only 43% of parents with children under 18 years of age who own a gun keep that gun safely locked. An estimated 1.2 million elementary-aged, latchkey children have access to guns in their homes. Parents must take more responsibility for their children's actions and their children's safety.

The measures taken by schools to curb the flow of guns into schools have been largely ineffective. Metal detectors, both hand-held and walk-through, provide little resistance to students determined to bring a gun to school. Most schools lack sufficient funds to purchase or enact adequate security measures.

Moreover, metal-detector searches are time-consuming, especially considering that to be entirely effective, hundreds and even thousands of students must be processed through a single checkpoint. In short, metal detectors are both inefficient and ineffective, but little else has been proposed to prevent guns from entering schools.

As of October 1995, 47 states adopted policies of mandatory suspension for students who bring a gun to school, and preliminary findings reveal there has been a decrease in the incidence of guns in schools since such policies were established. While the zero-tolerance policy may reduce school violence, it does not address guns outside of school, where violence against youth is most likely to occur. Since it is impossible to separate the problem of kids and guns from the more general societal problem of gun violence, we should enact measures that more strictly regulate the sale, manufacture, transfer, and possession of handguns by all Americans and therefore kids, access to handguns as well. Although possession of handguns by minors is illegal, it is important to remember that every handgun a child obtains, through whatever means, was at one time produced, bought and sold legally. In order to cut off the flow of handguns to youths, we must do a better job in regulating the flow of handguns to adults.

Source: Coalition to Stop Gun Violence, web site: http://www.gunfree.inter.net

In the following entry, the author argues that the youth homicide rate has increased because of the "recruitment of young people into illicit drug markets. Because those markets are illegal, the participants must arm themselves for self-protection."

DOCUMENT 186: "Youth Violence, Guns, and the Illicit-Drug Industry," Alfred Blumstein (1995)

A . . . facet causing concern is the greater degree to which homicide by the young is committed against strangers. Drive-by shootings are particularly distressing in this regard, because it may appear that the target was chosen at random and that innocent bystanders may be hit. Any person's concern about his vulnerability is heightened . . .

Today, murders by young people are more likely to target strangers. For example, analysis of the FBI's Supplementary Homicide Reports for 1991, reveals that 28% of the homicides committed by people under twenty-five were against strangers, whereas only 18% of those committed by offenders twenty-five or older were against strangers. Thus, the perception of the increasingly random nature of murders is reinforced by this difference in the relationship between offender and victim associated with the shift to the younger offenders.

Another salient factor intensifying concern about homicides is the increasing involvement of guns in young people's homicides. Again, this can engender fear because of the sense that young people are less likely to exercise the necessary restraint in handling dangerous weapons, especially rapid-fire assault weapons . . .

It is also important to address the illegal gun markets that are selling guns to young people. There are important illegal markets selling two dangerous products—drugs and guns. The nation has directed major attention and resources (tens of billions of dollars per year) to the illegal drug markets, but has paid little attention to the illegal gun markets. It might be easier to make some progress with the gun markets by using information from the youngster carrying the gun to work up the distribution chain, and by using the gun serial number to work down the distribution chain.

Source: The Journal of Criminal Law and Criminology 86 (Fall 1995): 10–36.

DOCUMENT 187: "Gun Ownership and Gang Membership," Beth Bjerregaard and Alan J. Lizotte (1995)

Recently, researchers discovered some alarming trends in the gangs they have studied: the gangs of today appear to be more violent in nature than the gangs of the first half of the century. The activities that gangs participate in appear to be changing; gang members now engage more frequently in serious crimes, drug-related behavior, and firearms use. While all these changes are of great concern to policymakers and criminal justice professionals, it is the latter of these changes, the increased use of firearms by gang members, that creates perhaps the most disturbing scenario . . .

Not only have researchers revealed an increase in the availability of firearms in gangs, but they also point out that weapons today are far more sophisticated and lethal than the weapons of the past. . . . This changing nature of weaponry has influenced the very nature of gang behavior. . . . Researchers have found that gang members are being arrested in increasingly large numbers for violent offenses such as assault with a deadly weapon, shooting incidence, batteries, and homicides. . . . Today, gang shootings tend to be unplanned and spontaneous events. The rumbles of yesteryear have been replaced by activities such as drive-by shootings . . .

While gangs do appear to influence gun ownership, the nature of that influence is slightly more complex than previous researchers have acknowledged. Those youths who eventually join a gang display slightly inflated rates of both gun ownership and delinquency before they become gang members. There are two possible explanations for this observation. First it may be that gangs recruit juveniles who already show a propensity for involvement in these delinquent activities. Second, it may be that the youths who are involved in the illegal firearms subculture and delinquent behavior are also the same youths who are likely to be attracted to a gang.

Source: The Journal of Criminal Law and Criminology, 86 (Fall 1995): 37–58.

A study in the Journal of the American Medical Association recently reported results from a school-associated violent death study.

DOCUMENT 188: "School-Associated Violent Deaths in the United States, 1992 to 1994," S. Patrick Kachur, M.D., M.P.H., et al. (June 12, 1996)

In a 2-year period, 105 school-associated violent deaths were identified. The estimated incidence of school-associated violent deaths was 0.09 per 100,000 student-years. Students in secondary schools, students of minority racial and ethnic backgrounds, and students in urban school districts had higher levels of risk. The deaths occurred in communities of all sizes in 25 different states. Homicide was the predominant cause of death (80.9%), and firearms were responsible for a majority (77.1%) of the deaths. Most victims were students (72.4%). Both victims and offenders tended to be young (median ages, 16 and 17 years, respectively) and male (82.9% and 95.6%, respectively). Approximately equal numbers of deaths occurred inside school buildings (29.5%), outdoors but on school property (35.2%), and at off-campus locations while the victim was in transit to or from school (35.2%). Equal numbers of deaths occurred during classes or other school activities (43.8%) and before or after official school activities (43.8%) . . .

School-associated violent deaths were more common than previously estimated. The epidemiologic features of these deaths were similar to those of homicides and suicides that occur elsewhere. A comprehensive approach that addresses violent injury and death among young people at school and elsewhere in the community is suggested.

Source: S. Patrick Kachur, M.D., M.P.H., Gail M. Stennies, M.D., M.P.H., Kenneth E. Powell, M.D., M.P.H., William Modzeleski, Ronald Stephens, Ed.D., Rosemary

Murphy, Ph.D., Marcie-jo Kresnow, M.S., David Sleet, Ph.D., and Richard Lowry, M.D. *Journal of the American Medical Association* 275 (1996): 1729–1733.

President Clinton weighed in with comments on youth violence recently.

DOCUMENT 189: Remarks by President Clinton to Launch the Alcohol, Tobacco and Firearms Youth Crime Gun Interdiction Initiative (July 8, 1996)

[A]s we take on this problem of youth violence, if we're serious about it we cannot avoid dealing with one of its most terrifying elements— teens with guns. This is an amazing fact—listen to this: The number of teenagers committing crimes without guns is the same today as it was in the 1970s two decades ago. Let me say that again: The number of teenagers in the United States today committing crimes without guns is the same today as it was 20 years ago. The number of homicides by teens who have guns has tripled.

Today, if a gang member is caught committing a crime with a smoking gun in his hand, often as not, the gun is simply put in the police locker with little further investigation. Yet, we know that gangs often buy in bulk from a single, shadowy supplier, a criminal network that channels an arsenal of weapons to young criminals or would-be criminals.

We need a national campaign to cut off the flow of guns to teens who commit crimes. Today, I am directing the Department of the Treasury and the Department of Justice to work with local law enforcement in a new nationwide initiative.

In 17 cities . . . we will, for the first time, see that every time that a gun is used in a crime and seized by law enforcement, it will be tracked through a national tracing system to find out where it came from. We will use that information to target those criminal gun-running networks that are peddling guns to our teenagers.

Local and national prosecutors have agreed to work together to break up these criminal gangs. And the new data from these 17 cities will give us a much better idea of how the black market in guns actually operates and how to break it. Police on the beat, prosecutors in the court room, federal investigators in the crime lab—they'll all work together in a genuine national team to take on the gun-runners.

Those who illegally peddle guns to our children will get a simple message: We will find you, we will prosecute you, and we will punish you.

We have to give the future back to all of our children. We cannot permit the United States to go into the 21st century the richest, the most powerful country in the world, with more opportunities available to more young people to live out their dreams than ever before, and keep allowing our young people to die before their dreams ever have a chance to take shape.

Source: Press release from the Office of the Press Secretary, White House, 8 July 1996.

GUNS, SCHOOLS, AND THE SUPREME COURT

In an effort to stem gun violence near schools, Congress passed a bill called the Gun Free School Zones Act in 1990 (Document 192). The Supreme Court overturned that law in a case called *U.S. v. Lopez* (see Documents 193 and 194). But that Court decision does not affect a similar-sounding law, the Gun-Free Schools Act of 1994 (Document 195). The two laws were similar in their goals—to keep people from bringing guns into or near schools.

However, the two laws differed in their approach. Congress is limited in its law-making abilities—it cannot usurp the power of the individual states. So federal laws must be shown to have a national relevance. Congress can do this in various ways, for example, through appropriations bills connecting federal funding to a certain action. Another way to accomplish this is by relying on the Interstate Commerce Clause of the U.S. Constitution.

DOCUMENT 190: Interstate Commerce Clause, U.S. Constitution

The Congress shall have the power . . . to regulate commerce with foreign nations, and among the several States, and with the Indian tribes.

Source: U.S. Constitution, Article 1, section 8, clause 3.

The Gun Free School Zones Act (Document 192) tried to establish that a good education is a kind of interstate commodity because the country relies on an educated work force. The Supreme Court did not believe that argument was convincing. However, it is important to note that the Supreme Court overturned the law only because the connection to interstate commerce was not clear. This was not a Second Amendment case. Indeed, the lawsuit leading up to the Court's decision is what prompted the revamped law in 1994.

The later Gun-Free Schools Act of 1994 tied its mandatory expulsion rule—or "zero tolerance policy"—to federal funding. It is a simpler concept, saying states risk losing their federal funding for education if such a zero tolerance policy is not in place. It is not tied to interpretation of the Interstate Commerce Act.

Sen. Dianne Feinstein of California details the difference between the two laws.

DOCUMENT 191: Statement of Sen. Dianne Feinstein (April 27, 1995)

Yesterday, the Supreme Court overturned the Gun Free Schools Zones Act, a 1990 law sponsored by Senator Kohl and others that made it a felony to bring a gun within 1,000 feet of a school. The case revolves around a San Antonio youth who was tried for bringing a .38 caliber to school, and the decision has ignited widespread debate because it reverses decades of Supreme Court precedent.

However, as a result of this controversy, it is extremely important to clarify the status of a separate, recently passed law, which has a similar name—the Gun-Free Schools Act of 1994—but remains firmly in place.

Parents, teachers, and school officials must know that gun possession on campus cannot be tolerated, that the Gun-Free Schools Act of 1994 remains in place, and that in order to receive Federal education funds every school district in the Nation must soon have in place and functioning a policy that assures that any youngster who brings a gun to school will be expelled for not less than 1 year.

The following points must be clearly understood:

First, the Gun-Free Schools Act of 1994 was not struck down by the Supreme Court yesterday.

Instead, the Court struck down a 1990 criminal law with a similar-sounding name—but a different legal status.

Second, the Gun-Free Schools Act of 1994 will not be swept away by the Court's decision.

By simply requiring schools to have a zero tolerance policy as a condition of receiving Federal education funds, the Gun-Free Schools Act does not rely on the commerce clause for its authority.

Third, the Gun-Free Schools Act remains in place, and zero tolerance policies are already showing positive results.

Many school districts such as New York, Los Angeles, and San Diego that have already implemented zero tolerance policies are seeing fewer guns brought to school, and as a result fewer student expulsions.

In San Diego, gun possession on campus was cut in half during 1993, the first year of that district's policy, and there have been only 5 gun possession cases during this year.

Under the Gun-Free Schools Act, States have until October 1995 to enact or revise their own zero tolerance policies for school districts, requiring that students caught with guns on campus be expelled for not less than a year.

Fourth, the Court's decision to revoke Federal law does not affect State laws outlawing gun possession on campus.

Forty States, including California, have their own criminal statutes making gun possession on or near a school a State crime. California's statute, signed into law by Pete Wilson, makes possession of a gun within 1,000 feet of a school a felony crime . . .

There have been 105 violent school-related deaths in just the last two years, according to the Centers for Disease Control—caused by guns, knives, and other weapons [Document 188].

In a nationwide survey, the CDC also found that 1 in 12 students brought a gun to school in 1993—up from 1 in 24 just three years before. However, in too many school districts students who bring guns to school are simply given a short suspension, counseling, or transferred to another school.

By requiring that offenders be expelled from the regular school program, the Gun-Free Schools Act mirrors policies in a growing number of State education codes and urban school district policies.

School violence—especially deadly violence—must be the Nation's top educational priority.

Sixty-five students and six school employees were shot and killed at U.S. schools during 1985–90, according to the Center To Prevent Handgun Violence.

Without being safe in school, neither teachers nor students can be expected to focus on learning.

Source: Congressional Record, 27 April 1995.

The language of the Gun Free School Zones Act of 1990 follows. The code exempts law enforcement and persons or programs approved by the school, as well as those persons traveling through school property with guns locked away and private property near school grounds.

DOCUMENT 192: Gun Free School Zones Act of 1990

(q)(1) The Congress finds and declares that—

(A) crime, particularly crime involving drugs and guns, is a pervasive, nationwide problem;

(B) crime at the local level is exacerbated by the interstate movement of drugs, guns, and criminal gangs;

(C) firearms and ammunition move easily in interstate commerce and have been found in increasing numbers in and around schools, as documented in numerous hearings in both the Judiciary Committee of the House of Representatives and Judiciary Committee of the Senate;

(D) in fact, even before the sale of a firearm, the gun, its component parts, ammunition, and the raw materials from which they are made have considerably moved in interstate commerce;

(E) while criminals freely move from State to State, ordinary citizens and foreign visitors may fear to travel to or through certain parts of the country due to concern about violent crime and gun violence, and parents may decline to send their children to school for the same reason;

(F) the occurrence of violent crime in school zones has resulted in a decline in the quality of education in our country;

(G) this decline in the quality of education has an adverse impact on interstate commerce and the foreign commerce of the United States;

(H) States, localities, and school systems find it almost impossible to handle gun-related crime by themselves; even States, localities, and school systems that have made strong efforts to prevent, detect, and punish gun-related crime find their efforts unavailing due in part to the failure or inability of other States or localities to take strong measures; and

(I) Congress has power, under the interstate commerce clause and other provisions of the Constitution, to enact measures to ensure the integrity and safety of the Nation's schools by enactment of this subsection.

(2)(A) It shall be unlawful for any individual knowingly to possess a firearm at a place that the individual knows, or has reasonable cause to believe, is a school zone.

(3)(A) Except as provided in subparagraph (B), it shall be unlawful for any person, knowingly or with reckless disregard for the safety of another, to discharge or attempt to discharge a firearm at a place that the person knows is a school zone.

(4) Nothing in this subsection shall be construed as preempting or preventing a State or local government from enacting a statute establishing gun-free school zones as provided in this subsection.

Source: 18 U.S. Code 922, section q.

The following two entries are the writings of two Supreme Court justices in the case, *U.S. v. Lopez*, which overturned the 1990 act mentioned above. The first is the opinion of the majority; the second is a dissenting opinion.

DOCUMENT 193: *U.S. v. Lopez*, Chief Justice William H. Rehnquist (April 26, 1995)

On March 10, 1992, respondent, who was then a 12th-grade student, arrived at Edison High School in San Antonio, Texas, carrying a concealed .38 caliber handgun and five bullets. Acting upon an anonymous tip, school authorities confronted respondent, who admitted that he was carrying the weapon. He was arrested and charged under Texas law with firearm possession on school premises. The next day, the state charges were dismissed after federal agents charged respondent by complaint with violating the Gun Free School Zones Act of 1990.

Respondent moved to dismiss his federal indictment on the ground that 922(q) is unconstitutional as it is beyond the power of Congress to legislate control over our public schools. The District Court denied the motion, concluding that 922(q) is a constitutional exercise of Congress' well-defined power to regulate activities in and affecting commerce, and the "business" of elementary, middle and high schools . . . affects interstate commerce. . . .

On appeal, respondent challenged his conviction based on his claim that 922(q) exceeded Congress' power to legislate under the Commerce Clause. The Court of Appeals for the Fifth Circuit agreed and reversed respondent's conviction. It held that, in light of what it characterized as insufficient congressional findings and legislative history, section 922(q), in the full reach of its terms, is invalid as beyond the power of Congress under the Commerce Clause. 2 F. 3d 1342, 1367–1368 (1993).

. . . 922(q) is not a regulation of the use of the channels of interstate commerce, nor is it an attempt to prohibit the interstate transportation of a commodity through the channels of commerce; nor can 922(q) be justified as a regulation by which Congress has sought to protect an instrumentality of interstate commerce or a thing in interstate commerce. Thus, if 922(q) is to be sustained, it must be under the third category as a regulation of an activity that substantially affects interstate commerce.

Section 922(q) is a criminal statute that by its terms has nothing to do with "commerce" or any sort of economic enterprise, however broadly one might define those terms. Section 922(q) is not an essential part of a larger regulation of economic activity, in which the regulatory scheme could be undercut unless the intra-state activity were regulated. It cannot, therefore, be sustained under our cases upholding regulations of activities that arise out of or are connected with a commercial transaction, which viewed in the aggregate, substantially affects interstate commerce. Second, 922(q) contains no jurisdictional element which would ensure, through case-by-case inquiry, that the firearm possession in question affects interstate commerce. . . .

The Government admits, under its "costs of crime" reasoning, that Congress could regulate not only all violent crime, but all activities that might lead to violent crime, regardless of how tenuously they relate to interstate commerce. . . . Similarly, under the Government's "national productivity" reasoning, Congress could regulate any activity that it found was related to the economic productivity of individual citizens: family law, for example. Under the theories that the government presents in support of 922(q), it is difficult to perceive any limitation on federal power, even in areas such as criminal law enforcement or education where States historically have been sovereign. Thus, if we were to accept the government's arguments, we are hard-pressed to posit any activity by an individual that Congress is without power to regulate . . .

We do not doubt that Congress has authority under the Commerce Clause to regulate numerous commercial activities that substantially affect interstate commerce and also affect the educational process. That authority, though broad, does not include the authority to regulate each and every aspect of local schools.

Source: U.S. v. Lopez, 115 S. Ct. 1624 131L.Ed 2d 626 (1995).

DOCUMENT 194: *U.S. v. Lopez, Dissenting Opinion*, Justice Stephen G. Breyer (April 26, 1995)

The question before us, as the Court recognizes, is not whether the "regulated activity sufficiently affected interstate commerce," but rather, whether Congress could have had "a *rational basis*" for so concluding . . .

Applying these principles to the case at hand, we must ask whether Congress could have had a *rational basis* for finding a significant (or substantial) connection between gun-related school violence and interstate commerce. Or, to put the question in the language of the explicit finding that Congress made when it amended this law in 1994: Could Congress rationally have found that "violent crime in school zones," through its effect on the "quality of education," significantly (or substantially) affects "interstate" or "foreign commerce"? . . . The answer to this must be yes . . .

Specifically, Congress could have found that gun-related violence near the classroom poses a serious economic threat (1) to consequently inadequately educated workers who must endure low paying jobs . . . and (2) to communities and businesses that might (in today's "information society") otherwise gain from a well-educated work force, an important commercial advantage. . . . Congress has written that "the occurrence of violent crime in school zones" has brought about a "decline in the quality of education" that "has an adverse impact on interstate commerce and the foreign commerce for the United States." The violence-related facts, the educational facts, and the economic facts, taken together, make this conclusion rational . . .

For one thing, this statute is aimed at curbing a particularly acute threat to the educational process—the possession (and use) of life-threatening firearms in, or near, the classroom. The empirical evidence that I have discussed above unmistakably Documents the special way in which guns and education are incompatible. . . . For another thing, the immediacy of the connection between education and the national economic well-being is Documented by scholars and accepted by society at large in a way and to a degree that may not hold true for other social institutions . . .

Source: Dissenting Opinion in *U.S. v. Lopez*, 115 S. Ct. 1624 131L.Ed 2d 626 (1995).

Excerpts from the Gun-Free Schools Act follow. The law also requires that each educational agency reports to the state confirming its adherence to the policy as well as details of any expulsions that occur as a result of the law.

DOCUMENT 195: Gun-Free Schools Act of 1994

. . . Each State receiving Federal funds under this chapter shall have in effect a State law requiring local educational agencies to expel from school for a period of not less than one year a student who is determined to have brought a weapon to a school under the jurisdiction of local educational agencies in that State, except that such State law shall allow the chief administering officer of such local educational agency to modify such expulsion requirement for a student on a case-by-case basis.

... Nothing in this subchapter shall be construed to prevent a State from allowing a local educational agency that has expelled a student from such a student's regular school setting from providing educational services to such student in an alternative setting.

Source: 20 United States Code, subchapter VIII, section 8921.

COURT WATCH

The assault weapons ban and the Brady bill are also under scrutiny by the courts. The Government Accounting Office outlined the legal challenges to Brady in its report.

DOCUMENT 196: *Gun Control: Implementation of the Brady Handgun Violence Prevention Act,* **General Accounting Office (January 25, 1996)**

Generally, the law enforcement community has strongly supported Brady, as evidenced by public endorsements from the International Association of Chiefs of Police and other organizations.

Nonetheless, some sheriffs have filed federal lawsuits essentially contending, among other things, that the phase I background check provision of Brady is beyond the scope of Congress' Commerce Clause powers and is inconsistent with the Tenth Amendment. Eight of the nine court cases that had been initiated against the Brady Act through December 31, 1995, resulted from separate filings by individual sheriffs—each having jurisdictional responsibility for one county or parish in his respective state—whereas the ninth and most recent case was filed by the Wyoming Sheriff's Association. By December 1994, federal district courts had ruled in favor of the respective sheriff in five of the six cases decided. All six cases were appealed to U.S. circuit courts. In September 1995, the U.S. Court of Appeals for the Ninth Circuit reversed two of the federal district courts' decisions, saying the federal government can require state and local law enforcement agencies to check records of prospective handgun buyers. As of October 1995, the four remaining federal district court cases were still under appeal. ...

The first decision in the several challenges to Brady was Printz v. United States [854 F. Supp. 1503 (D. Mont. 1994)]. In that May 1994 decision, for example, the Federal District Court for Montana ruled that the phase I background check provision substantially commandeers state executive officers and indirectly commandeers the legislative processes of the states to administer an unfunded federal program. The court observed that the chief law enforcement officers are indirectly required to allocate their resources to implement Brady instead of using those resources to address problems important to their constituents. In so ruling, the court rejected the federal government's argument that the phase I background check provision was discretionary.

Source: General Accounting Office, *Gun Control: Implementation of the Brady Handgun Violence Prevention Act* (Washington, D.C.: Government Printing Office, 25 January 1996).

On June 17, 1996, the U.S. Supreme Court decided it would consider challenges to the Brady law in its next term. The court will decide on two cases together, *Mack v. United States* and *Printz v. United States*, filed by sheriffs in Arizona and Montana, respectively, who have challenged the federal law.

DOCUMENT 197: "High Court Plans Review of Brady Handgun Law," *Washington Post* (June 18, 1996)

The Supreme Court announced that it would decide whether a federal law that requires sheriffs to run background checks on handgun purchasers unconstitutionally burdens local officials and infringes on the domain of the states.

The high court's review of the 1993 Brady Handgun Violence Prevention Act will bring together some of the hottest issues of the day: debate over crime control and gun ownership and the shifting balance between federal and state powers. In recent decisions, the court has found in favor of states that have complained about Washington usurping their powers . . .

Source: Joan Biskupic, *Washington Post*, p. A5.

However, at least one rather unusual case has resulted from Brady. In *Roy v. Kentucky State Police*, 1995, WL, 146989 (W.D. Ky. 1995), four Kentucky sheriffs have sued the Kentucky State Police for usurping their right under Brady to do the background checks. In that case, the court decided that should qualified local police or sheriffs want to do their own background checks, they should be allowed to do so. The case was reported in the spring 1995 issue of the *Firearms Litigation Reporter.*

The assault weapons ban has also been challenged in courts, as the following press release from the Second Amendment Foundation explains.

DOCUMENT 198: "Federal Lawsuit Filed against Clinton's Gun Ban Today," Second Amendment Foundation Press Release (March 23, 1995)

A lawsuit challenging the constitutionality of the Clinton Crime Bill's so-called "assault weapon" ban was filed today by two of the impacted firearms manufacturers. The precedent setting legal complaint presented to the District of Columbia federal court is being funded by the Second Amendment Foundation.

"The anti-gun, Clinton Congress left themselves wide open to legal challenges on numerous fronts," declared Alan Gottlieb, founder of the Second Amendment Foundation. "It will be a pleasure to defeat this illegal ban on guns just as other recent firearm legislation has been declared unconstitutional," added Gottlieb.

The thrust of this challenge is threefold: first, Congress exceeded its delegated powers; second, the gun ban is a Bill of Attainder and therefore specifically prohibited under Article I. Section 9 of the U.S. Constitution; and third, the law is unconstitutionally vague.

"Overstepping their delegated powers has cost Congress several prized pieces of legislation, including the federal gun-free school zones," reminded Alan Gottlieb. "The gun-free school zone law was declared unconstitutional when Congress failed to indicate under what authority it enacted such a law. Congress similarly failed to declare what power it was exercising in enacting Section 922(v)(I) and Section 922(w)(I) of the Clinton Crime Bill," Gottlieb continued.

Several courts have thrown out previous so-called "assault weapon" bans for unconstitutional vagueness. A recent example is last year's 6th Circuit decision in *Springfield Armory v. City of Columbus*, 29 F. 2D 250.

"This is one of the most poorly written laws I've ever seen. In addition to being unconstitutionally vague in several areas, this unnecessary assault on gun owners and manufacturers is too specific in other areas," proclaimed Alan Gottlieb. His statement refers to the fact that by specifically targeting individual companies, this law became a Bill of Attainder.

Two of the hardest hit businesses are Intratec and Penn Arms, the two named manufacturers in the lawsuit. Intratec produced the TEC DC9 and TEC 22 handguns which are listed by name on the ban list. Penn Arms manufactured the "Striker 12" shotgun which is also specifically listed under the ban.

"This law is the product of a trial by Congress of Intratec and Penn Arms. Unlike defendants in a judicial trial, these businesses had no voice to defend themselves in Congress. This is exactly the evil kind of legislation that the Framers of our Constitution sought to prevent," continued Gottlieb.

Source: Press release from Second Amendment Foundation, 23 March 1995.

To date, the assault weapons ban stands.

However, lawsuits stemming from federal and state assault weapons bans are growing. Consider the following story in the *Firearms Litigation Reporter*, a publication of the Firearms Litigation Clearinghouse project of the Educational Fund to End Handgun Violence.

DOCUMENT 199: "California Judge Allows Suit against Assault Gun Maker," *Firearms Litigation Reporter* (1995)

In a potentially landmark decision, [a] San Francisco Superior Court Judge . . . has ruled that victims of an outlawed assault weapon have a cause of action against the gun's manufacturer, even though the shooter legally purchased it in another state . . .

The cases comprising this action arise out of the July 1, 1993 massacre in the San Francisco law firm of Pettit & Martin and neighboring offices, when former client Gian-Luigi Ferri randomly opened fire with two Navegar TEC-DC9 semiautomatic assault weapons, equipped with 30-cartridge magazines made by USA. Ferri killed eight people, including himself, and wounded six. Ferri had purchased these weapons from a pawnbroker in Las Vegas, Nevada in April, 1993 . . .

Fundamental to the opinion is the premise that California's public policy is to prohibit assault weapons within its borders, as mandated by the 1989 passage of the California Assault Weapons Control Act (AWCA). The AWCA banned the manufacture, sale, advertising, or possession of assault weapons, including the Navegar TEC-9, and any other models which are only variations of those weapons . . .

According to the complaints, Navegar made minor modifications to the TEC-9 after passage of the AWCA and renamed it the TEC-DC9, ostensibly to avoid the ban. Plaintiffs also allege that Navegar markets the gun to criminals and takes pride in its appeal to criminals, by touting its resistance to fingerprints and claiming it is "as tough as your toughest customer." The quoted ads appeared in publications in California . . .

Source: Firearms Litigation Reporter 9, no. 1 (Spring 1995).

ARE GUNS SAFE?

Another relatively new wrinkle in the gun control debate centers on whether guns are safe devices. These questions focus more on their design than how they are used, although there is obviously a crossover since guns are, ultimately, designed to kill.

In tort law, in which a person gains the right to sue for damages, it is being argued that manufacturers should be held responsible for injuries and deaths caused by the consumer products they create.

Indeed, the Federal Trade Commission was petitioned by the Center to Prevent Handgun Violence and the American Academy of Pediatrics to prohibit gun makers from implying in their ads that having a gun in the home leads to greater safety.

Citing statistics from public health studies found earlier in this volume, the petitioners say the ads are misleading because they do not mention the potential risks of bringing a handgun into the home.

If the FTC were to decide to prohibit such advertising, gun makers could be fined up to $10,000 for each ad that violates the rule, once established.

In the following entry, two plaintiff's attorneys—those who argue on behalf of victims of shootings—explain the concept of strict liability. They note that "three developments in strict liability law have set the stage for its application to handgun suppliers." The first concept is bystander recovery, which means that right to compensation goes beyond the purchaser of the product. In other words, a passenger who is injured in a car with faulty brakes should not be denied recovery just because he or she was not the one who bought the car. The second concept is called foreseeable environment of use, meaning that manufacturers and suppliers should know what kind of environment their products will be used in and design and market them accordingly. The third concept is that the plaintiff must prove that the product has some kind of a defect. Comments on the latter two points are included below.

DOCUMENT 200: "Strict Tort Liability of Handgun Suppliers," Windle Turley, J.D., and Cliff Harrison, J.D. (1983)

The social policy goals underlying strict tort liability are two-fold: first, to discourage distribution of dangerous products by imposing economic responsibility upon the suppliers of such products; second, to shift the economic cost of injuries and death from the often innocent victim and the state, to the manufacturers and suppliers who can more readily absorb the cost, and who are in a better position to discover and guard against the harm. By placing the cost upon the manufacturers and suppliers, the costs of injuries are ultimately borne not by society at large, as they would be if the costs were paid by medical insurance and government health care programs, but by those consumers who exercise their freedom of choice to purchase these same products. Through higher consumer prices for the particular product, necessitated by the supplier's increased insurance premiums, the true product cost to society is soon known. The free marketplace then determines whether the product is worth that cost to society. . . .

[On foreseeable environment.] Handgun suppliers contend that their products are meant for law enforcement, hunting, sport shooting and "self-protection," and not for criminal misuse, suicide or accidental shooting. Spokesmen for the handgun industry even have suggested they cannot possibly know that their products are being so used. The alarming frequency with which such events occur, however, makes it inconceivable that the industry should take this "ostrich" approach. . . . Handgun suppliers must face the fact that their products represent the second leading cause of unnatural death in this country . . .

[On product design.] Simply because the product is designed as technologically safe as possible does not make it an acceptable, although "unavoidably unsafe," product. It is a universal rule that a product may perform precisely as it was designed and intended, yet be unreasonably dangerous and accordingly subject to a [strict tort] liability. . . . Even so-called unavoidably unsafe products must demonstrate a benefit that outweighs the hazards of the product as designed and marketed. While it may be conceded that many handguns are made as safe as any handgun can be made, if the surrounding danger incident to the over-the-counter manner in which it is marketed outweighs any acceptable usefulness, then the handgun is "defective" and unreasonably dangerous rather than "unavoidably unsafe."

Source: Hamline Law Review 6 (July 1983): 285–312.

In an article in the violence theme issue of the *Journal of the American Medical Association*, a physician (and researcher) explains the rationale, from a public health perspective, on why he feels tort liability can influence safer gun designs.

The following document was written by Howard L. Siegel, J.D., the attorney who successfully represented Olen Kelly, a grocery store manager who was shot by a .38 special handgun, described as a cheap, easily concealable Saturday Night Special. *Kelly v. Roehn* was the first case in which a gun manufacturer was held liable under this standard of strict liability. The entry was written before the case was won.

DOCUMENT 201: "Liability of Manufacturers for the Negligent Design and Distribution of Handguns," Howard L. Siegel, J.D. (1983)

Perhaps the most frequent and inane comparison offered by the pro-handgun forces involves convincing us that handguns are really no different than knives or rifles, the bow and arrow, baseball bats or ice cream cones. In theory, the argument is that any one of these implements can be used to perpetrate crime or cause injury when accidentally misused. After all, you can stick an ice cream cone in somebody's eye and do serious damage.

But, not one of these products is specifically designed to accomplish that purpose, and that's the difference. What does the designer have in mind, we have to ask, when he designs a .38 caliber revolver with a two-inch barrel? I suppose it could be argued that handguns have become a convenience item like pocket calculators, and that is exactly right. They are small enough to put in your pocket, they are concealable, and you can conceal something when you want to surprise someone, like President Reagan and Jim Brady, or the thousands of others who are injured and maimed and killed every year. . . .

Is there any other product which is mass produced and sold to the general public that embodies such excessive danger and is designed to kill people? I have only been able to discover a few. . . .

There is no greater perversion of the free enterprise system than that which seeks to reap profits from human suffering. Who should bear the cost when the products sold by these merchants of destruction accomplish exactly what they are intended to accomplish? It's time to make them pay for the wrongs which a sane society can no longer tolerate. If the notions of morality, conscience and common sense are not enough to restrain these corporations, then just maybe redistributing some of their dollars to the innocent victims of crime will suffice.

Source: Hamline Law Review (July 1983): 321–32.

DOCUMENT 202: "Handgun Injuries: The Epidemiologic Evidence for Assessing Legal Responsibility," Stephen P. Teret, J.D., M.P.H., and Garen J. Wintemute, M.D., M.P.H. (1983)

Even if a product mechanically functions exactly as the product's designer intended, and even if the danger of the product is not hidden, a product's design may be inherently defective so as to render it unreasonably dangerous. In litigation involving handguns, factors bearing upon a finding that the product is unreasonably dangerous and defective in design are the foreseeability of injury from handguns and the risk/benefit ratio of handguns. Evidence bearing upon the issues of foreseeability and risk/benefit ratio concerning handguns comes from the field of injury control and injury epidemiology.

Injuries, like diseases, are not purely chance occurrences; they have clearly defined risk factors, patterns of occurrence, and methods of prevention. Frequently, the most effective methods of prevention, and the greatest degree of foreseeability, depend more on the nature of a product than on the modification of the consumer's behavior. . . .

For more than a decade, there has been a growing body of literature which describes the tremendous impact of firearms, particularly handguns, on the public's health. This literature is based not on polemics but on sound epidemiologic data. Manufacturers of handguns are chargeable with knowledge of these data and, therefore, can foresee the carnage wrought by their products.

When the risks of handguns are balanced against their benefits, using population based data, the result is a clear demonstration that handguns are unreasonably dangerous to society as a whole, and to their owners. These data form a body of relevant and compelling evidence available to the plaintiff's trial lawyer in a handgun product liability lawsuit. Such lawsuits, which will impose the same level of responsibility on handguns manufacturers as is imposed on other product manufacturers, can lead to a reduction in handgun fatalities.

Source: Hamline Law Review 6 (July 1983): 341–50.

As with nearly every other area of the gun control debate, the idea that gun manufacturers should be held responsible for injuries resulting from the use or misuse of their products is hotly contested. Attorney Stephen P. Halbrook summarizes the opposite view in the following document. Interestingly, he details a case in which a consumer sued a gun manufacturer and won because the hunting rifle he purchased specifically for a safari to India failed. As a result, the plaintiff, who had relied on the company's advertisements that this was an appropriate rifle for big game hunting, was unable to shoot a Bengal tiger.

DOCUMENT 203: "Tort Liability for the Manufacture, Sale, and Ownership of Handguns?" Stephen P. Halbrook, J.D. (1983)

A new strategy has been devised by those who would ban the ownership of handguns by common citizens. Proponents are beginning to file suits against manufacturers, distributors, and owners of pistols and revolvers where those instrumentalities are employed by third parties in wrongful injury of death. It is projected that standards of either strict liability or negligence per se will make it financially impossible to make, sell, or own handguns, should suppliers and consumers of this product be required to absorb all losses of all persons victimized with handguns.

Under this theory, whenever a handgun has been sold to the general public, it would be said to be transformed into an unreasonably dangerous, and hence defective, product. Whenever an injury has been occasioned by the reckless or criminal use of a handgun, regardless of whether it had been innocently transferred to or stolen by the perpetrator, the owner and every person responsible for its previous transfer and manufacture would be liable for all damages. Manufacturers and dealers would be responsible for placing the weapon into the channels of commerce, and purchasers would be responsible since they support the industry.

The same theory asserts that handguns have no social utility for self-defense, and that citizens would be better off never resisting robbery, assaults, or rape. Allegedly designed solely as an instrument of death, the handgun, in some animistic fashion, appears to proponents of this theory as the proximate cause of death and injury. . . .

The law of products liability, premised originally on express and implied warranties, has progressed through negligence theories and, perhaps most importantly today, strict liability theories. Strict liability may be imposed when a product performs differently than a reasonable user

would expect. Products liability suits alleging accidental injuries due to
defective firearms for the most part result from barrel explosions, pre-
mature firing, and failure of the safety mechanism. Similar suits which
allege defective cartridges, shells or other ammunition normally result
from delayed discharge.

Probably the most commonly alleged defect in strict liability handgun
cases relates to traditionally designed single action revolvers which are
loaded in all six chambers and discharge upon being dropped. As a
safety precaution, the chamber under the hammer of a single action
should never be loaded. Some consumers may be unaware of the need
for this precaution since modern double action revolvers may be fully
loaded safely . . .

The purpose of existing tort law is to enable members of the general
public to enjoy the use of safe and reliable handguns, not to deprive
them of that use.

Further, the proposed theory that principles of strict liability or negligence per se should be applied is contrary to constitutional limitations
on tort law. Like the first amendment, the second amendment (both in
conjunction with the fourteenth), according to the ruling of the United
States Supreme Court and the intent of the respective framers, protects
from infringement the right [to] have [a] handgun. Adoption of a rule
of tort law which would make it financially impossible to manufacture,
sell, or own handguns would create an environment in which this constitutional right could not survive.

A constitutionally protect[ed] right has social utility as a matter of law,
and the utility of a handgun owned by a common citizen is no more of
a jury question than is the utility of the doctrines of atheists or Jehovah's
Witnesses. Legal considerations aside, the handgun is nothing more than
a product of evolving technology prompted by man's natural quest for
those tools known as arms. While all other animals are born with defensive weapons which they cannot remove, humans are born with the capacity for the reason and the physical ability to make tools, enabling
them to produce more versatile arms to protect themselves . . .

Given the utter impossibility of expecting a police force with a mo-
nopoly on legal handgun[s] to protect every citizen at all times and
places from attack, members of the general public will continue to own
handguns. Pistols and revolvers are part and parcel of the many useful
tools which characterize modern technological development. The recent
"discovery" that this tool, used by the public for the last half millennium,
has an unreasonably dangerous design and should not be entrusted to
common citizens appears to be a far belated form of Luddism. [The Lud-
dites were a group of British workmen, who, fearing progress, attempted
to prevent the use of labor-saving machinery by destroying it.]

Source: Hamline Law Review 6 (July 1983): 351–82.

In the following entry, attorney Joshua M. Horwitz suggests that the arguments used in *Kelly* can be applied to assault gun makers.

DOCUMENT 204: *"Kelly v. R. G. Industries, Inc.:* A Cause of Action for Assault Weapons," Joshua M. Horwitz, J.D. (1989)

The decision in *Kelly v. R. G. Industries, Inc.*, created a framework for establishing liability against the makers and sellers of cheap, easily concealable handguns that injure innocent victims during the course of a crime. . . . Whether or not there is merit to the criticism [of *Kelly*] as it applies to handguns, the cause of action is particularly well suited to holding manufacturers and marketers of semi-automatic assault weapons liable to innocent persons injured by these weapons during the course of a crime . . .

The court in *Kelly* held the manufacturers and marketers of Saturday Night Specials liable, in part, because the societal risk of those weapons outweighed their utility. Similarly, strong evidence of the lack of utility of assault weapons is their failure to pass the sporting purpose test of [the United States Code]. Sales of these weapons reflect intended use outside the traditional sporting application. Since assault weapons are anti-personnel and [are] designed to be used as offensive weapons, one of their most obvious non-sporting applications is in the criminal arena . . .

In *Kelly*, the court determined that the manufacturer or marketer that has knowledge of the potential harm of its product can be held liable. . . . A manufacturer consistently identified as a maker of assault weapons cannot claim ignorance of its product's classification as an assault weapon and its foreseeable use. . . .

. . . [T]he *Kelly* cause of action, as applied to assault weapons, should be particularly insulated from these criticisms [of the *Kelly* decision] . . .

Courts have criticized the *Kelly* opinion because a factor in finding manufacturers and marketers of Saturday Night Specials liable was the low cost of this class of guns. Basing liability on cost, it is argued, would discriminate against low income purchasers.

This writer proposes that all assault weapons, not just inexpensive and poorly made ones, should be subject to the *Kelly* cause of action. Hence, a duty would be imposed not by the price and quality of the weapons, but rather through the design. Manufacturers and marketers that make and sell weapons that fall into the design category of assault weapons, well made or poorly made, cheap or expensive, will all have the same burden. . . .

Liability should be fashioned on the three criteria of *Kelly v. R. G. Industries, Inc.* These criteria are that: (1) assault weapons are more of a risk to society than a benefit; (2) the manufacturers and marketers have knowledge of this risk; and (3) between the innocent victim and the merchant profiting from the sale of such a product the merchant is more at fault.

Source: University of Dayton Law Review 15 (1989): 125–39.

Epilogue

It is not hard to see why the debate over gun control has lasted so long. It is based on compelling but conflicting ideals.

Many supporters of gun ownership cite as part of their argument a mistrust of centralized government. They consider an armed citizenry as one check against a too-powerful federal authority. It is an argument they trace from our nation's earliest days to more recent events such as Waco and Ruby Ridge. Others argue that it should not be the government's call to limit how people can protect themselves or their families.

Yet proponents of limiting gun ownership point to the cost in human lives that guns have taken. They argue that one reason the United States leads the world in homicide rates is because of widespread gun ownership. Homicide is the leading cause of death for young black men aged 15 to 34 years and the second overall leading cause of death nationwide for individuals aged 15 to 24 years. And guns are the weapon used in the vast majority of these homicides. That is why some public health professionals are now calling firearms injuries and deaths a public health emergency.

Although these are opposing views, they are not necessarily exclusive. Hunters can support some additional gun control laws just as gun control supporters can have as their hobby target shooting. But the debate tends to be dominated by those at opposite ends of the issue. We can expect that the gun control debate will rise to the forefront of public opinion nearly every time there is a heinous act of gun violence. Both sides of the issue will mourn the loss of life involved, but each side often sees the event in terms of bolstering its cause.

Are these deaths a tragic, yet acceptable, price to pay so that law-abiding citizens can retain the privilege to protect themselves as they choose, or are they are an outrage and indicative of an absence of strong laws?

With each act of violence and new law proposed, the gun control debate will return to center stage. If new laws are passed, they will almost assuredly be challenged in the courts.

Since so much of the gun control debate is played out in the court of public opinion, however, it is important that we stay updated with the scholarship on this issue. Some of that research might confirm our beliefs; other research can make us question our own conclusions. Either way, periodic review of our own opinions will help us to contribute to a meaningful debate.

APPENDIX A

State Constitutional Clauses on the Right to Keep and Bear Arms

The constitutions or bill of rights in 43 states contain a "right to bear arms" clause. The seven states that do not have a constitutional provision are California, Iowa, Maryland, Minnesota, New Jersey, New York, and Wisconsin.

Alabama: That every citizen has a right to bear arms in defense of himself and the state. Alabama Constitution: Article I, section 26.

Alaska: A well-regulated militia being necessary to the security of a free state, the right of the people to keep and bear arms shall not be infringed. Alaska Constitution: Article I, section 19.

Arizona: The right of the individual citizen to bear arms in defense of himself or the State shall not be impaired, but nothing in this section shall be construed as authorizing individuals or corporations to organize, maintain, or employ an armed body of men. Arizona Constitution: Article II, section 26.

Arkansas: The citizens of this State shall have the right to keep and bear arms for their common defense. Arkansas Constitution: Article II, section 5.

Colorado: The right of no person to keep and bear arms in defense of his home, person and property, or in aid of the civil power when thereto legally summoned, shall be called in question; but nothing herein contained shall be construed to justify the practice of carrying concealed weapons. Colorado Constitution: Article II, section 13.

Connecticut: Every citizen has a right to bear arms in defense of himself and the state. Connecticut Constitution: Article I, section 15.

Delaware: A person has the right to keep and bear arms for the defense of self, family, home and State, and for hunting and recreational use. Delaware Constitution: Article I, section 20.

Florida: The right of the people to keep and bear arms in the defense of themselves and of the lawful authority of the state shall not be infringed, except that the manner of bearing arms may be regulated by law. Florida Constitution: Article I, section 8.

Georgia: The right of the people to keep and bear arms shall not be infringed, but the General Assembly shall have the power to prescribe the manner in which arms may be borne. Georgia Constitution: Article I, section I, paragraph VIII.

Hawaii: A well-regulated militia being necessary to the security of a free state, the right of the people to keep and bear arms shall not be infringed. Hawaii Constitution: Article I, section 15.

Idaho: The people have the right to keep and bear arms, which right shall not be abridged; but this provision shall not prevent the passage of laws to govern the carrying of weapons concealed on the person, nor prevent passage of legislation providing minimum sentences for crimes committed while in possession of a firearm, nor prevent passage of legislation providing penalties for the possession of firearms by a convicted felon, nor prevent the passage of legislation punishing the use of a firearm. No law shall impose licensure, registration or special taxation on the ownership for possession of firearms or ammunition. Nor shall any law permit the confiscation of firearms, except those actually used in the commission of a felony. Idaho Constitution: Article I, section 11.

Illinois: Subject only to the police power, the right of the individual citizen to keep and bear arms shall not be infringed. Illinois Constitution: Article I, section 22.

Indiana: The people shall have a right to bear arms, for the defense of themselves and the State. Indiana Constitution: Article I, section 32.

Kansas: The people have the right to bear arms for their defense and security; but standing armies, in time of peace, are dangerous to liberty, and shall not be tolerated, and the military shall be in strict subordination to the civil power. Kansas Bill of Rights: section 4.

Kentucky: All men are, by nature, free and equal, and have certain inherent and inalienable rights, among which may be reckoned: . . .
   Seventh: The right to bear arms in defense of themselves and of the state, subject to the power of the general assembly to enact laws to prevent persons from carrying concealed weapons. Kentucky Bill of Rights: section I, paragraph 7.

Louisiana: The right of each citizen to keep and bear arms shall not be abridged, but this provision shall not prevent the passage of laws to prohibit the carrying of weapons concealed on the person. Louisiana Constitution: Article I, section 11.

Maine: Every citizen has a right to keep and bear arms and this right shall never be questioned. Maine Constitution: Article I, section 16.

Massachusetts: The people have a right to keep and bear arms for the common defense. And as, in time of peace, armies are dangerous to liberty, they ought not to be maintained without the consent of the legislature; and the military power shall always be held in an exact subordination to the civil authority, and be governed by it. Massachusetts Declaration of Rights: Part I, Article XVII.

Michigan: Every person has a right to keep and bear arms for the defense of himself and the state. Michigan Constitution: Article I, section 6.

Mississippi: The right of every citizen to keep and bear arms in the defense of his home, person, or property, or in aid of the civil power when thereto legally summoned, shall not be called in question, but the legislature may regulate or forbid carrying concealed weapons. Mississippi Constitution: Article 3, section 12.

Missouri: That the right of every citizen to keep and bear arms in defense of his home, person and property, or when lawfully summoned in aid of the civil power, shall not be questioned; but this shall not justify the wearing of concealed weapons. Missouri Constitution: Article I, section 23.

Montana: The right of any person to keep or bear arms in defense of his own home, person, and property, or in aid of the civil power when thereto legally summoned, shall not be called in question, but nothing herein contained shall be held to permit the carrying of concealed weapons. Montana Constitution: Article II, section 12.

Nebraska: All persons are by nature free and independent, and have certain inherent and inalienable rights; among these are . . . the right to keep and bear arms for security or defense of self, family, home, and others, and for lawful common defense, hunting, recreational use, and all other lawful purposes, and such rights shall not be denied or infringed by the state or any subdivision thereof. Nebraska Constitution: Article I, section I.

Nevada: Every citizen has the right to keep and bear arms for security and defense, for lawful hunting and recreational use and for other lawful purposes. Nevada Constitution: Article 1, section II, paragraph 1.

New Hampshire: All persons have the right to keep and bear arms in defense of themselves, their families, their property, and the state. New Hampshire Constitution: Part 1, Article II-a.

New Mexico: No law shall abridge the right of the citizen to keep and bear arms for security and defense, for lawful hunting and recreational use and for other lawful purposes, but nothing herein shall be held to permit the carrying of concealed weapons. No municipality or county shall regulate, in any way, an incident of the right to keep and bear arms. New Mexico Constitution: Article II, section 6.

North Carolina: A well regulated militia being necessary to the security of a free State, the right of the people to keep and bear arms shall not be infringed; and as standing armies in time of peace are dangerous to liberty, they shall not be maintained, and the military shall be kept under strict subordination to, and governed by, the civil power. Nothing herein shall justify the practice of carrying concealed weapons, or prevent the General Assembly from enacting penal statutes against that practice. North Carolina Constitution: Article I, section 30.

North Dakota: All individuals are by nature equally free and independent and have certain inalienable rights, among which are . . . to keep and bear arms for the defense of their person, family, property, and the state, and for lawful hunting, recreational, and other lawful purposes, which shall not be infringed. North Dakota Constitution: Article I, section 1.

Ohio: The people have the right to bear arms for their defense and security; but standing armies, in time of peace, are dangerous to liberty, and shall not be kept up; and the military shall be in strict subordination to the civil power. Ohio Constitution: Article I, section 4.

Oklahoma: The right of a citizen to keep and bear arms in defense of his home, person, or property, or in aid of the civil power when thereunto legally summoned, shall never be prohibited; but nothing herein contained shall prevent the Legislature from regulating the carrying of weapons. Oklahoma Constitution: Article II, section 26.

Oregon: The people shall have the right to bear arms for the defense of themselves, and the State, but the Military shall be kept in strict subordination to the civil power. Oregon Constitution: Article I, section 27.

Pennsylvania: The right of the citizens to bear arms in defense of themselves and the State shall not be questioned. Pennsylvania Constitution: Article I, section 21.

Rhode Island: The right of the people to keep and bear arms shall not be infringed. Rhode Island Constitution: Article I, section 22.

South Carolina: A well regulated militia being necessary to the security of a free State, the right of the people to keep and bear arms shall not be infringed. As, in times of peace, armies are dangerous to liberty, they shall not be maintained without the consent of the General Assembly. The military power of the State shall always be held in subordination to the civil authority and be governed by it. No soldier shall in time of peace be quartered in any house without the consent of the owner nor in time or war but in the manner prescribed by law. South Carolina Constitution: Article I, section 20.

South Dakota: The right of the citizens to bear arms in defense of themselves and the state shall not be denied. South Dakota Constitution: Article VI, section 24.

Tennessee: That the citizens of this State have a right to keep and to bear arms for their common defense; but the Legislature shall have power, by law, to regulate the wearing of arms with a view to prevent crime. Tennessee Constitution: Article I, section 26.

Texas: Every Citizen shall have the right to keep and bear arms in lawful defense of himself or the State; but the Legislature shall have power, by law, to regulate the wearing of arms, with a view to prevent crime. Texas Constitution: Article I, section 23.

Utah: The individual right of the people to keep and bear arms for security and defense of self, family, others, property, or the State, as well as for the other lawful purposes shall not be infringed; but nothing herein shall prevent the legislature from defining the lawful use of arms. Utah Constitution: Article I, section 6.

Vermont: That the people have a right to bear arms for the defense of themselves and the State—and as standing armies in time of peace are dangerous to liberty, they ought not to be kept up; and that the military should be kept under strict subordination to and governed by the civil power. Vermont Constitution: Chapter I, Article XVI.

Virginia: That a well regulated militia, composed of the body of the people, trained to arms, is the proper, natural, and safe defense of a free state, therefore, the right of the people to keep and bear arms shall not be infringed; that standing armies, in time of peace, should be avoided as dangerous to liberty; and that in all cases the military should be under strict subordination to, and governed by, the civil power. Virginia Constitution: Article I, section 13.

Washington: The right of the individual citizen to bear arms in defense of himself, or the state, shall not be impaired, but nothing in this section shall be construed as authorizing individuals or corporations to organize, maintain, or employ an armed body of men. Washington Constitution: Article I, section 24.

West Virginia: A person has the right to keep and bear arms for the defense of self, family, home and state, and for lawful hunting and recreational use. West Virginia Constitution: Article III, section 22.

Wyoming: The right of citizens to bear arms in defense of themselves and of the state shall not be denied. Wyoming Constitution: Article I, section 24.

APPENDIX B

State Gun Control Laws

State laws regarding gun possession and carrying can change. State laws are posted on several Internet sites. Many states have their own Web sites, as do several of the organizations involved in the gun control debate—see sources, Appendix III.

All states are subject to federal laws, such as the ban on the sale of semiautomatic assault weapons. Many states have received exemptions from following the provisions of the Brady law. As states develop an instant background check or suitable alternative, they become eligible for exemption. For other states, the Brady law establishes a five-working-day waiting period to provide police a chance to assess an applicant's background to ensure he or she is not prohibited from buying a handgun.

General definitions of the terms used in the synopses below include the following:

Licensing/Required Permits require a gun purchaser to apply for a license or permit. Preemption means that localities are preempted or not allowed to pass gun laws that are stricter than those in place at the state level. (A "yes" following the preemption entry means that such a law exists in the state.)

Purchasing Limits: Some states limit the number of guns per time interval that can be sold to an individual.

Registration requires a gun purchaser to register the gun with a local or state authority.

Waiting period: the time between filing required paperwork and being able to actually purchase the gun. (Note that states with a "no" or "none" entry are subject to the provisions of a five-day federal waiting period and mandatory background check as detailed in the Brady act. Only those states with a permit system or instantaneous background check are exempt from those provisions.)

Alabama

Concealed Carry: Alabama has permissive laws allowing citizens to carry concealed weapons (Alabama law enforcement has some discretionary power).

Licensing/Required Permits: Yes

Preemption: Yes, with regards to handguns

Registration: None

Purchasing Limits: None

Waiting Period: Yes, 48 hours for pistols

Alaska

Concealed Carry: Alaska has permissive laws allowing citizens to carry concealed weapons.

Licensing/Required Permits: None

Preemption: Yes, but preemption may be overridden by local referendum.

Purchasing Limits: None

Registration: None

Waiting Period: None

Arizona

Concealed Carry: Arizona has permissive laws allowing citizens to carry concealed weapons.

Felons: Arizona automatically restores first time felons the ability to own firearms.

Licensing/Required Permits: None

Preemption: Yes

Purchasing Limits: None

School Grounds: Possession of a deadly weapon on school grounds is an act of criminal misconduct.

Waiting Period: None

Arkansas

Concealed Carry: Arkansas has permissive laws allowing citizens to carry concealed weapons.

Licensing/Required Permits: None

Preemption: Yes

Purchasing Limits: None

School Grounds: Possession of a firearm on school grounds is a felony offense.

Waiting Period: None

California

Armor-piercing Bullets: Possession of any ammunition designed to penetrate metal or armor is a criminal offense.

Bans: Assault Weapons

Concealed Carry: California has restrictive laws allowing citizens to carry concealed weapons only when need is demonstrated.

Licensing/Required Permits: Permit required for purchase of any type of firearm. For a concealable firearm, purchaser must present a firearm safety certificate.

Preemption: Yes, with respect to handguns

Purchasing Limits: None

Registration: Dealers are required to keep detailed information on firearms sales.

Waiting Period: 15-day waiting period for handgun purchases, so state is exempt from provisions of the Brady act. As of January 1996, the law calls for a 15-day waiting period for concealable guns, 10 days for all others.

Numerous local restrictions, including restrictions on firearms dealers.

Colorado

Concealed Carry: Colorado has restrictive laws allowing citizens to carry concealed weapons only when need is demonstrated.

Licensing/Required Permits: None

Preemption: None

Purchasing Limits: None

Waiting Period: None, state has an instant check system, exempting it from the federal Brady bill.

Some localities have added restrictions.

Connecticut

Bans: Assault weapons (recently ruled constitutional by Connecticut Supreme Court)

Concealed Carry: Connecticut has permissive laws allowing citizens to carry concealed weapons.

Licensing/Required Permits: Permit required to carry concealed weapons.

Preemption: No

Waiting Period: For handgun purchase; no waiting period for persons with a permit; two weeks without permit. For purchase of shotguns or rifles, no waiting period for holders of a valid hunting license; two-week waiting period without a hunting license.

State is exempt from provisions of Brady.

Several localities have greater restrictions.

Delaware

Concealed Carry: Delaware has restrictive laws allowing citizens to carry concealed weapons only when need is demonstrated.

Licensing/Required Permits: None

Preemption: No

Purchasing Limits: None

Registration: None

Waiting Period: Three days for purchase of handguns and rifles; the state is exempt from following the provisions of the Brady law.

Florida

Concealed Carry: Florida has permissive laws allowing citizens to carry concealed weapons.

Licensing/Required Permits: None

Possession by Minors: It is unlawful to store or leave a firearm in any place within the reach or easy access of a minor (person under 16 years of age).

Preemption: Yes

Purchasing Limits: None

Registration: None

Waiting Period: Florida has an instant background check system in place, so it is exempted from the federal Brady law.

Georgia

Concealed Carry: Georgia has permissive laws allowing citizens to carry concealed weapons.

Licensing/Required Permits: None

Possession by Minors: Providing a pistol to a person under 21 years of age is a misdemeanor.

Preemption: Yes

Waiting Period: Georgia is in the process of establishing an instant background check system. Once in place, the state will be exempted from federal Brady law requirements.

Several counties and cities have more restrictive gun laws on the books, but the state's preemption clause means many cannot be enforced.

Hawaii

Bans: Assault weapons and silencers

Concealed Carry: Hawaii has restrictive laws allowing citizens to carry concealed weapons only when need is demonstrated.

Licensing/Required Permits: A permit and firearms safety instruction are required for the purchase of all firearms.

Preemption: No

Purchasing Limits: No

Registration: Registration required for all firearms.

Waiting Period: Up to 16 days for all firearms, so the state has been exempted from the federal Brady law.

Idaho

Concealed Carry: Idaho has permissive laws allowing citizens to carry concealed weapons.

Licensing/Required Permits: No

Preemption: Yes

Registration: None

Waiting Period: State is establishing an instant background check system; once in place, the state will be exempted from the federal Brady law.

Illinois

Bans: Short-barreled rifles and shotguns, silencers, and hollow point and armor-piercing ammunition

Concealed Carry: Carrying of concealed weapons is not allowed.

Licensing/Required Permits: Owners of firearms must have a Firearm Owner's Identification Card.

Possession by Minors: Persons under the age of 18 are prohibited from possessing any concealable firearm. Persons under the age of 21 who have been convicted of a misdemeanor other than a traffic offense are prohibited from possessing firearms or ammunition.

Preemption: No

Purchasing Limits: None

Registration: Dealers who sell concealable guns must keep a register of all firearm sales.

Waiting Period: 72 hours for concealable guns and 24 hours for long guns; Illinois is exempted from provisions of the federal Brady law.

Numerous local restrictions, including handgun bans in Chicago, Morton Grove, East St. Louis, and Evanston.

Indiana

Bans: Armor-piercing handgun ammunition. Dealing in (but not possession of) a sawed-off shotgun.

Concealed Carry: Indiana has permissive laws allowing citizens to carry concealed weapons.

Dealers: Dealers must possess a state license.

Licensing/Required Permits: Application is required for transfer of ownership of firearms.

Preemption: Local governments are prohibited from creating a gun registry.

Waiting Period: Seven working days, no waiting period for those with a permit to carry a concealed weapon; the state is exempted from provisions of the federal Brady law.

Gary and East Chicago have bans on assault weapons.

Iowa

Concealed Carry: Iowa has restrictive laws allowing citizens to carry concealed weapons only when need is demonstrated.

Licensing/Required Permits: Annual permit required for pistols and revolvers.

Possession by Minors: Firearm ownership prohibited for persons under 21 years of age.

Preemption: Yes

Purchasing Limits: None

Waiting Period: A 3-day waiting period exists for the annual permit.

Kansas

Concealed Carry: Carrying of concealed weapons is not allowed.

Licensing/Required Permits: None

Possession by Minors: Firearm ownership is prohibited for persons under 18 years of age.

Preemption: No

Purchasing Limits: None

Registration: None

Waiting Period: No

Several localities have passed stricter gun laws, including bans on short-barreled rifles and silencers.

Kentucky

Bans: Armor-piercing ammunition

Concealed Carry: Kentucky has permissive laws allowing citizens to carry concealed weapons.

Licensing/Required Permits: None

Preemption: Yes

Purchasing Limits: None

Registration: None

Waiting Period: No

Louisiana

Bans: Armor-piercing ammunition

Concealed Carry: Louisiana has permissive laws allowing citizens to carry concealed weapons.

Dealers: Dealers must keep records of firearm sales.

Licensing/Required Permits: Permit required for manufacturers, importers, businesses, and dealers.

Possession by Minors: Sales to persons under age of 18 are prohibited.

Preemption: Yes

Purchasing Limits: None

Registration: No registration except for a few specific cases including sawed-off shotguns and rifles, any firearm that has had its serial number or mark of identification obliterated, grenade launchers, bazooka, rocket launchers, flame throwers, and so forth.

Waiting Period: No

Several localities have stricter laws in place.

Maine

Bans: Armor-piercing ammunition

Concealed Carry: Maine has permissive laws allowing citizens to carry concealed weapons. Persons convicted of a crime may apply for restoration of their ability to carry a concealed weapon five years after they have completed their sentence.

Dealers: Dealers must keep records of firearm sales and must provide a firearm safety brochure with every purchase.

Licensing/Required Permits: None

Minors: Furnishing a gun to a person under 16 is a crime.

Preemption: Yes

Purchasing Limits: None

Storage: Leaving a gun or ammunition accessible to a child is a crime.

Waiting Period: No

Maryland

Bans: Assault pistols and Saturday Night Specials (all handguns must be approved for sale and possession in Maryland by the Handgun Roster Board).

Concealed Carry: Maryland has restrictive laws allowing citizens to carry concealed weapons only when need is demonstrated.

Dealers: A state license is required to sell handguns.

Gun Shows: Firearm sales at gun shows are subject to the waiting period and application process.

Licensing/Required Permits: An application is required for all sales and transfers of handguns. The application has a $10 fee.

Preemption: Yes, with exceptions for local regulations that govern firearm ownership by minors in places of public assembly.

Purchasing Limits: None

Waiting Period: Seven-day period for handguns and assault rifles; the state is exempt from provisions of the federal Brady law.

Several localities have stricter laws in place.

Massachusetts

Concealed Carry: Massachusetts has restrictive laws allowing citizens to carry concealed weapons only when need is demonstrated.

Dealers: Records of sales required.

Licensing/Required Permits: A license to carry or one-time permit to purchase is required in addition to a firearms identification card for firearm purchase.

Possession by Minors: Minors under the age of 15 cannot acquire a firearms identification card. Persons over 15 but under 18 may get a firearms identification card with the written permission of a parent or guardian.

Preemption: None

Purchasing Limits: None

Registration: Within seven days, the purchaser shall register the firearm and report the conditions of sale in writing to the commissioner of public safety.

Waiting Period: Seven-day waiting period for first-time permit applicants; the state is exempt from provisions of the federal Brady law.

Boston has a ban on replica firearms.

Michigan

Bans: Armor-piercing ammunition

Concealed Carry: Michigan has restrictive laws allowing citizens to carry concealed weapons only when need is demonstrated.

Dealers: Register of firearm sales required.

Licensing/Required Permits: For every firearm purchase, purchaser is required to obtain a license to purchase from local police. Applicant must pass a basic firearm safety test. One copy of the license must be returned to the police within 10 days after purchase is completed. License expires 10 days after issuance.

Pawnbrokers: Accepting a pistol for resale is a misdemeanor.

Preemption: Yes

Purchasing Limits: None

Resident Requirements: Only residents of the state or contiguous states may purchase rifles or shotguns. Michigan residents may purchase rifles and shotguns within the state or contiguous states.

Waiting Period: None, because of the state's licensing system, it is exempt from provisions of the federal Brady law.

Minnesota

Bans: Possession and manufacture of Saturday Night Specials

Concealed Carry: Minnesota has restrictive laws allowing citizens to carry concealed weapons only when need is demonstrated.

Licensing/Required Permits: A transferee permit is required for transfers of ownership of pistols and semiautomatic weapons. A permit to carry also satisfies the permit requirement.

Preemption: Yes

Purchasing Limits: None

Registration: None

Resident Requirements: Only residents of Minnesota or contiguous states may purchase rifles or shotguns. Minnesota residents only may purchase rifles and shotguns within the state or contiguous states.

Waiting Period: Seven-day waiting period for purchase of all firearms. The waiting period may be waived by the sheriff or chief of police for purchasers of rifles or shotguns who have a valid transferee permit or permit to carry. For purchasers of handguns, the federal five-day waiting period mandated by the Brady bill is always in effect.

Mississippi

Concealed Carry: Mississippi has permissive laws allowing citizens to carry concealed weapons.

Dealers: Records of firearm and ammunition sales required.

Licensing/Required Permits: None

Preemption: Yes

Purchasing Limits: None

Registration: None

Waiting Period: No

Missouri

Concealed Carry: Carrying of concealed weapons is not allowed.

Licensing/Required Permits: Permit required for transfers of ownership of concealable firearms.

Preemption: None

Purchasing Limits: None

Registration: None

Waiting Period: Up to seven working days for concealable weapons; the state is exempt from provisions of the Brady law.

Local Legislation: Dealers in St. Louis must have a local firearms dealers license.

Montana

Bans: Silencers, sawed-off shotguns

Concealed Carry: Montana has permissive laws allowing citizens to carry concealed weapons.

Licensing/Required Permits: None

Possession by Minors: Minors under the age of 14 are prohibited from handling guns except under the supervision of a parent/guardian or qualified firearms instructor.

Preemption: Yes

Purchasing Limits: None

Registration: None

Waiting Period: No

Nebraska

Concealed Carry: Carrying of concealed weapons is not allowed.

Licensing/Required Permits: Certificate required for purchase of handguns.

Preemption: None

Purchasing Limits: None

Registration: None

Waiting Period: State has an instant criminal history record check, exempting it from provisions of the federal Brady law.

Some local restrictions exist.

Nevada

Bans: Metal-penetrating handgun ammunition, short-barreled rifles and shotguns

Concealed Carry: Nevada has permissive laws allowing citizens to carry concealed weapons.

Dealers: Dealers must keep records of weapon sales.

Licensing/Required Permits: None

Possession by Minors: Minors under the age of 14 are prohibited from controlling a gun except under the supervision of an adult. It is a misdemeanor for an adult to aid or permit minors to gain access to guns. The sale of concealable weapons to persons under 18 years of age is prohibited.

Preemption: No

Purchasing Limits: None

Registration: None

School Grounds: Possession of a dangerous weapon on school grounds is a misdemeanor.

Waiting Period: No

A few localities have stricter regulations.

New Hampshire

Bans: Armor-piercing ammunition

Concealed Carry: New Hampshire has permissive laws allowing citizens to carry concealed weapons.

Dealers: Records of sales must be kept.

Licensing/Required Permits: Yes, sales to nonresidents are subject to the laws of their state of residence.

Preemption: None

Purchasing Limits: None

Registration: None

Residence Requirements: Nonresidents are subject to the laws of their state of residence.

Waiting Period: No

New Jersey

Bans: Assault weapons, armor-piercing ammunition

Concealed Carry: New Jersey has restrictive laws allowing citizens to carry concealed weapons only when need is demonstrated.

Dealers: Records of handgun sales required.

Licensing/Required Permits: Permit to carry required for handguns; Firearm Purchaser ID card required for shotguns and rifles.

Preemption: Yes

Purchasing Limits: Only one handgun can be purchased per permit.

Registration: Dealers must keep register of handgun sales.

School Grounds: Possession of a gun on school property is a criminal offense.

Waiting Period: Seven-day waiting period to acquire a handgun permit; state is exempt from provisions of federal Brady law.

New Mexico

Concealed Carry: Carrying of concealed weapons is not allowed.

Licensing/Required Permits: None

Preemption: None

Purchasing Limits: None

Registration: None

Waiting Period: No state-mandated waiting period; the Brady Bill is in effect.

New York

Concealed Carry: New York has restrictive laws allowing citizens to carry concealed weapons only when need is demonstrated.

Dealers: Record keeping of transactions is required for firearms dealers and gunsmiths.

Licensing/Required Permits: License required for possession and carrying of firearms. Permits are good for a maximum of three years.

Possession by Minors: Firearm sales to persons under 19 who are not licensed to possess firearms are prohibited.

Preemption: Yes, however, New York City is exempted from state preemption law.

Purchasing Limits: None

Registration: Dealers and gunsmiths must keep register of gun sales.

Waiting Period: Up to six months for permit; state is exempt from provisions of federal Brady law.

Several local restrictions apply, especially in New York City, which requires its own permit; permits issued elsewhere in the state are not valid in the city.

North Carolina

Concealed Carry: North Carolina's new permissive concealed carrying law went into effect in December 1995.

Dealers: Record keeping of firearm sales required. State dealer's license required.

Licensing/Required Permits: Permit required for sale of firearms.

Possession by Minors: A firearm cannot be stored so that it is accessible to a minor.

Preemption: State's preemption law went into effect in 1996.

Purchasing Limits: None

Registration: None

Waiting Period: Up to 30 days for issuance of a permit; however, the Brady bill is in effect to allow for background check on handgun purchases.

Several localities require dealer licenses.

North Dakota

Concealed Carry: North Dakota has permissive laws allowing citizens to carry concealed weapons.

Licensing/Required Permits: None

Possession by Minors: Persons under 18 years of age may not possess a handgun except under direct supervision of an adult for handgun safety training, target shooting, or hunting.

Preemption: Yes

Purchasing Limits: None

Registration: None

Waiting Period: No state-mandated waiting period; the Brady law is in effect with exceptions for persons who have been issued a permit to carry within the last five years.

Ohio

Concealed Carry: Carrying of concealed weapons is not allowed.

Licensing/Required Permits: License required.

Possession by Minors: Sales of firearms prohibited to persons under 18 years of age. Sales of handguns prohibited to persons under 21 years of age. Persons under 18 may be furnished a firearm for hunting, safety instruction, or marksmanship only under supervision of an adult.

Preemption: None

Purchasing Limits: None

Registration: None

Waiting Period: No

About a dozen localities have stricter laws in place that range from weapons ban on school grounds to record-keeping requirements and bans on Saturday Night Specials and assault weapons.

Oklahoma

Bans: Armor-piercing ammunition

Concealed Carry: Oklahoma has permissive laws allowing citizens to carry concealed weapons.

Licensing/Required Permits: None

Possession by Minors: Sale of pistols and revolvers to minors is prohibited.

Preemption: Yes

Purchasing Limits: None

Registration: None

Waiting Period: No

Oregon

Bans: Armor-piercing ammunition, silencers, and short-barreled rifles and shotguns

Concealed Carry: Oregon has permissive laws allowing citizens to carry concealed weapons.

Dealers: Records of firearm sales are required. No state license is required.

Possession by Minors: Possession of handguns by persons under 18 years of age is prohibited. Parents and guardians may transfer possession of shotguns and rifles to a minor under their care.

Preemption: Yes. Law was passed in 1995, nullifying local restrictions. The bill was vetoed by the governor, but a legislative override put it on the books.

Purchasing Limits: None

Registration: Dealers are required to keep register of firearm sales. However, Oregon state law specifically forbids the compilation of information on lawful purchases of firearms for any reason other than to determine if the firearm is stolen or has been used in the commission of a crime.

School Grounds: Discharge or attempt to discharge a weapon on school grounds is a felony offense.

Waiting Period: Oregon has a 15-day waiting period and background check system. However, the legislature has approved an instant background check system; the state is exempt from provisions of the federal Brady law.

Two localities require local dealer's licenses.

Pennsylvania

Bans: Armor-piercing ammunition

Concealed Carry: Pennsylvania has permissive laws allowing citizens to carry concealed weapons.

Dealers: A dealer license is required to sell firearms. License is renewed annually. Records of firearm sales must be kept.

Licensing/Required Permits: Yes, for purchase of any type of firearm.

Loans of Firearms: Loaning or giving a firearm to any person without following laws on transfer of firearm ownership is prohibited.

Possession by Minors: Delivery of firearms to persons under the age of 18 years is prohibited. To sell, give, or otherwise furnish a "starter pistol" to a person under 18 years of age is prohibited.

Preemption: Yes

Purchasing Limits: None

Registration: None

Waiting Period: 48-hour waiting period on all firearm sales; federal five-day waiting period on handgun purchases mandated by Brady is in effect with exemptions for those persons with a valid permit to carry a concealed weapon.

Several localities require local permits or local dealer's licenses. Philadelphia has a ban on military-style weapons.

Rhode Island

Bans: Silencers, armor-piercing ammunition

Concealed Carry: Rhode Island has restrictive laws allowing citizens to carry concealed weapons only when need and ability is demonstrated.

Dealers: Dealers must be licensed to sell handguns. Handgun dealer license is renewed on an annual basis. Dealers are required to keep registry of firearm sales.

Licensing/Required Permits: Gun safety education course is required for handgun purchases.

Possession by Minors: Sale of firearms and ammunition to persons under 18 years of age is prohibited except with parental or guardian's consent. Sale of pistols and revolvers to persons under 21 years of age is prohibited. Persons under 15 may possess or use firearms only if minor has a permit and is in the presence of a qualified adult.

Preemption: Yes

Purchasing Limits: None

Registration: None—expressly prohibited

Resident Requirements: Only state residents and members of the armed forces stationed in Rhode Island may purchase handguns. Citizens of Rhode Island must fill out a Rhode Island (RI) handgun purchase application and go through a background check even when purchasing a concealable firearm from a dealer in another state.

Waiting Period: Seven days for handgun purchases; the mandated criminal background check specified in Brady is in effect.

South Carolina

Bans: Saturday Night Specials, sawed-off shotguns and rifles, teflon-coated (armor-piercing) ammunition

Concealed Carry: South Carolina's legislature in June 1996 passed a right-to-carry law, making it the 31st state to have a permissive concealed carry policy.

Dealers: State dealers license required for sale of pistols.

Licensing/Required Permits: Purchasers of pistols must fill out application prior to purchase.

Possession by Minors: Sale and possession of pistols to persons under 22 years of age is prohibited except for temporary possession under the supervision of a parent or adult instructor.

Preemption: Yes

Purchasing Limits: Persons may purchase no more than one pistol per month.

Resident Requirements: Only South Carolina residents and members of the armed forces may buy pistols in South Carolina.

Registration: None

Waiting Period: No

South Dakota

Bans: Silencers, short-barreled shotguns

Concealed Carry: South Dakota has permissive laws allowing citizens to carry concealed weapons.

Licensing/Required Permits: Pistol permit application or permit to carry required for purchase.

Possession by Minors: None

Preemption: Yes

Purchasing Limits: None

Registration: None

Waiting Period: State mandates a 48-hour waiting period for the purchase of pistols; however, the five-day wait mandated by Brady is in effect. Persons with a valid permit to carry a concealed pistol are exempted from the waiting period.

Tennessee

Bans: Silencers, short-barreled rifles and shotguns, hollow-point ammunition

Background Check: A background check is required for all firearm transfers including transactions involving pawnbrokers and transactions between private individuals.

Concealed Carry: Tennessee has permissive laws allowing citizens to carry concealed weapons. Firearms are prohibited where alcohol is sold.

Dealers: Firearms dealers must be licensed by the state.

Licensing/Required Permits: Purchasers must fill out an application and submit to a background check to purchase a pistol.

Possession by Minors: The sale, loan, or gift of a firearm to a minor is prohibited except as a loan or gift for hunting or sporting activity.

Preemption: Yes, except ordinances enacted prior to April 8, 1986.

Purchasing Limits: None

Registration: None

Resident Requirements: Tennessee residents eligible to purchase a rifle or shotgun may purchase a rifle or shotgun in a contiguous state. Residents of a contiguous state may purchase a rifle or shotgun in Tennessee providing they are eligible to do so under the laws of their resident state, Tennessee, and the federal government.

Waiting Period: State mandates a waiting period of up to 15 days for a background check; it is exempt from provisions of the Brady law.

Several localities have stricter laws, such as Chattanooga's prohibition on sale of pistols and a few three-day waiting periods on gun sales.

Texas

Bans: Short-barreled rifles and shotguns, silencers, armor-piercing ammunition, and zip guns

Concealed Carry: Texas has permissive laws allowing citizens to carry concealed weapons.

Licensing/Required Permits: None

Possession by Minors: The loan, sale, or gift of a firearm to a person under 18 years of age is prohibited except when the minor's parent or guardian has given consent.

Preemption: Yes

Purchasing Limits: None

Registration: None

Waiting Period: No

Utah

Concealed Carry: Utah has permissive laws allowing any citizen to carry concealed weapons; no license required.

Licensing/Required Permits: None

Possession by Minors: Possession of weapons prohibited for persons under 14 years of age except when accompanied by a parent or guardian or for persons under 18 with the permission of parent or guardian.

Preemption: Yes

Purchasing Limits: None

Registration: None

Waiting Period: An instant criminal background check system exempts the state from provisions of the Brady law.

Silencers are banned in Salt Lake County.

Vermont

Concealed Carry: Vermont has permissive laws allowing citizens to carry concealed weapons.

Dealers: Records of firearm sales must be kept. Record keeping requirement also applies to pawnbrokers.

Licensing/Required Permits: None

Possession by Minors: To sell or furnish a firearm to a person under the age of 16 years is a criminal offense. The possession of a handgun by a person under 16 years of age without the consent of a parent or guardian is prohibited.

Preemption: Yes

Purchasing Limits: None

Registration: None

Waiting Period: No

Virginia

Bans: Toy guns that discharge objects (other than cap pistols), plastic guns, and "Street Sweepers"

Concealed Carry: Virginia has permissive laws allowing citizens to carry concealed weapons.

Dealers: Dealers shall keep a register of all short-barreled rifles and shotguns handled by him.

Gun Shows: Gun shows are regulated.

Licensing/Required Permits: Purchaser must submit to background check.

Possession by Minors: Transfer of pistols to minors prohibited, except by family members for sporting purposes.

Preemption: Yes

Purchasing Limits: One gun per month, but purchasers can petition the police to have the limit waived if need is demonstrated.

Registration: None

Waiting Period: An instant criminal background check system exempts the state from provisions of the federal Brady law.

Numerous localities have passed stricter gun control laws, many of which cannot be enforced because of the state preemption law.

Washington

Concealed Carry: Washington has permissive laws allowing citizens to carry concealed weapons.

Dealers: A state license is required to sell firearms and ammunition. Dealers must notify police of every firearm purchase. Dealers must be licensed to do business in the state of Washington.

Liability: The state and local government are immune from liability if anyone approved for pistol purchase is in fact ineligible.

Licensing/Required Permits: Application required for purchase of pistols. Applicants for concealed carry license must submit to background check.

Possession by Minors: Persons between the ages of 18 and 21 may own a pistol only.

Preemption: Yes

Purchasing Limits: None

Waiting Period: 30-day waiting period for a concealed carry license; federal 5-day waiting period on handgun purchases is in effect.

Washington, D.C.

Bans: City prohibits the private ownership of all firearms, with narrow exceptions for military, police, and security personnel.

Brady Bill: Not applicable

Concealed Carry: Carrying of concealed weapons is not allowed.

Licensing/Required Permits: Permit required for purchase of any firearm.

Possession by Minors: Not allowed under 18 years, ages 18–21 only with parental permission.

Preemption: Not applicable

Registration: All firearms must be registered.

Waiting Period: For sale of regulated pistols, 48 hours

West Virginia

Concealed Carry: West Virginia has permissive laws allowing citizens to carry concealed weapons.

Licensing/Required Permits: Permit required for high-powered rifles.

Possession by Minors: None

Preemption: Yes, with regards to regulations limiting ownership

Purchasing Limits: None

Registration: None

Waiting Period: No

Wisconsin

Bans: Short-barreled rifles, shotguns, and silencers

Concealed Carry: Carrying of concealed weapons is not allowed.

Licensing/Required Permits: Background check required for handgun purchases.

Possession by Minors: It is a criminal offense to keep a loaded firearm within easy access of a minor. Minors may possess a firearm with a barrel 12 inches in length or longer.

Preemption: Yes

Purchasing Limits: None

Registration: None

Waiting Period: For handgun purchase, 48-hours from receipt of confirmation number on background check. State is exempt from provisions of the federal Brady law, except that the federal five-day waiting period is in effect on handgun purchases from pawnbrokers.

Several localities have stricter gun laws in effect, including dealer and permit requirements and a ban on handguns in Madison.

Wyoming

Concealed Carry: Wyoming has permissive laws allowing citizens to carry concealed weapons.

Dealers: Dealers must keep registry of firearm sales.

Licensing/Required Permits: None

Possession by Minors: None

Preemption: None
Purchasing Limits: None
Registration: None, but dealers must keep records of firearm sales.
Waiting Period: No

APPENDIX C
Summary of Federal Gun Regulations

The following summary of federal gun regulations was compiled by the Coalition to Stop Gun Violence. The organization cautions that laws are subject to change and these are only summaries, not intended to be used as legal advice. Nor do these summaries include the penalties prescribed in the law.

ARMOR-PIERCING AMMUNITION

A 1986 law makes it unlawful to manufacture, import, sell, or deliver armor-piercing ammunition. This law has an exemption for law enforcement. This legislation also excludes ammunition designed for sporting rifles.

The Violent Crime Control and Law Enforcement Act of 1994 creates a new definition of armor-piercing ammunition that is aimed at eliminating new types of bullets. Now, handgun ammunition made of tungsten alloys, steel, iron, brass, bronze, beryllium, copper, or depleted uranium or handgun ammunition larger than .22 caliber where the jacket weighs more than 25 percent of the bullet is banned.

ASSAULT WEAPONS

The Violent Crime Control and Law Enforcement Act of 1994 prohibits the future manufacture, transfer, and possession of semiautomatic assault weapons and ammunition magazines that hold more than 10 rounds. This law has an exemption for law enforcement.

The Violent Crime Control and Law Enforcement Act of 1994 defines assault weapons as (1) 19 named weapon types (see listing below) and (2) guns that have specific assault weapon characteristics.

Named Weapons

1. Norinco, Mitchell, and Poly Technologies Automat Kalashnikovs (all models)
2. Action Arms Israeli Military Industries UZI and Galil
3. Berretta Ar70 (SC-70)
4. Colt AR-15
5. Fabrique National FN/FAL, FN/LAR, and FNC
6. SWD M-10, M-11, M-11/9, and M-12
7. Steyr AUG
8. INTRATEC TEC-9, TEC-DC9, and TEC-22
9. Revolving cylinder shotguns, such as (or similar to) the Street Sweeper and Striker 12

The Gun Control Act of 1968 outlaws the importation of guns that are not "generally recognized as particularly suitable for, or readily adaptable to sporting purposes." Under this section of the statute, ATF has set up guidelines to determine which weapons can be imported. In 1989, the importation of several makes of assault rifles was suspended.

FEDERAL TAXES

There is a 10 percent excise tax on handgun sales, and an 11 percent excise tax on long gun and ammunition sales. The tax applies only to the first sale of the gun or ammunition by a manufacturer or importer. Revenues generated by the tax benefit a hunter education and land conservation program.

IMPORTATION OF NON-SPORTING WEAPONS (SATURDAY NIGHT SPECIALS)

The Gun Control Act of 1968 outlaws the importation of guns that are not "generally recognized as particularly suitable for, or readily adaptable to sporting purposes." Under this section of the statute, ATF has set up guidelines about which weapons can be imported.

1. Inexpensive, short-barreled handguns with no sporting purpose made from inferior materials, commonly known as Saturday Night Specials, are permanently excluded from importation.
2. Imported versions of the Street Sweeper are barred from importation.
3. In 1989 the importation of several makes of assault rifles was suspended.

The 1986 Firearms Owners' Protection Act bans the importation of barrels for Saturday Night Specials.

LICENSING OF MANUFACTURERS

The Gun Control Act of 1968 requires that firearms manufacturers obtain a federal license and pay a fee of $50 per year unless the manufacturer makes "destructive devices" or "armor-piercing ammunition," in which case the fee is $1,000 per year. The manufacturer must allow the ATF to inspect the premises (including places of storage). Licensed manufacturers must renew their license every three years.

The Gun Control Act of 1968 requires that ammunition manufacturers obtain a federal license and pay a $10 fee per year unless the manufacturer makes "destructive devices" or "armor-piercing ammunition," in which case the fee is $1,000 per year.

LICENSING OF GUN DEALERS

The Gun Control Act of 1968 requires that firearms dealers obtain a federal license. The Brady Handgun Violence Prevention Act of 1993 increases the Federal Firearms Licensee (FFL) fee to $200 for three years with an additional $90 for a three-year renewal. Prior to the 1993 law the fee was $10 per year.

In order to obtain an FFL, the applicant must be 21 years old. The applicant must not fall into any of the categories of individuals to whom the sale of a firearm is prohibited (see the section, "Persons to Whom Sale of a Firearm Is Prohibited"). The applicant must also intend to engage in the business of selling firearms.

The Violent Crime Control and Law Enforcement Act of 1994 requires that FFLs now be photographed and fingerprinted. This law also increases the amount of time the ATF has to complete a background investigation of gun dealer applicants from 45 to 60 days. It also requires that applicants be in compliance with all state and local laws. The ATF now has access to a dealer's records whenever a crime gun is traced to that dealer. Dealers must report any theft within 48 hours and respond to trace requests immediately. The chief law enforcement officer in each jurisdiction will receive a list from ATF of gun dealers within his/her jurisdiction.

MACHINE GUNS

The 1934 National Firearms Act requires registration and thorough background checks for those who manufacture, buy, and sell machine guns and sawed-off shotguns.

An amendment to the Firearms Owners' Protection Act of 1986 generally outlaws the sale, transfer, and possession of new machine guns. The transfer of machine guns that were manufactured before May 1986 is permitted, but a fee of $200 is required.

PROHIBITIONS ON FIREARM SALES

Persons to Whom Sale of Firearms Is Prohibited

It is unlawful for any person to sell or otherwise dispose of any firearm or ammunition to

1. a person under indictment for, or who has been convicted in, any court of a crime punishable by over a year in prison
2. a fugitive from justice
3. an unlawful user of any controlled substance or a person addicted to any controlled substance
4. a person who has been adjudicated as a mental defective or has been committed to any mental institution
5. a person illegally or unlawfully in the United States
6. a person dishonorably discharged from the Armed Forces
7. a citizen of the United States who has renounced his/her citizenship
8. a person subject to a court order that restrains him/her from "harassing, stalking or threatening an intimate partner . . . or child or such intimate partner . . ."

Sale to Juveniles

Shotguns, rifles, and the ammunition for shotguns or rifles can be sold to anyone over 18 years old. It is unlawful for any licensed importer, manufacturer, dealer, or collector to sell or deliver any other type of firearm or ammunition to someone younger than 21 years.

The Violent Crime Control and Law Enforcement Act of 1994 made it unlawful for any person to sell, deliver, or otherwise transfer a handgun or ammunition only suitable for a handgun to anyone younger than 18 years old. It is also illegal for persons under the age of 18 to knowingly possess a handgun or ammunition only suitable for a handgun.

BACKGROUND CHECKS AND WAITING PERIODS

The Brady Handgun Violence Prevention Act of 1993 requires that the backgrounds of prospective handgun purchasers be checked to ensure that the sale of a handgun to the prospective purchaser is legal. The law provides a five-day waiting period so that law enforcement has time to run these background checks. This provision sunsets in five years (1998) when a national instant check system should be established. States that already require background checks that meet ATF's minimum standard are exempt. In five years, when the national instant check system is installed, states that wish to maintain a waiting period may do so.

The Brady Handgun Violence Prevention Act of 1993 authorizes spending $200 million a year over five years to computerize criminal background information and create a national instant check system.

GUN-FREE SCHOOLS ACT OF 1994

States receiving federal education funds are required to pass a law that local school agencies will expel for a minimum of one year any student who brings a gun to school.

APPENDIX D

Major Provisions of Brady II under Consideration by Congress

Introduced by Sen. Howard M. Metzenbaum and Rep. Charles E. Schumer, the sponsors of the Brady law, Brady II addresses many aspects of gun violence. The following provisions are in the legislation being considered. (Language and provisions in bills under consideration are subject to considerable change before [and should] they become law.)

Title I—Licensing and Registration. Establishes a system of state-based licensing and registration and makes it illegal for anyone, including a private citizen, to sell a handgun to anyone who does not possess a valid state handgun license. Seven days must elapse before the sale can be completed and a registration form must be sent to the appropriate state law enforcement authority.

The state license must be issued by the state's chief law enforcement authority and be valid for a period of no more than two years. The license must contain the licensee's name, address, date of birth, physical description, a license number, and a photograph of the licensee.

In order to receive a license, the applicant must: (1) be at least 21 years of age; (2) present valid identification and proof of residence; (3) pass a name and fingerprint-based background check; and (4) complete a required state handgun safety course.

States are authorized to charge appropriate fees and the bill authorizes $200 million in federal grants to states for the start up costs associated with establishing a system of licensing and registration.

Title II—Restrictions on Firearms Possessions. Establishes new restrictions on the possession of firearms. Anyone who has been indicted or convicted of a violent offense (or who is under a court restraining order because of a threat of physical violence) may not purchase or possess a firearm.

With certain limited exceptions, anyone under the age of 21 may not possess a handgun, and anyone under the age of 16 may not possess a long gun. Adults are prohibited from transferring firearms to juveniles, and adults with children under the age of 16 must not allow juveniles access to loaded guns.

A new Federal Arsenal License requirement is established for those who possess more than 20 firearms or more than 1,000 rounds of ammunition. Applicants for an arsenal license must pass a name and fingerprint-based background check and receive clearance from local law enforcement.

Title III—Restrictions on Gun Sellers. Raises the annual Federal Firearms Licensee (FFL) fee for the nation's 286,000 gun dealers to $1,000 per year; increases federal supervision of gun dealers; and imposes new restrictions on their operations.

The Bureau of Alcohol, Tobacco and Firearms (ATF) is given more time (180 days) to complete the required background check on applicants, and the number of unannounced inspections permitted each year under the law is raised from one to three.

FFLs are required to (1) sell exclusively from their licensed premises (thus, barring sales at gun shows); (2) respond immediately to gun traces conducted by ATF; and (3) report thefts or losses within 24 hours of their discovery. FFL employees must be at least 18 years of age and undergo a background check. FFLs are liable in Federal court for damages proximately caused by the sale, delivery or transfer of a firearm in violation of federal law.

Federal law is changed to provide that only FFLs may sell ammunition.

Title IV—Prohibited Weapons. Makes it illegal for anyone to manufacture, except for government use, the following prohibited weaponry: (1) a silencer; (2) a short-barreled shotgun; (3) a short-barreled rifle; (4) a destructive device; (5) a semi-automatic assault weapon; (6) a Saturday night special handgun; (7) non-sporting ammunition; and (8) a large capacity (6 rounds or more) ammunition magazine.

Prohibited weapons lawfully possessed prior to the effective date of the ban may be retained, but if they are transferred they are subject to the registration and transfer tax requirements presently imposed on the transfer of automatic weapons by the National Firearms Act of 1934.

Persons convicted of using a prohibited weapon in the commission of a crime of violence or a drug trafficking crime are subject to an additional prison term of 10 years.

Manufacturers of firearms are required, within one year of enactment, to meet tough new safety standards, including handgun load indicators and a mechanism preventing a firearm from firing once the magazine has been removed.

Source: Handgun Control, Inc.

APPENDIX E

Additional Resources

The following are several of the key organizations involved in the gun control debate. Internet Web site addresses for several organizations are provided.

American Firearms Association
% Macdonald & Associates
4020 University Drive, Suite 207
Fairfax, VA 22030
http://www.firearms.org/afa/index.html

Center to Prevent Handgun Violence
1225 Eye Street NW, Suite 1100
Washington, DC 20005
Telephone: (202) 289–7319

Citizens' Committee for the Right to Keep and Bear Arms
Liberty Park
12500 NE 10th Place
Bellevue, WA 98005
Telephone: (206) 454–4911

Coalition to Stop Gun Violence (CSGV)
1000 16th Street NW, Suite 603
Washington, DC 20036
Telephone: (202) 530–0340
http://www.gunfree.inter.net

The Educational Fund to End Handgun Violence (EFEHV)
1000 16th Street NW, Suite 603
Washington, DC 20036
Telephone: (202) 530–0340
http://www.gunfree.inter.net

Gun Owners of America
8001 Forbes Place, Suite 102
Springfield, VA 22151
Telephone: (703) 321–8585

Handgun Control, Inc. (HCl)
1225 Eye Street, NW, Suite 1100
Washington, DC 20005
Telephone: (202) 898–0792

National Rifle Association
11250 Waples Mill Road
Fairfax, VA 22030
Telephone: (703) 267–1000
http://www.nra.org

The Second Amendment Foundation
12500 NE 10th Place
Bellevue, WA 98005
Telephone: (206) 454–7012

The Violence Policy Center (VPC)
1300 N Street NW
Washington, DC 20005
Telephone: (202) 783–4071
http://www.inter.net

Violence Prevention Research Program
University of California, Davis
2315 Stockton Blvd.
Sacramento, CA 95817
http://edison.ucdmc.ucdavis.edu.80/research/vprp/

APPENDIX F
Statements of Key Organizations in the Gun Control Debate

STATEMENT OF THE NATIONAL RIFLE ASSOCIATION

Founded in 1871, the National Rifle Association of America today has more than 3.4 million members and nearly 15,000 affiliated clubs. Through its Institute for Legislative Action (ILA), NRA works to protect the constitutional right of American citizens to keep and bear arms.

NRA-ILA fights mainly restrictive firearm legislation, but it is also involved in related issues that affect firearm ownership and use. ILA's *CrimeStrike* Division, for example, unites victims, prosecutors, police and concerned citizens in an effort to fight for measures that save lives and reduce violent crime.

When Americans choose to exercise their Second Amendment right to use or own a firearm, NRA—the oldest civil rights organization in the country—is beside them all the way, defending their constitutional right to make such a choice and continually reaffirming that right through a commitment to safety, education and responsibility.

Since NRA and the state of New York jointly developed the first Hunter Safety Program, more than 20 million Americans have been trained to be safe and responsible hunters. NRA also conducts safety and marksmanship programs for youth in cooperation with the Boy Scouts, 4-H, the American Legion and many others.

The NRA Personal Protection Course has given hundreds of thousands of people a firm foundation in safe gun handling, storage, shooting and self-defense. NRA's Eddie Eagle Gun Safety Program has brought the message of gun safety to more than 6.5 million children grades pre-K through sixth.

STATEMENT OF THE AMERICAN FIREARMS ASSOCIATION

This can be found in Document 66.

STATEMENT OF THE COALITION TO STOP GUN VIOLENCE

The Coalition to Stop Gun Violence (CSGV) was founded in 1974 to combat the growing gun violence problem in the United States. CSGV is a unique coalition of more than forty religious, professional, labor, medical, educational, and civic organizations. The Coalition also counts more than 100,000 individual members nationwide.

The goal of CSGV is the orderly elimination of the private sale of handguns and assault weapons in the United States. CSGV seeks to ban handguns and assault weapons from importation, manufacture, sale, and transfer by the general American public with reasonable exceptions made for police, military and security personnel, gun clubs where guns are secured on club premises, and gun dealers and collectors trading in antique and collectible firearms in inoperable condition. Hunting weapons, such as shotguns and rifles, would be unaffected by these bans because they do not pose a large threat to the American public in the way handguns and assault weapons do.

In addition to a ban, the Coalition supports intermediate steps to reduce gun violence. These steps include limiting the availability of gun dealers' licenses, increasing gun dealers' license fees, restrictively licensing and registering gun owners, and increasing handgun and ammunition taxes to offset health care costs, imposing strict liability on gun manufacturers and dealers, regulating firearms as consumer products, banning Saturday Night Specials, and establishing a national one-handgun-per-month purchase limit.

To accomplish these goals, CSGV engages in a vigorous program of lobbying the US Congress and state legislatures. CSGV provides technical support to activist organizations across the country and is building the Ceasefire Action Network, a national network of grass-roots activists dedicated to stopping gun violence.

STATEMENT OF HANDGUN CONTROL, INC. (HCI)

Handgun Control, Inc., has a comprehensive program to combat gun violence.

Federal Legislation

Goal: Enact a federal gun control policy to reduce gun violence; protect existing gun laws.

Key Initiatives: Pass Brady II; defend key gun control laws against weakening or repeal.

State Legislation

Goal: Enact state legislation to reduce gun violence; protect existing gun laws.

Defeat gun lobby's legislation to allow the carrying of concealed weapons.

Enact handgun waiting period laws.

Ban semiautomatic assault weapons.

Require adults to keep guns inaccessible to children.

Community Outreach

Goal: Build a national grass-roots movement in support of gun control by mobilizing national organizations, state and local gun control groups, and individual activists.

Identify, enlist, and mobilize new constituencies.

Work with other allied organizations to make gun control a priority.

Recruit activists.

Voter Education Fund

Goal: Elect public officials who support responsible gun control laws.

Support pro-gun control candidates currently in office and challengers to gun control opponents.

Educate the public about candidates' positions on gun control.

Media Relations

Goal: Advance the goals of both organizations (HCI and the Center to Prevent Handgun Violence) by spreading our message to the public through the media.

Produce public service announcements and paid advertising campaigns.

Hold news conferences on major initiatives.

Reach out to national, state and local press.

Develop and distribute press materials on targeted issues.

Law Enforcement

Goal: Work with law enforcement to help pass federal and state legislation; coordinate state and local gun violence reduction campaigns with law enforcement.

Coordinate lobbying efforts by police in states and Washington, DC.

Hold press conferences on key issues.

Develop gun interdiction strategies with local police departments.

Produce public service announcements with law enforcement leaders.

Develop and distribute *Handgun Safety Guidelines* brochure.

Index

About the Editor

MARJOLIJN BIJLEFELD is a freelance writer and editor. Until 1990, she worked with the Coalition to Stop Gun Violence and served as the director of the Educational Fund to End Handgun Violence.